T0261997

Encyclopedia of MATLAB: Science and Engineering Volume II

Edited by **Louis Young**

LANRYE
INTERNATIONAL

New Jersey

Published by Clanrye International,
55 Van Reypen Street,
Jersey City, NJ 07306, USA
www.clanryeinternational.com

Encyclopedia of MATLAB: Science and Engineering
Volume II
Edited by Louis Young

International Standard Book Number: 978-1-63240-190-8 (Hardback)

This book contains information obtained from authentic and highly regarded sources. Copyright for all individual chapters remain with the respective authors as indicated. A wide variety of references are listed. Permission and sources are indicated; for detailed attributions, please refer to the permissions page. Reasonable efforts have been made to publish reliable data and information, but the authors, editors and publisher cannot assume any responsibility for the validity of all materials or the consequences of their use.

The publisher's policy is to use permanent paper from mills that operate a sustainable forestry policy. Furthermore, the publisher ensures that the text paper and cover boards used have met acceptable environmental accreditation standards.

Trademark Notice: Registered trademark of products or corporate names are used only for explanation and identification without intent to infringe.

Printed in the United States of America.

Contents

Preface   VII

Image and Signal Processing   1

Chapter 1   **Artificial Human Arm Driven by EMG Signal**   3
Mohammed Z. Al-Faiz and Abbas H. Miry

Chapter 2   **Analysis and Modeling of Clock-Jitter
Effects in Delta-Sigma Modulators**   31
Ramy Saad, Sebastian Hoyos and Samuel Palermo

Chapter 3   **Image Reconstruction Methods for MATLAB Users –
A Moore-Penrose Inverse Approach**   61
S. Chountasis, V.N. Katsikis and D. Pappas

Chapter 4   **Matlab-Based Algorithm for Real Time Analysis of
Multiexponential Transient Signals**   81
Momoh-Jimoh E. Salami, Ismaila B. Tijani,
Abdussamad U. Jibia and Za'im Bin Ismail

Chapter 5   **Digital FIR Hilbert Transformers:
Fundamentals and Efficient Design Methods**   103
David Ernesto Troncoso Romero and Gordana Jovanovic Dolecek

Chapter 6   **Position Estimation of the PMSM High Dynamic
Drive at Low Speed Range**   141
Konrad Urbanski

Chapter 7   **Detection of Craters and Its Orientation on Lunar**   165
Nur Diyana Kamarudin, Kamaruddin Abd. Ghani,
Siti Noormiza Makhtar, Baizura Bohari and Noorlina Zainuddin

Permissions

List of Contributors

Preface

It is often said that books are a boon to mankind. They document every progress and pass on the knowledge from one generation to the other. They play a crucial role in our lives. Thus I was both excited and nervous while editing this book. I was pleased by the thought of being able to make a mark but I was also nervous to do it right because the future of students depends upon it. Hence, I took a few months to research further into the discipline, revise my knowledge and also explore some more aspects. Post this process, I begun with the editing of this book.

This book analyzes applications of MATLAB in roughly every division of science. The text covers applications, image and signal processing based on the engineering of MATLAB as a tool for computing. The book has several chapters dealing with numerous professional fields and can be utilized by experts for their researches.

I thank my publisher with all my heart for considering me worthy of this unparalleled opportunity and for showing unwavering faith in my skills. I would also like to thank the editorial team who worked closely with me at every step and contributed immensely towards the successful completion of this book. Last but not the least, I wish to thank my friends and colleagues for their support.

Editor

Image and Signal Processing

Artificial Human Arm Driven by EMG Signal

Mohammed Z. Al-Faiz and Abbas H. Miry

Additional information is available at the end of the chapter

1. Introduction

This chapter presents the anatomy of Electromyography (EMG) signal, measurement, analysis, and it's processing. EMG is the detection of the electrical activity associated with muscle contraction. It is obtained by measurement of the electrical activity of a muscle during contraction. EMG signals are directly linked to the desire of movement of the person.

Robot arms are versatile tools found in a wide range of applications. While the user moves his arm, (EMG) activity is recorded from selected muscles, using surface EMG electrodes. By a decoding procedure the muscular activity is transformed to kinematic variables that are used to control the robot arm. EMG signals have been used as control signals for robotics devices in the past. EMG signals, which are measured at the skin surface, are the electrical manifestations of the activity of muscles. It provides an important access to the human neuromuscular system. It has been well recognized as an effective tool to generate control commands for prosthetic devices and human-assisting manipulators. Up to the present, a number of EMG-based human interfaces have been proposed as a means for elderly people and the disabled to control powered prosthetic limbs, wheelchairs, teleoperated robots, and so on. The core part of these human–robot interfaces is a pattern classification process, where motions or intentions of motions are classified according to features extracted from EMG signals. Commands for device control are then generated from the classified motions (Bu et al., 2009).

It has been proposed that the EMG signals from the body's intact musculature can be used to identify motion commands for the control of an externally powered prosthesis. Information extracted from EMG signals, represented in a feature vector, is chosen to minimize the control error. In order to achieve this, a feature set must be chosen which maximally separates the desired output classes. The extraction of accurate features from the EMG signals is the main kernel of classification systems and is essential to the motion command identification (Park &Lee, 1998).

2. EMG signal fundamentals

EMG is the recording of the electrical activity produced within the muscle fibers. The relation of surface EMG to torque makes EMG an attractive alternative to direct muscle tension measurements, necessary in many physical assessments. However, the complexity of the EMG signal origin has been a barrier for developing a quantitative description of this relation. The EMG signal origin and character is necessary background to understand the difficulty of establishing a relationship between surface EMG and torque.

The nervous system controls the voluntary movement of various body parts in humans by contracting and relaxing various skeletal muscles. To instantiate a contraction, a neuron generates a small electrical potential on the surface of the muscle fiber. This electrical potential causes depolarization of the muscle fiber tissue and a following depolarization waveform. This waveform travels the length of the muscle fiber and is known as the Action Potential (AP). Fig. 1 depicts the generation of electric fields in muscle fibers.

Muscle fibers are excited by nerve branches by one motoneuron in groups known as motor units. These motor units are defined as the fundamental unit of contraction and can range from a few muscle fibers for small muscles such as those in the hand and fingers, to thousands of muscle fibers in large muscles such as those in skeletal muscle. Because each motor unit contains a number of muscle fibers that are attached to the motor neuron at various points, the electrical signal of a motor unit is the summation of the action potential of each muscle fiber, which may be phase shifted from the other muscle fibers in that unit (Perry & Bekey,1981).

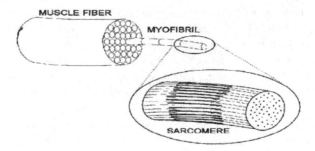

Figure 1. Muscle Fibers Composition

This notion is reinforced in Fig. 2. The electrical potential due to contraction of all fibers in a motor unit during a single activation is referred to as the Motor Unit Action Potential (MUAP). This MUAP can be recorded by using electrodes placed on the surface of the skin above the muscle. Also, a muscle is not typically excited by only one action potential. In order to hold a contraction for any length of time, the motor units must be repeatedly activated. This repeated activation gives rise to a series of MUAPs that can be modeled as a pulse train in classical signal processing terms. This series of MUAPs that is produced is referred to as a Motor Unit Action Potential Train (MUAPT). When the electromyography measured using a surface electrode, the electromyography can be defined as the superposition of numerous MUAPTs firing asynchronously. Fig. 3 reinforces the notion that the superposition of motor unit action potentials gives rise to surface EMG. The surface electromyography signal typically does not exceed 5-10 mV in amplitude with the majority of signal information being contained between the frequencies of 15 and 400 Hz. As a result, the amplitude of the EMG contains a great deal of the signal information which can be modeled as a Gaussian random process. The EMG amplitude can thus be defined as the time-varying standard deviation of the EMG signal and is a measure of the activity level of the muscle under observation.

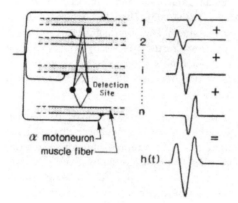

Figure 2. MUAP with Phase shifted from the other muscle fibers

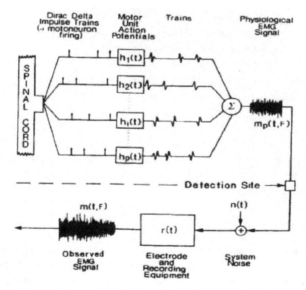

Figure 3. Superposition of Motor Unit Action Potential Gives Rise to Surface EM

3. Prosthetic limb developments

As previously discussed EMG signals provide a non-invasive measure of ongoing muscle activity. Therefore, EMG signals can be potentially used for controlling robotic prosthetic devices. Most prosthetic devices that are currently available usually only have one degree-of-freedom. As a result, these devices provide nowhere near the amount of control as the original limb which they are intending to replace. Through clinical research, it has been shown that amputees and partially paralyzed individuals typically have intact muscles that they can exercise varying degrees of control over. As a result, research is being conducted in regards to utilizing the signals from these intact muscles to control robotic devices with multiple degrees of freedom (Beau 2005). The EMG has been used in two manners in the area of prosthetic limb development. The first approach is for the subject to exert a force with a particular muscle. This force results in a steady-state EMG signal amplitude estimate. A degree of freedom of a robotic limb is then moved in proportion to the EMG amplitude. This described approach is used in the control of a standard prosthetic gripper that has one degree-of-freedom (Beau 2005).

The second manner that EMG signals are used involves discrete actions. When a discrete action is performed, such as the quick movement of the hand or arm, the surface EMG is obtained from various muscle cites. The temporal structure of the transient EMG activity is then analyzed. Upon analyzing the transient EMG activity, various movements can be classified. Hence, EMG signals can be used in the development of advanced prosthetic devices that have various degrees-of-freedom.

4. Muscle anatomy

Agonist-antagonist muscles exist in many human joint. Such human joint is usually activated by many muscles .The following is a summary of the muscles that are responsible for the movement of the arm, wrist, and hand. Abduction of the arm is performed by the deltoid. Human elbow is mainly actuated by two antagonist muscles: biceps and triceps, although it consists of more muscles. Consequently, biceps and a part triceps are bi-particular muscles. By adjusting the amount of force generated by these muscles, the elbow angle and impedance can be arbitrary controlled (Kiguchi et al., 2001). Contraction of the biceps brachii flexes the elbow. Contraction of triceps brachii extends the elbow. Most of the muscles that move the forearm and hand originate within the forearm. The extensor carpi radialis produces extension and abduction of the wrist. The flexor carpi ulnaris flexes and adducts the wrist (Elliott,1998).

5. Feature parameters

EMG classification is one of the most difficult pattern recognition problems because there exist large variations in EMG features. Especially, it is difficult to extract useful features from the residual muscle of an amputee. So far, many researches proposed many kinds of EMG feature to classify posture and they showed good performance. However, how to select a feature subset with the Best discrimination ability from those features is still an issue for classifying EMG signals (Huang et al., 2003). The success of any pattern classification system depends almost entirely on the choice of features used to represent the raw signals. It is desirable to use multiple feature parameters for EMG pattern classification since it is very difficult to extract a feature parameter which reflects the unique feature of the measured signals to a motion command perfectly. But the inclusion of an additional feature parameter with a small separability may degrade overall pattern recognition performance. The feature parameters of EMG signal are listed in Table .1 .

Feature Parameters (Phinyomark & Baraani ,2009)	
1. Integrated EMG	$IEMG = \sum_{n=1}^{N} \lvert h_n \rvert$
2. Mean Absolute Value	$MAV = \dfrac{1}{N} \sum_{n=1}^{N} \lvert h_n \rvert$
3. Modified Mean Absolute Value	$MMAV = \dfrac{1}{N} \sum_{n=1}^{N} \lvert h_n \rvert W_n \qquad W_x = \begin{cases} 1 & 0.25N \le n \le 0.75N \\ 0.5 & otherwise \end{cases}$
4. Variance of EMG	$VAR = \dfrac{1}{N-1} \sum_{n=1}^{N} h_n^2$
5. Waveform Length	$WL = \sum_{n=1}^{N-1} \lvert h_{n+1} - h_n \rvert$
6. Wilson Amplitude(WAMP)	$WAMP = \sum_{n=1}^{N-1} f(\lvert h_{n+1} - h_n \rvert), \quad f(x) = \begin{cases} 1 & x \ge threshold \\ 0 & otherwise \end{cases}$

Table 1. Feature Parameters of EMG signal

The MATLAB code of this action is:

```
%% program of Building Data Base
function data_base =build_data_base
global mscl1 mscl2 mscl3 mscl4 mscl5
ths=50;interval=1600;
IIEMGT=IEMGT';IIEMGT=IIEMGT(:);
VVARR=VARR';VVARR=VVARR(:);
MMAV=MAV';MMAV=MMAV(:);
MMMAVT1=MMAV1';MMMAVT1=MMMAVT1(:);
WWAMPT=(WAMP(ths))';WWAMPT=WWAMPT(:);
WLTT=WL'; WLTT=WLTT(:);
data_base =[IIEMGT';VVARR';MMAV';MMMAVT1';WWAMPT';WLTT'];
```

6. K-nearest neighbor (KNN) algorithm

The K-nearest neighbor (KNN) classification rule is one of the most well-known and widely used nonparametric pattern classification methods. Its simplicity and effectiveness have led it to be widely used in a large number of classification problems. When there is little or no prior knowledge about the distribution of the data, the KNN method should be one of the first choices for classification. It is a powerful non-parametric classification system which bypasses the problem of probability densities completely.

Nearest Neighbor (NN) is a "lazy" learning method because training data is not preprocessed in any way. The class assigned to a pattern is the class of the nearest pattern known to the system, measured in terms of a distance defined on the feature (attribute) space. On this space, each pattern defines a region (called its Voronoi region). When distance is the classical Euclidean distance, Voronoi regions are delimited by linear borders. To improve over 1-NN classification, more than one neighbor may be used to determine the class of a pattern (K-NN) or distances other than the Euclidean may be used. The KNN rule classifies χ by assigning it the label most frequently represented among the K nearest samples; this means that, a decision is made by examining the labels on the K-nearest neighbors and taking a vote KNN classification was developed from the need to perform discriminate analysis when reliable parametric estimates of probability densities are unknown or difficult to determine (Parvin et al., 2008).

 K-NN is the most usable classification algorithm. This algorithm operation is based on comparing a given new record with training records and finding training records that are similar to it. It searches the space for the k training records that are nearest to the new record as the new record neighbors. In this algorithm nearest is defined in terms of a distance metric such as Euclidean distance. Euclidean distance between two records (or two points in n-dimensional space) is defined by:

If $\chi_1 = (\chi_{11}, \chi_{12}, ..., \chi_{1n})$ and $\chi_2 = (\chi_{21}, \chi_{22}, ..., \chi_{2n})$ then

$$dist(\chi_1, \chi_2) = \sqrt{\sum_{i=1}^{n} (\chi_{1i} - \chi_{2i})^2} \tag{1}$$

Where χ_1 and χ_2 are two records with n attributes. This Formula measures the distance between two patterns χ_1 and χ_2 (Moradian & Baraani, 2009). The K-nearest neighbor classifier is a supervised learning algorithm where the result of a new instance query is classified based on majority of the K-nearest neighbor category. The training samples are described by n-dimensional numeric attributes. Each sample represents a point in an n-dimensional pattern space. In this way, all of the training samples are stored in an n-dimensional pattern space.

The following discussion introduces an example demonstrating the general concept of this algorithm in detail. The K nearest neighbor algorithm is very simple. It works based on minimum distance from the query instance to the training samples to determine the nearest neighbors. After we gather K nearest neighbors, we take simple majority of these K-nearest neighbors to be the prediction of the query instance. The data for KNN algorithm consists of several multivariate attributes names that will be used to classify the object Y. Suppose that the K factor is set to be equal to 8 (there are 8 nearest neighbors) as a parameter of this algorithm. Then the distance between the query instance and all the training samples is computed. Because there are only quantitative , the next step is to find the K-nearest neighbors. All training samples are included as nearest neighbors if the distance of this training sample to the query is less than or equal to the Kth smallest distance. In other words, the distances are sorted of all training samples to the query and determine the Kth minimum distance. The unknown sample is assigned the most common class among its k nearest neighbors. As illustrated above, it is necessary to find the distances between the query and all training samples. These K training samples are the closest k nearest neighbors for the unknown sample. Closeness is defined in terms of Euclidean distance (Bawaneh et al., 2008).

Let us consider a set of patterns $\chi = \{\chi_1, ..., \chi_N\} \subseteq R^P$ of known classification where each pattern belongs to one of the classes $CR = \{CR_1, CR_2, ..., CR_S\}$. The nearest neighbor (NN) classification rule assigns a pattern Z of unknown classification to the class of its nearest neighbor, where $\chi_i \in \chi$ is the nearest neighbor to Z if

$$Dist(\chi_i, Z) = \min\{Dist(\chi_l, Z) \quad l = 1, 2, ..., N\} \tag{2}$$

Dist is the Euclidean distance between two patterns in R^P . This scheme is called the 1-NN rule since it classifies a pattern based on only one neighbor of Z. The k-NN rule considers the k-nearest neighbors of Z and uses the majority rule. Let t_l where l=1, 2,..,s be the number of neighbors from class l in the k-nearest neighbors of Z (Pal & Ghosh, 2001).

$$\sum_{l=1}^{s} t_l = k \tag{3}$$

Then Z is assigned to class j if

$$t = \underbrace{Max\{t_l\}}_{l} \tag{4}$$

Here is step by step on how to compute KNN algorithm:

1. Determine parameter K = number of nearest neighbors.
2. Calculate the distance between the query-instance and all the training samples.
3. Sort the distance and determine nearest neighbors based on the K-th minimum distance.
4. Gather the category Y of the nearest neighbors.
5. Use simple majority of the category of nearest neighbors as the prediction value of the query instance.These steps are summarized in Fig.4.

The MATLAB program of K-NN is :

```
%%%%  main program of KNN
Dst=dist(IF,DB);nn=6;[a ,b]=sort(Dst);
st=floor(b/nn)+1;
kk=15;y=st(1:kk)';x=ones(length(y),1);
a1= y ==1;b1=sum(x(a1));
a2= y ==2;b2=sum(x(a2));
a3= y ==3;b3=sum(x(a3));
a4= y ==4;b4=sum(x(a4));
a5= y ==5;b5=sum(x(a5));
bb=[b1 b2 b3 b4 b5];
[a ,b]=sort(bb);af=fliplr(a);bf=fliplr(b);
result=bf(1)
```

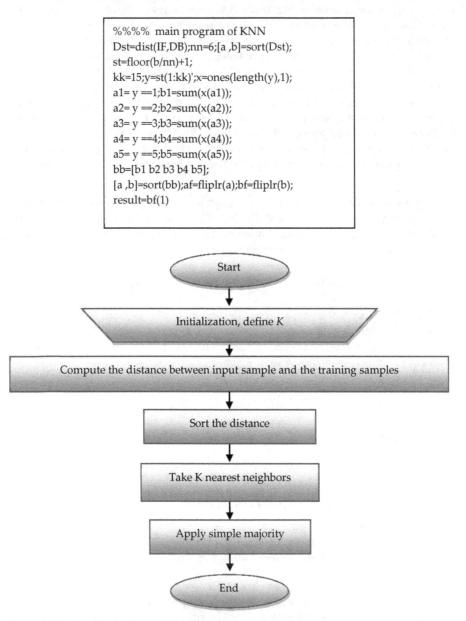

Figure 4. Flowchart for the K- nearest neighbors

7. Measurement of Real EMG signal

EMG signal has two main sources, one of them is measured real EMG and the other one is generated EMG by EMG Simulator. Every one of them has advantage and disadvantage with respect to accuracy and reliability. There are many problems in real measurement system as follows: The first stage is the sensor of EMG signal (electrodes), there are two problems related with the considered structure. The first problem related with the electrode types, that is a needle type. This problem can be summarized as follows: the procedure for using this type by inserting the needle in proper placement on muscle to touch the fiber and sensing the EMG signal. One disadvantage of this needle type is caused high pain to human and it has side affect if using for long times, and it is used only with up normal muscle to check the activity or response of nerve that supply this muscle. Another problem is fixing the needle on the skin, where at any movement of muscle the needle will go out. To overcome the above mentioned problems, the needle may be replaced by either surface electrode or integral surface electrode. The main advantage for using the needle electrode is the amplitude of measured signal where it is better than using another types. In the needle case, the EMG signal is measured directly from MU. The second problem of obtaining EMG signals measured by a needle is only one channel exist for measuring in the same time. This is huge problem in the design where it needs number of channels equal to number of muscles that caused the required recognized movements. If one likes to recognize the wrist joint movement he needs four channels. To overcome the problems in real measuring system, the user can use the generation of EMG signal by EMG simulator.

8. Simulation for EMG signal generation (EMG simulator)

The best modeling of clinical EMG signals was achieved in algorithm by A. Hamilton and D. W. Stashuk at 2005 (Hamilton & Stashuk ,2005). This algorithm is simulated by using MATLAB software and using the GUI approach to get full mathematical simulated model for generating real EMG signal of a specific human arm muscle as shown in Fig. 5 .

This simulator has many options used with rearrangement to generate EMG signal for human arm muscle. The option of the simulator can be summarized as:

Muscle: This popup shows the muscle being simulated. One can select from the list (which adding for human arm muscles), of already defined muscles or select "Custom." to define a new one. Clicking the edit button allows one to modify the muscle parameters. Helping for specification of human arm muscles is added to this window to help the user to generate EMG data more nearest to clinical data, Fig. 6 shows the window for this option.

Electrode: This popup shows the electrode being simulated. The user can select from the list of already defined electrodes or select "Custom..." to define a new one. Clicking the edit button allows the user to modify the electrode parameters. The "Electrode" panel allows the user to save new or modified sets of electrode parameters. Selecting "Multiple Electrodes" allows the user to simulate simultaneous recordings from more than one electrode. Select "Add" from the number popup to add a new electrode. Each electrode can be of a different type. If the user specifies multiple electrodes, then the program creates separate data files for each electrode. The signal from the first electrode is still named filename.dat, and the signals from the other electrodes are named filenameI.dat, where "I" is the electrode number. Fig .7 shows the window for this option.

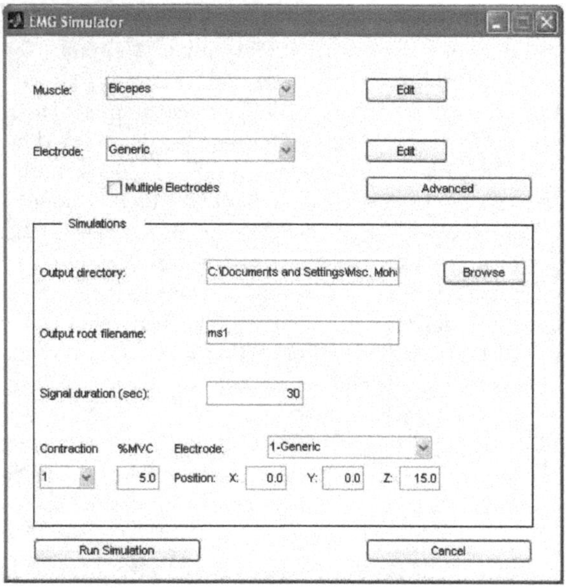

Figure 5. The EMG Signal Simulator.

Advanced: This allows the user to specify some advanced simulation preferences. Include all units: This causes the firing patterns of all the active motor units to be included in the annotation file, not just the ones closest to the electrode.

Output directory: Specifies the directory in which to write the data files. The default directory is the data subdirectory in the simulator directory.

Output root filename: Specifies the root filename for the output files.

Signal duration: Specifies the length of each signal, in seconds.

Contraction: Selects a contraction. To add additional contractions select "Add" from the popup.

%MVC: Specifies the contractile level for the selected contraction.

Position: Specifies the x, y, and z electrode locations (in mm) for the selected contraction. The z coordinate is the distance from the muscle endplate along the muscle axis. Use the "electrode" popup to specify locations for multiple electrodes. Note that you can specify different locations for each electrode in each contraction.

Delete: Deletes the current contraction.

Run Simulation. Runs the specified set of simulations (one simulation per electrode per contraction). The simulations can take a fair amount of time, depending on the specified signal duration. The trace statements from the simulation routines are displayed in the command window.

Cancel. Quits the simulator and returns to MATLAB.

After press the " Run Simulation " button , each simulation may take a minute or more. The program creates the following files for each contraction:

Filename.dat →→ EMG signal, Filename.hea →→ header file (allows signals to be read by software).,Filename.eaf. →→ annotation file, These files can be used to analysis the EMG signal. The real value of the muscle parameters can be obtained by studying the anatomy of muscles in detail. Depending on the practical data obtained from medical table and consultation with the specialist, the muscle parameters adopted are as shown in table 2. Fig.5 represents the generation of EMG signal by EMG simulator. There are two choices to get the EMG data. The first one is by EMG simulator with specified values for the parameters of the muscle as shown in figure 6. The second choice is used to produce data of EMG signal by selecting a specific muscle of the human arm as shown in figure 7. The data are calculated by selecting the specification of normal human body as given in table 2

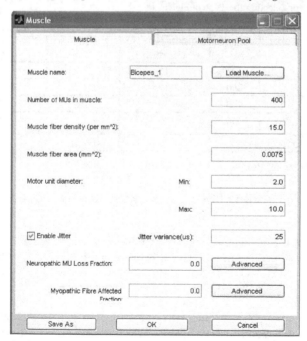

Figure 6. Window for the Selection or Design of Human arm Muscle

Figure 7. Window for Selecting the Type of Electrode

Muscle name	No. of MU	Fiber Density (per mm²)	Fiber Area (mm²)	Range MU diameter (mm)
biceps	400	15	0.0075	2 - 10
triceps	350	10	0.0055	2 – 9
deltoid	450	20	0.0085	3 - 11
extensor carpi radial	250	8	0.0035	1.5 – 8
flexor carpi ulna	100	5	0.0015	2 – 6

Table 2. Standard Parameters of Muscle Human Arm

9. Simulation for reading EMG signals generated by EMG simulator (EMG Lab)

The program, which explains the graphic of the files obtained from the EMG simulator, is called EMGlab (EMGLAB software,2008). This program is built in MATLAB software and the description of run EMGlab in MATLAB command window as follows. The program runs in a single MATLAB window, which is divided into five panels: At the top is the signal panel, which displays a segment of the EMG signal. Below that is the template panel, which displays the MUAP templates. Below that on the left is the firing panel, which displays the firing patterns of the identified MUs. To the right is the close-up panel, which displays a section of the EMG signal at an expanded scale. At the very bottom is the navigation panel which displays a thumbnail of the EMG signal. The buttons on the edges of the panels are used to change the display characteristics .

Fig. 8 shows the output of EMGlab with data of EMG signal. It receives the data that are generated by EMG simulator and the practical measured data and explain the decomposition of the signal and register the data of this signal. The inserted symbols in the window are:

+, - zoom in or out vertically

<, > scroll left or right, and | |, | | zoom in or out horizontally

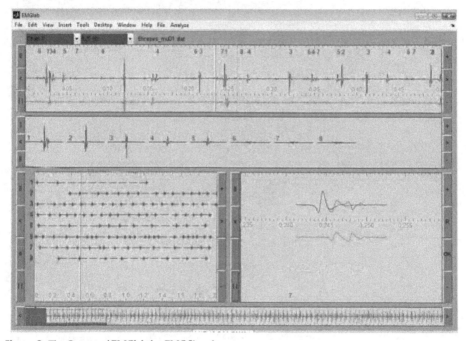

Figure 8. The Output of EMGlab for EMG Signal

10. Human arm movements recognition based on k-nearest neighbor algorithm

The discrimination of the EMG signal into the correct class of movement is a fundamental element of the system. The precision of a classifier lies on its capability to give the correct answers in spite of some inaccuracies that may occur during the process of detection of the EMG signal.

To improve precision of a classifier with decrease of the training time, a recognition system based K-NN algorithm is used. The success of any pattern classification system depends almost entirely on the choice of features used to represent the raw signals. In the proposed system multiple feature parameters for EMG pattern classification are used since it is very difficult to extract a feature parameter which reflects the unique feature of the measured signals to a motion command perfectly.

Five kinds of arm motion are recognized: Abduction of the arm, flexion the elbow, extension the elbow, extension and abduction of the wrist and flexes and adducts the wrist .These motions are produced by contraction of five muscles. Therefore ,if the EMG signal of muscle is recognized then the specified motion of this muscle is recognized. The proposed method is outlined in Fig. 9 and the stages of proposed system are discussed below:

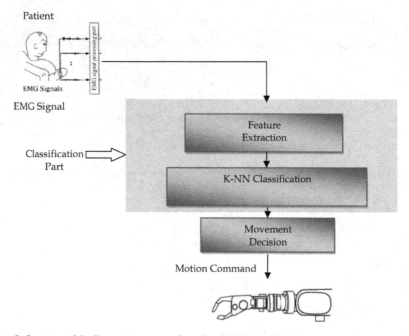

Figure 9. Structure of the Recognition system based on K-NN classifier

10.1. Data bases building with multiple feature parameters

Training of the system involves the partitioning of the feature space to represent different classes of separable motions. In this state, data base is constrained with five muscles (biceps, triceps, deltoid, extensor carpi radialis and flexor carpi ulnaris). This stage has the following steps:

Step 1. Take six frames from each muscle as shown in Fig. 10 to produce thirty frames.

Step 2. Six features (which were introduced in section (4)) are extracted from each frame. In this step thirty vectors are billed as a basic Data Base, each vector has six elements. See Fig.11.

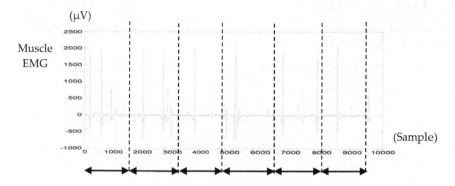

Frame 1 Frame 2 Frame 3 Frame 4 Frame 5 Frame 6

Figure 10. EMG Signal frames.

$$DB_{ij}=\{IEMG_{ij}\ MAV_{ij}\ MMAV_{ij}\ VAR_{ij}\ WAMP_{ij}\ WL_{ij}\} \tag{5}$$

$i=1,\dots,30\ ,j=1,\dots,6$

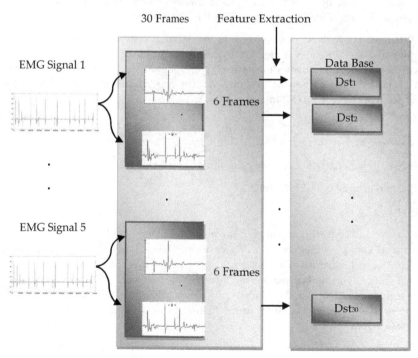

Figure 11. Building Data Base from EMG signals

10.2. Recognition of EMG signals based on k-nearest neighbor algorithm

The data for EMG are generated by EMG simulator then processing will be applied to this signal such as feature extraction.

The recognition system of EMG patterns consists of the following steps:

Step 3. In this step take the feature extraction of input signal to produce Input Feature (IF) which has six elements. Now, there is one vector and it is required to be classified to which type of EMG signal included with thirty frame found in data base, step 2-6 represent K-NN algorithm as shown in Fig. 12.

Step 4. Take Euclidean distance between IF and DB to produce set of distance elements $(Dst_1, Dst_2,…, Dst_{30})$

$$Dst_i = \{ Dist(DB_i, IF) \quad i=1,2,…,30\} \tag{6}$$

Step 5. Take the nearest neighbors to IF by sorting the distance elements ascendant to produce sorted elements $(S_1, S_2,…,S_{30})$, where S_1 is nearest element to IF.

Step 6. Take the first K^{th} elements from sorted elements $(S_1, S_2,…,S_K)$.

Step 7. Assign sorted elements to its original frames of EMG signals.

Step 8. Apply Majority Rule (Which EMG signals has largest number of neighbors from input signal in the K-Nearest Neighbors frames?). The input signal is assigned the most common class of EMG signal among its k nearest neighbors.

As illustrated above, it is necessary to find the distances between the query and all training samples and the closeness is defined in terms of Euclidean distance. Each muscle have specified motion therefore after recognize the EMG signal the command is sent to prosthetic arm to perform the motion of this muscle. The performance index for the Recognition Accuracy (RA) is given by (Momen et al.,2008):

$$RA = \frac{co}{tn} x100 \tag{7}$$

Where: co is the number of correctly classified EMG signals.

tn is the total number of EMG signals.

Case study:

The simulated data are generated from an EMG signal simulator. Several motions are recognized based on classification of five input EMG signals. In the present study, the accuracy for each participant is simply calculated by averaging the performance indices over all movements. To simulate real noise, different noise is considered, i.e. random noise. The noise is added to EMG signals which produce new EMG signal with lower SNR. Now some noised EMG signals are classified using Artificial Neural Network (ANN) and k-Nearest Neighbor algorithm.

Table 3 gives the comparison results of the K-NN with different K values with the back propagation neural network (BP-NN). The structure of BP-NN is (6-20-5). Where the input nodes equal to the number of the features and output nods equal to the number of classified EMG signals.

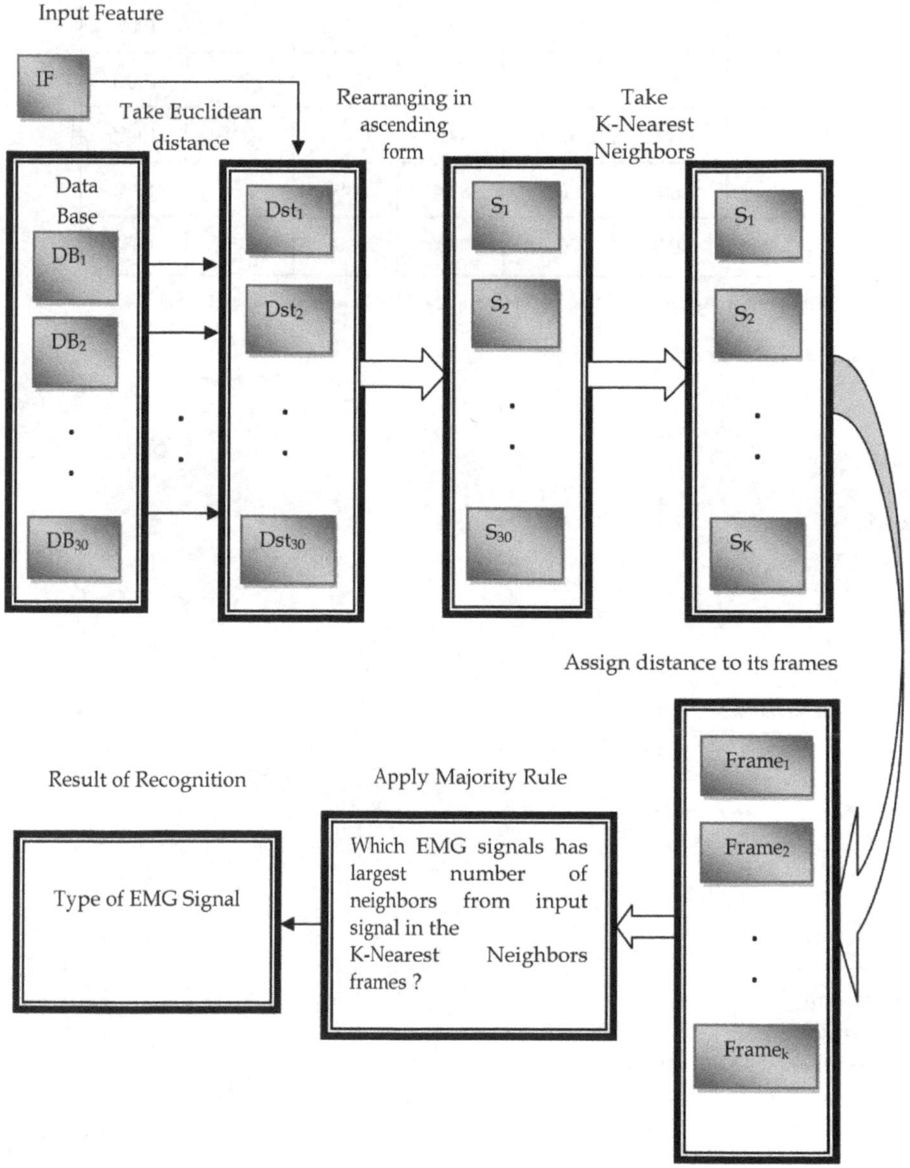

Input Feature

Figure 12. K-NN Classification Process

SNR (dB)	ANN	K-NN K=7	K-NN K=9	K-NN K=13	K-NN K=15	K-NN K=17
25	83%	100%	100%	100%	100%	100%
11	66%	100%	100%	100%	100%	100%
9	66%	100%	100%	100%	100%	100%
7	66%	80%	83%	88%	90%	83%
5	50%	70%	73%	80%	83%	80%

Table 3. Recognition Accuracy of Neural Network and K-NN Method with Noisy Signal.

The MATLAB program is given below:

```
%%%%%%% main program of EMG recognition
clear
clc
load mscl2
%--------------------
%  test signal
%--------------------
 interval=1600;
ths=50;v=120;
DB=build_data_base;
%%%%%%%%% chose second EMG signal as test signal with added noise
x=mscl2(1,:);
xold=x;
x = x'+v*randn(size((x')));
r = SNR(x, xold');
 %--------------------
%  featur extraction
%--------------------
 mx=mean(abs(x));
vx=var(abs(x));
mavx=mean(abs(x))/interval;
w=.5*ones(1,interval);w(1,.25*interval:.75*interval)=1;
mmavt1=mean((w.*abs(x'))')/interval;
wwamp=WAMPsingle(x',ths);
wl=Wlsingle(x');
IF=[mx vx mavx mmavt1 wwamp wl];
```

```
%--------------------
% apply k-nn
%--------------------
Dst=dist(IF,DB);
nn=6;
[a ,b]=sort(Dst);
st=floor(b/nn)+1;
kk=15;
Frame=st(1:kk)';
x=ones(length(Frame),1);
a1= Frame ==1;
b1=sum(x(a1));
a2= Frame ==2;
b2=sum(x(a2));
a3= Frame ==3;
b3=sum(x(a3));
a4= Frame ==4;
b4=sum(x(a4));
a5= Frame ==5;
b5=sum(x(a5));
bb=[b1 b2 b3 b4 b5];
[a ,b]=sort(bb);
af=fliplr(a);bf=fliplr(b);
result=bf(1)
```

11. Proposed model and vr simulation for artificial human arm

The simulator was built using MATLAB with Virtual Reality Toolbox. MATLAB provides powerful engineering tool including frequently used mathematical functions. It is easy to implement control algorithm including visualization of data used in the algorithm. In addition, by using Virtual Reality Toolbox, it is convenient to treat 3D objects defined with Virtual Reality Modeling Language (VRML). Thus, it is possible to build a simulator within a relatively short period. virtual reality is a system which allows one or more users to move and react in a computer generated environment. The basic VR systems allow the user to visual information using computer screens. The simulation contain two part ,first ,building model for human arm in VRML, second, call and run the model of human arm using virtual reality toolbox in the MATLAB.

To realize the VRML model for Human arm save the file as HumanArm.wrl file, which is the file format for Virtual Reality software, the VRML model of the human arm is designed in V-Realm Builder 2.0 . Fig.13 presents the VRML model of the human arm.

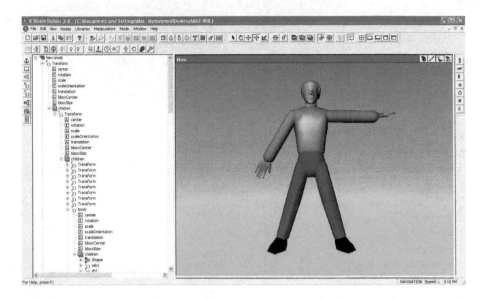

Figure 13. The VRML model of the Human arm

The MATLAB program is given as:

```
%% control of human arm as MATLAB code
world=vrworld('HumanArm.wrl', 'new');
open(world);
fig=vrfigure(world);
elbow=vrnode(world, 'elbow');
k=0;
for theta=pi/2:-pi/100:0
  k=k+1;
  x(k)=theta;
  pause(0.05)
  elbow.rotation=[0 0 theta theta];
  vrdrawnow;
end
```

12. EMG simulator based GUI

The method of recognition based K-NN algorithm and technique of virtual reality are introduced, now the simulation which connect between the EMG recognition system and virtual reality is presented.

From MATLAB, the user can set the positions and properties of VRML objects, create callbacks from Graphical User Interfaces (GUI), and map data to virtual objects. The user can also view the world with a VRML viewer, determine its structure, and assign new values to all available nodes and their fields. The Virtual Reality Toolbox includes functions for retrieving and changing the virtual world properties and for saving the VRML files corresponding to the actual structure of a virtual world. MATLAB provides communication for control and manipulation of virtual reality objects using MATLAB objects.

This part concerns with the simulation of human arm movement using EMG Signal as shown in the fig 14 .

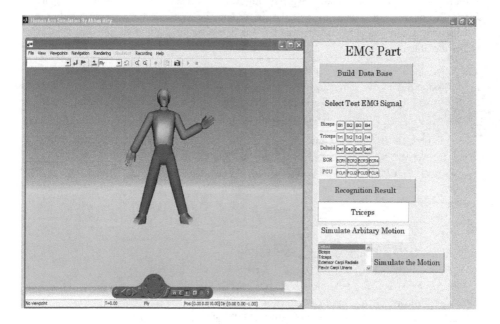

Figure 14. Recognition Result Windows

It has the following stages:

6. **Build Data Base**: This stage represents the training state in which data base is constrained with five muscles (biceps, triceps, deltoid, extensor Carpi radialis and flexor carpi ulnaris). More details found in subsection (10.1).
7. **Select Test EMG Signal**: Select the type of EMG signal to recognize with added noise to test the equality of proposed method with different noise level. Five muscle are tested (biceps,triceps, deltoid, extensor carpi radialis and flexor carpi ulnaris)are tested with four level of noise to produce four noised EMG signals for each muscle.

8. **Recognition Result:** In this stat the K-NN algorithm is applied to recognize the EMG signal in order to produce the motion provided by this EMG signal in virtual reality. The details of this stage can be found in subsection (10.2).
9. **Simulate Arbitrary Motion:** In this part of simulation any motion can be chosen by selecting the muscles which produce this motion.
10. **Simulate the Motion:** After pressing on this button the human arm is moves in the virtual reality.

The recognition algorithm consists of following steps. Firstly, a nearest neighbor algorithm is applied to compute the distance between the feature extraction of input motion to be recognized and each of the 30 feature extraction representing the recognizable motions, which were collected in a Data Base. The algorithm then sorts the motion indexes starting from the nearest candidate in descending order. The distance between two patterns is computed in the feature extraction as the Euclidean distance between the two vectors of feature extraction.

The basic motions types are executed to test the model's performance: a Abduction of the arm, flexion the elbow, extension the elbow, extension and abduction of the wrist and flexes and adducts the wrist. For all motions, the system will receive an EMG signal of human arm.The MATLAB program, which executes this algorithm, is given as:

```
function EMGGUI(hObject,eventdata)
 fh2 = figure('MenuBar','none','Name',' Artificial Human Arm Driven by EMG Signal
','NumberTitle','off','Position',[0 0 1300 800]);
 v1=10;
 v2=20;
 v3=30;
 v4=200;
 ph = uipanel('Parent',fh2,'Position',[.65 .05 .3 .9]);
 e1 = uicontrol(fh2,'style','text','string','EMG Part','Position',[875 625 250
75],'FontName','Century Schoolbook','FontSize',24);
 database = uicontrol(fh2,'style','pushbutton','string','Build Data Base
','BackgroundColor','c','Position', [850 600 260 50],'callback',@Data_Base,'FontName','Century
Schoolbook','FontSize',14);
 e2 = uicontrol(fh2,'style','text','string','Select Test EMG Signal ','Position',[850 500 250
60],'FontName','Century Schoolbook','FontSize',14);
 XX7=480;
 e3 = uicontrol(fh2,'style','text','string','Biceps','Position',  [850 XX7 50
25],'BackgroundColor','Y','FontName','Century Schoolbook','FontSize',10);
 e4 = uicontrol(fh2,'style','pushbutton','string','Bi1','Position', [900 XX7 25
25],'callback',@Biceps1);
 e5 = uicontrol(fh2,'style','pushbutton','string','Bi2','Position', [925 XX7 25
25],'callback',@Biceps2);
```

e6 = uicontrol(fh2,'style','pushbutton','string','Bi3','Position', [950 XX7 25
25],'callback',@Biceps3);

e7 = uicontrol(fh2,'style','pushbutton','string','Bi4','Position', [975 XX7 25
25],'callback',@Biceps4);

XX1=XX7-30;

e8 = uicontrol(fh2,'style','text','string','Triceps','Position', [850 XX1 50
25],'BackgroundColor','Y','FontName','Century Schoolbook','FontSize',10);

e9 = uicontrol(fh2,'style','pushbutton','string','Tr1','Position', [900 XX1 25
25],'callback',@Triceps1);

e10 = uicontrol(fh2,'style','pushbutton','string','Tr2','Position', [925 XX1 25
25],'callback',@Triceps2);

e11 = uicontrol(fh2,'style','pushbutton','string','Tr3','Position', [950 XX1 25
25],'callback',@Triceps3);

e12 = uicontrol(fh2,'style','pushbutton','string','Tr4','Position', [975 XX1 25
25],'callback',@Triceps4);

XX2=XX1-30;

e13 = uicontrol(fh2,'style','text','string','Deltoid','Position', [850 XX2 50
25],'BackgroundColor','Y','FontName','Century Schoolbook','FontSize',10);

e14 = uicontrol(fh2,'style','pushbutton','string','De1','Position', [900 XX2 25
25],'callback',@Deltoid1);

e15 = uicontrol(fh2,'style','pushbutton','string','De2','Position', [925 XX2 25
25],'callback',@Deltoid2);

e16 = uicontrol(fh2,'style','pushbutton','string','De3','Position', [950 XX2 25
25],'callback',@Deltoid3);

e17 = uicontrol(fh2,'style','pushbutton','string','De4','Position', [975 XX2 25
25],'callback',@Deltoid4);

XX3=XX2-30;

e18 = uicontrol(fh2,'style','text','string','ECR','Position',   [850 XX3 50
25],'BackgroundColor','Y','FontName','Century Schoolbook','FontSize',10);

e19 = uicontrol(fh2,'style','pushbutton','string','ECR1','Position', [900 XX3 30
25],'callback',@ECR1);

e20 = uicontrol(fh2,'style','pushbutton','string','ECR2','Position', [930 XX3 30
25],'callback',@ECR2);

e21 = uicontrol(fh2,'style','pushbutton','string','ECR3','Position', [960 XX3 30
25],'callback',@ECR3);

e22 = uicontrol(fh2,'style','pushbutton','string','ECR4','Position', [990 XX3 30
25],'callback',@ECR4);

XX4=XX3-30;

e23 = uicontrol(fh2,'style','text','string','FCU','Position',   [850 XX4 50
25],'BackgroundColor','Y','FontName','Century Schoolbook','FontSize',10);

e24 = uicontrol(fh2,'style','pushbutton','string','FCU1','Position', [900 XX4 30
25],'callback',@FCU1);

```
e25 = uicontrol(fh2,'style','pushbutton','string','FCU2','Position', [930 XX4 30
25],'callback',@FCU2);
e26 = uicontrol(fh2,'style','pushbutton','string','FCU3','Position', [960 XX4 30
25],'callback',@FCU3);
e27 = uicontrol(fh2,'style','pushbutton','string','FCU4','Position', [990 XX4 30
25],'callback',@FCU4);
 result1 = uicontrol(fh2,'style','pushbutton','string','Recognition Result
','BackgroundColor','c','callback',@test,'Position',[850 300 270 60],'FontName','Century
Schoolbook','FontSize',14);
result2 = uicontrol(fh2,'style','edit','Position',[850 250 250 50],'FontName','Century
Schoolbook','FontSize',14,'BackgroundColor','W');
e28 = uicontrol(fh2,'style','text','string','Simulate Arbitary Motion
','BackgroundColor','y','Position',[850 200 250 40],'FontName','Century
Schoolbook','FontSize',14);
e29 = uicontrol(fh2,'Style','listbox','String',{'Deltoid','Biceps','Triceps','Extensor Carpi
Radialis','Flexor Carpi Ulnaris'},'Max',5,'Min',0,'Value',[1],'Position',[850 125 150 70]);
e30 = uicontrol(fh2,'style','pushbutton','string','Simulate the Motion
','callback',@simulat_motion,'BackgroundColor','c','Position',[1000 125 200
50],'FontName','Century Schoolbook','FontSize',14);
 end
```

After execution of this program, its results will be given as in Fig. 14 .

As an examples the progress of the Abduction of the arm can be observed in Fig. 15.

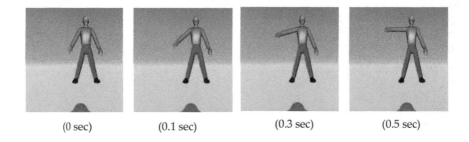

(0 sec)   (0.1 sec)   (0.3 sec)   (0.5 sec)

Figure 15. Abduction of the arm movements

The execution of the elbow flexion can be observed in Fig. 16 along with several of the arm states. At the initial position, the human arm is in extension. When flexion begins, the human arm opposition angle is controlled to the right position for the elbow flexion. After receiving the elbow flexion signal, the structure of the arm causes its joints to flex in a natural motion

The block diagram of the package for the human arm simulator is shown in Fig. 17. It enables testing of different control algorithms. The simulator uses MATLAB as this language both provides a virtual reality toolbox and an extensive mathematical library.

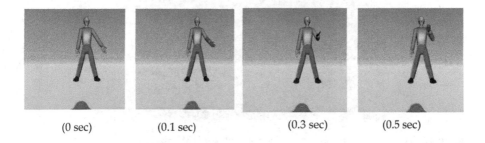

(0 sec)   (0.1 sec)   (0.3 sec)   (0.5 sec)

Figure 16. Flexion of the elbow movements.

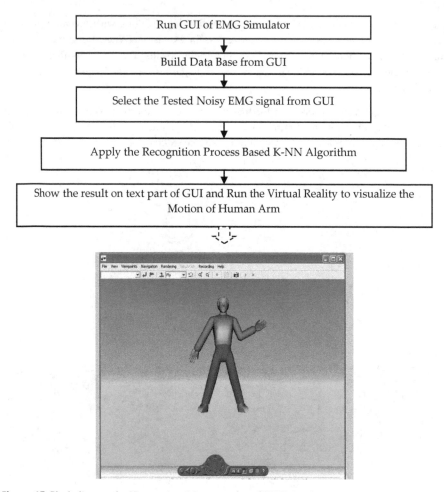

Figure 17. Block diagram for Human Arm Movement based EMG signal

13. Conclusions

In this chapter the motion classification simulations are carried out, in order to evaluate classification performance of the human arm movements recognition based on k-Nearest Neighbor algorithm. The simulated data were generated from an EMG signal simulator. Several motions are recognized based on classification of five input EMG signals. In the present study, the accuracy for each participant was simply calculated by averaging the performance indices over all movements.

The results illustrate that the recognition using K-NN presents better results than artificial neural network in term of recognition accuracy as shown Table 2. This table shows the result of recognition with noisy signal having lower SNR for the neural network and different values of k. It can be found that the K-NN method with the value of k=15 achieves better performance than neural network method and K-NN with the other values of k. The reason of successful of K-NN algorithm that, the input signal may be similar to other frames of EMG signal due to the effect of the noise, therefore ,it is necessary to check the input EMG signal with more frames of EMG signal to give good recognition result .

The possible reason for the poor results of ANN may be due to the simple decision function realized by this method. EMG signal has variation with time therefore necessary to check the input signal with more frame for each muscle as shown in K-NN which provides more accuracy in the recognition. The choice multiple features provide more information about the input signal, failer one of these features can be repaired by the other features.

This chapter also presents the simulation of human arm motion in virtual reality to test the algorithm of EMG recognition. It can be concluded that, The Virtual Reality is useful to test the viability of designs before the implementation phase on a virtual reality prototype. It found that, MATLAB a convenient platform for development of computational algorithms, and with the visualization functions of MATLAB Ver.R2009a a reasonable amount of visualization techniques are available.

Author details

Mohammed Z. Al-Faiz
Computer Engineering Department, Al-Nahrain University, Baghdad, Iraq

Abbas H. Miry
Electrical Engineering Department, AL-Mustansiriyah University, Baghdad, Iraq

14. References

Bawaneh, M.; Alkoffash, M. & Rabea, A.(2000). Arabic Text Classification using K-NN and Naive Bayes, *Journal of Computer Science*. ISSN 1549-3636, Vol.4 No.7, pp: 600-605.

Beau C. (2005), Real-Time Classification of Electromyographic Signals for Robotic Control, *Technical Report No. 2005-03-05, Department of Computer Science, University of Washington*

Bu, N.; Okamoto, M. & Tsuji, T. (2009).A Hybrid Motion Classification Approach for EMG-Based Human–Robot Interfaces Using Bayesian and Neural Networks, *IEEE Trans. on Robot.* Vol. 23, No. 3, pp. 502–511.

Elliott, R. (1998).Feature Extraction Techniques for Grasp Classification ", *Master Thesis, University of Canterbury.*

EMGLAB software Version 0.9 User's Guide, "The MathWorks, at www.mathworks.com, 2008.

Hamilton, A. & Stashuk, D. W. (2005).Physiologically based simulation of clinical EMG signals, *IEEE Trans. Biomed. Eng.,* Vol. 52, No. 2, PP:171-183, 2005.

Huang, H.; Liu, Y. & Wong, C.(2003).Automatic EMG Feature Evaluation for Controlling a
    Prosthetic Hand Using a Supervised Feature Mining Method :An Intelligent Approach,
    International Conference on Robotics & Automation, Taiwan, IEEE, pp:220-225, 2003.

Kiguchi, K.; Watanabe, S.; Izumi, K. & Fukuda, T. (2001).An Exoskeletal Robot for Human
    Elbow Motion Support—Sensor Fusion, Adaptation, and Control, *IEEE Trans on System,
    Man and Cybernetics*, Vol. 31, No.3, pp:353-361.

Momen K.; Krishnan, S. & Chau, T. (2007). Real-Time Classification of Forearm
    Electromyographic Signals Corresponding to User-Selected Intentional Movements for
    Multifunction Prosthesis Control, *IEEE Trans on Neural System and Rehabilitation
    Engineering*, Vol. 15, No. 4, pp:535-542.

Moradian, M. & Baraani, A.(2009). KNNBA: K-Nearest-Neighbor-Based-Association
    Algorithm. *Journal of Theoretical and Applied Information Technology*, Vol.6. No. 1, pp 123 –
    129.

Pal, N. & Ghosh, S. (2001).Some Classification Algorithms Integrating Dempster–Shafer
    Theory of Evidence with the Rank Nearest Neighbor Rules, *IEEE Trans on Systems, Man,
    and Cybernetics—Part A*, Vol. 31, No. 1, pp: 59-66.

Park, S. & Lee, S. (1998). EMG Pattern Recognition Based on Artificial Intelligence
    Techniques, *IEEE Trans on Rehabilitation Engineering*, Vol. 6, No. 4, pp:400-405.

Parvin, H; Alizadeh, H. & Bidgoli, B. (2008). MKNN: Modified K-Nearest Neighbor,
    Proceedings of the World Congress on Engineering and Computer Science, pp:831-834.

Perry, J.; Bekey, G. (1981).EMG-force relationships in skeletal muscle." *CRC Critical Rev. in
    Biomed. Eng.*, pp. 1-22.

Phinyomark, A.; Limsakul, C. & Phukpattaranont, P.(2009). A Novel Feature Extraction for
    Robust EMG Pattern Recognition, *Journal of Computing*, ISSN: 2151-9617, Vol.1, No. 1,
    pp:71-80.

Chapter 2

Analysis and Modeling of Clock-Jitter Effects in Delta-Sigma Modulators

Ramy Saad, Sebastian Hoyos and Samuel Palermo

Additional information is available at the end of the chapter

1. Introduction

The quest for higher data rates in state-of-the-art wireless standards and services calls for wideband and high-resolution data-converters in wireless transceivers. While modern integrated circuits (IC) technologies provide high cut-off frequencies (f_T) for transistors and hence allow the operation at higher speeds, the main limitation against increasing speed of operation of data-converters is the problem of clock-jitter. Clock-jitter is a common problem associated with clock generators due to uncertainty in the timing of the clock edges caused by the finite phase-noise (PN) in the generated clock waveform. Particularly, noise components induced by several noise sources in the system providing the clock (e.g. phase-locked loop, PLL) add to the clock waveform and cause uncertainty in the timing of the zero-crossing instants from cycle to cycle. Figure 1 shows a survey chart of the analog-to-digital converter (ADC) implementations reported in IEEE International solid-state circuits conference (ISSCC) and VLSI Symposium since 1997 [1]. The straight lines show the limitation on the achievable signal-to-noise ratio (SNR) by clock-jitter for jitter root-mean square (rms) values of 1ps and 0.1ps. As can be seen from the chart, the performance of most ADCs falls below the line corresponding to 1ps rms jitter, few ADCs reside in the range between 1ps and 0.1ps, and almost all ADC implementations reported so far are beyond the 0.1ps rms jitter line. This means that the main limitation on increasing the ADC performance in terms of SNR and speed is the specification on the clock-jitter of 0.1ps.

Delta-sigma ($\Delta\Sigma$) ADCs are the convenient choice in low power and state-of-the-art multi-standard wireless receivers for two main reasons. First, they trade DSP for relaxed analog circuit complexity. Particularly, $\Delta\Sigma$ ADC implementations span analog and digital domains ($\Delta\Sigma$ pulse density modulation + digital decimation and filtering, as shown in Figure 2) and hence exploit DSP to relax hardware requirements on analog blocks. Thus, the simplified analog part ($\Delta\Sigma$ modulator) and the digital filtering can be efficiently reconfigured to fulfill performance requirements of different standards at minimum power consumption. Second, $\Delta\Sigma$ modulators use oversampling and hence trade speed for resolution. Specifically, for a given $\Delta\Sigma$ modulator and channel bandwidth (BW), higher effective number of bits (ENOB) can be achieved by increasing the oversampling ratio (OSR). This qualifies $\Delta\Sigma$ ADCs to benefit from increasing speeds of operation offered by advanced deep submicron CMOS technologies (maximum cutoff-frequency $f_T > 300\,GHz$ in 45nm [2]) to meet higher resolution requirements for modern and future wireless services at minimum power overhead.

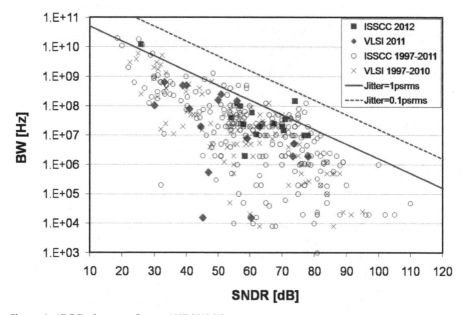

Figure 1. ADC Performance Survey 1997-2012 [1]

Continuous-time (CT) $\Delta\Sigma$ ADCs are widely used in wideband low power wireless receivers [3, 4]. The CT operation of the loop filter relaxes the requirements on the gain-bandwidth product (GBW) of the adopted amplifiers and hence allows the operation at higher speeds or lower power consumption compared to discrete-time (DT) implementations. Also, CT loop filters offer inherent anti-aliasing and thus save the need for explicit anti-aliasing filter before the ADC. The requirements on the sample-and-hold (S/H) circuitry are also relaxed because the sampling is performed after the loop filter and hence the sampling errors experience the maximum attenuation offered by the loop (similar to quantization noise). However, CT $\Delta\Sigma$ modulators suffer from high sensitivity to clock-jitter in the sampling-clock of the digital-to-analog converters (DACs) in the feedback.

In this context, this chapter is intended to provide a comprehensive background and study for the effects of clock-jitter in the sampling-clocks of $\Delta\Sigma$ modulators. Also, Matlab/Simulink models for additive errors induced by clock-jitter in ΔΣ modulators are given so that to help designers characterize the sensitivities of various types of ΔΣ architectures to clock-jitter. The material in this chapter is organized as follows. Section 2 gives a general background about the types of errors caused by clock-jitter in different classes of switched circuits and signal waveforms. The critical sources of jitter induced errors in a ΔΣ loop are identified for DT and CT ΔΣ modulators and a comparison between the two types, in terms of sensitivity to clock-jitter, is done in Section 3. Section 4 provides detailed sensitivity analysis for CT ΔΣ modulators to clock-jitter in the feedback DAC sampling-clock. In Section 5, Simulink models, based on the analysis of Section 4, for the additive errors generated by clock-jitter in CT ΔΣ modulators are shown and the robustness of these models is verified by CT simulations in Matlab/Simulink. Simulations results show good agreement with the theoretical expectations. Finally, conclusions are drawn in Section 6.

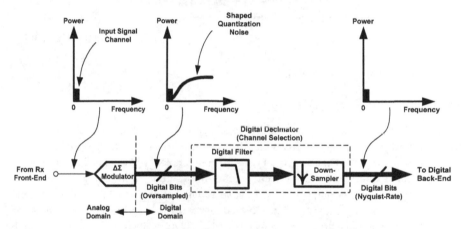

Figure 2. ΔΣ ADC (ΔΣ pulse density modulation + digital decimation and filtering).

2. Jitter problems: Background

Since digital data is always available in DT form, then any process of converting information from analog form to digital bit-stream or vice versa entails sampling. However, the clock signals driving sampling switches suffers clock-jitter due to the noise components that accompany the clock waveform. Figure 3 shows the PN density in a typical voltage-controlled oscillator (VCO)[1]. In the time-domain, the integrated effect of these noise components results in random variations in the phase of the generated clock signal. In data-converters, the problem of clock-jitter is a very critical issue and can significantly deteriorate the achievable SNR by several dBs. The problems resulting from clock-jitter are classified as follows:

---

[1] The design of clock generators and the mechanisms of PN generation in PLLs are not within the scope of the material given in this chapter.

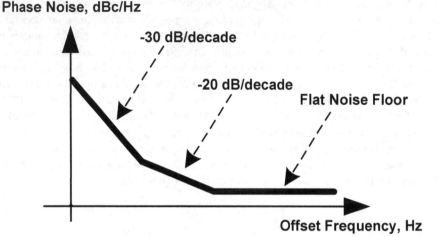

Figure 3. Typical Phase-Noise profile in a VCO.

2.1. Aperture jitter: Voltage sampling errors

In ADCs, it is desirable to convert CT voltage signals into DT form. Figure 4(a) shows a common track-and-hold (T/H) circuit based on a switch driven by a clock signal (sampling-clock) and a sampling capacitor C_S. Errors in the sampled voltage (during the tracking phase) value is one of the most common problems resulting from timing uncertainty Δt (clock-jitter) in the sampling-clock. Particularly, on sampling an input voltage signal, random variations in the timing of the clock edges can result in an incorrect sampled signal, as illustrated in Figure 4(b). This effect is called aperture jitter. The noise induced by aperture jitter can be illustrated as follows. Suppose that a sinusoidal signal $A\,sin(\omega t)$, where A is the amplitude and ω is the angular frequency, is to be sampled using a T/H circuit. Then, the error in the nth sample of the sampled signal due to a timing error $\Delta t(n)$ is given by

$$e(n\,T_s) = A\,\{sin[\omega(n\,T_s + \Delta t(n))] - sin(\omega\,n\,T_s)\}$$

$$\approx A\,\omega\,\Delta t(n)\,cos(n\,T_s). \tag{1}$$

where T_s is the sampling-period. If σ_j^2 is the variance of the timing error Δt, then the error power is given by

$$\sigma_e^2 = E(e^2) = \frac{(A\,\omega\,\sigma_j)^2}{2} \tag{2}$$

Since the signal power of the sinusoid is given by $A^2/2$, the SNR due to aperture jitter is given by

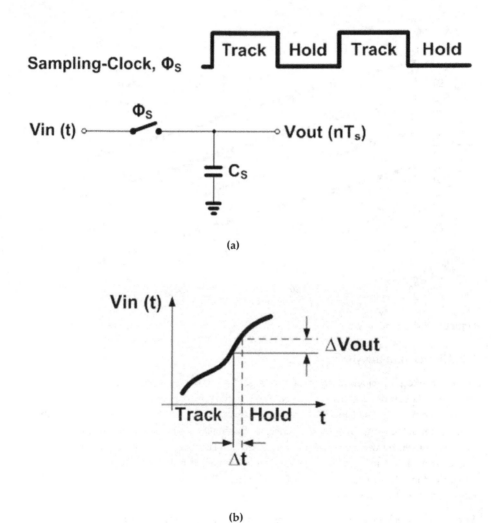

Figure 4. T/H Circuit. (a) Schematic view and clock waveform. (b) Effect of aperture jitter on sampled values.

$$SNR|_{Due\ to\ aperture\ jitter} = 10\ Log\ \left(\frac{1}{\omega^2\sigma_j^2}\right) = 10\ Log\ \left(\frac{1}{4\ \pi^2\ f^2\sigma_j^2}\right) \tag{3}$$

where $f = \omega/2\pi$ is the frequency. From (3) the SNR has the worst value at the edge of the signal band (largest value of frequency, f_{max}). The plots in Figure 5 show the limitation on the achievable SNR vs. the signal frequency due to aperture jitter for different values of the rms jitter σ_j.

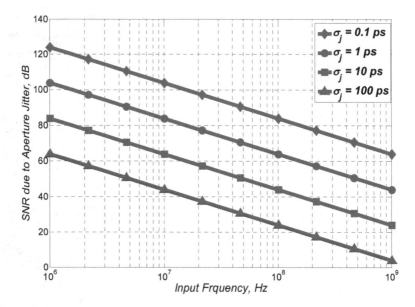

Figure 5. SNR variation with the input frequency due to aperture jitter for different rms jitter values.

2.2. Charge transfer jitter

Another effect of clock-jitter, called charge transfer jitter, shows up in circuits whose operation is based on charge transfer by switching. In particular, switched-capacitor (SC) circuits commonly used in DT ADCs and DACs suffer from charge transfer errors due to clock-jitter in the sampling clocks. Consider the simple non-inverting SC integrator in Figure 6(a). As shown by the time-domain waveforms in Figure 6(b), during integrating phase $\emptyset_2$, the charge stored in a sampling capacitor C_S is transferred to an integrating capacitor C_I through the ON resistance (R_{ON}) of the switch. The discharging of C_S takes place in an exponentially-decaying rate.

For a given clock-cycle n, the instantaneous exponentially-decaying current $I_n(t)$ resulting from the charge transfer from C_S to C_I can be derived as follows:

$$I_n(t) = \begin{cases} I_p\, e^{\frac{-(t-\alpha)T_S}{\tau}} & , \quad \alpha T_S < t < \beta T_S, 0 \leq \alpha \leq \beta \leq 1 \\ 0 & , \qquad\qquad otherwise \end{cases} \qquad (4)$$

where I_p is the value of the peak current at the beginning of the pulse, α and β are the start and end times of the exponentially-decaying pulse normalized to the sampling period T_S and τ is the discharging time-constant and is given by the product $R_{ON}C_S$. The values of α and β are determined by the duty-cycle of the clock. In typical SC circuits, $\alpha = 0.5$ and $\beta =$

1. Recall that the input voltage is sampled on C_S during the first clock half-cycle (when $\emptyset_1$ is high) and then the charge on C_S is transferred to C_I during the second clock half-cycle (when $\emptyset_2$ is high). For a total charge of Q_n to be transferred during $\emptyset_2$ of clock-cycle n,

$$Q_n = \int_{\alpha T_s}^{\beta T_s} I_n(t)\, dt = \int_{\alpha T_s}^{\beta T_s} I_p\, e^{\frac{-(t-\alpha)T_s}{\tau}}\, dt = -\tau A\, e^{\frac{-(t-\alpha)T_s}{\tau}} \Big|_{\alpha T_s}^{\beta T_s} = \tau A \left(1 - e^{\frac{-(\beta-\alpha)T_s}{\tau}}\right) \qquad (5)$$

Thus,

$$I_p = \frac{Q_n}{\tau\left(1 - e^{\frac{-(\beta-\alpha)T_s}{\tau}}\right)}. \qquad (6)$$

Substituting with (6) in (4) yields

$$I_n(t) = \begin{cases} \dfrac{Q_n}{\tau\left(1 - e^{\frac{-(\beta-\alpha)T_s}{\tau}}\right)} e^{\frac{-(t-\alpha)T_s}{\tau}}, & \alpha T_s < t < \beta T_s, 0 \le \alpha \le \beta \le 1. \\[2em] 0, & otherwise. \end{cases} \qquad (7) \qquad (7)$$

However, in presence of timing error $\Delta t(n)$ in the pulse-width of the discharging phase $\emptyset_2$, the resulting error in the integrated charge in the nth clock-cycle is given by

$$e_j(n) = \frac{Q_n}{\tau\left(1 - e^{\frac{-(\beta-\alpha)T_s}{\tau}}\right)} \int_{\beta T_s}^{\beta T_s + \Delta t(n)} e^{\frac{-(t-\alpha)T_s}{\tau}}\, dt = \frac{-Q_n}{\left(1 - e^{\frac{-(\beta-\alpha)T_s}{\tau}}\right)} e^{\frac{-(t-\alpha)T_s}{\tau}} \Big|_{\beta T_s}^{\beta T_s + \Delta t(n)}$$

$$= \frac{Q_n}{\left(1 - e^{\frac{-(\beta-\alpha)T_s}{\tau}}\right)} \left[e^{\frac{-(\beta-\alpha)T_s}{\tau}} - e^{\frac{-(\beta-\alpha)T_s - \Delta t(n)}{\tau}} \right]$$

$$= \frac{Q_n}{\left(1 - e^{\frac{-(\beta-\alpha)T_s}{\tau}}\right)} e^{\frac{-(\beta-\alpha)T_s}{\tau}} \left[1 - e^{-\frac{\Delta t(n)}{\tau}} \right], \qquad (8)$$

which for $\Delta t_n \ll \tau$ can be approximated by

$$e_j(n) \approx \frac{Q_n}{\tau\left(1 - e^{\frac{-(\beta-\alpha)T_s}{\tau}}\right)} e^{\frac{-(\beta-\alpha)T_s}{\tau}} \Delta t(n). \qquad (9)$$

If σ_j^2 the variance of the timing error $\Delta t(n)$, then the error power is given by

$$\sigma_e^2 = E(e^2) = \left(\frac{Q_{rms}}{\tau\left(1 - e^{\frac{-(\beta-\alpha)T_s}{\tau}}\right)} e^{\frac{-(\beta-\alpha)T_s}{\tau}} \right)^2 \sigma_j^2, \qquad (10)$$

where Q_{rms} is the rms charge sampled on the sampling capacitor C_S. Thus, the SNR due to charge transfer jitter caused by charge transfer jitter is given by

$$SNR|_{Due\ to\ charge\ transfer\ jitter} = 10\,Log\left(\frac{Q_{rms}^{2}}{\left(\dfrac{Q_{rms}}{\tau\left(1-e^{\frac{-(\beta-\alpha)T_s}{\tau}}\right)}\,e^{\frac{-(\beta-\alpha)T_s}{\tau}}\right)^{2}\sigma_j^{2}}\right)$$

$$= 10\,Log\left(\frac{\tau^{2}\left(1-e^{\frac{-(\beta-\alpha)T_s}{\tau}}\right)^{2}}{\left(e^{\frac{-(\beta-\alpha)T_s}{\tau}}\right)^{2}}\frac{1}{\sigma_j^{2}}\right). \tag{11}$$

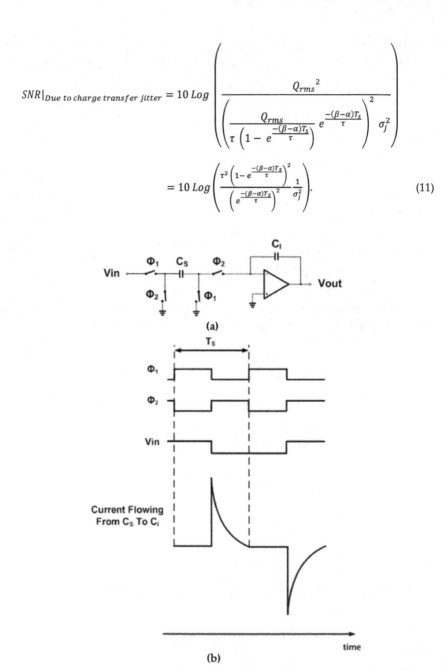

Figure 6. (a) Non-inverting switched-capacitor discrete-time integrator. (b) Time-domain waveforms for clock phases, input signal, and charge flow from C_S to C_I.

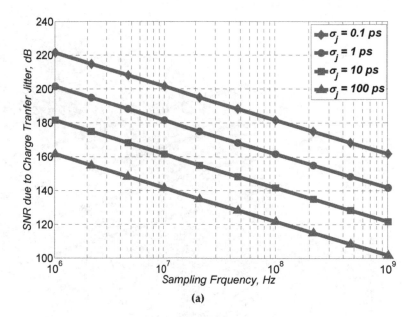

(a)

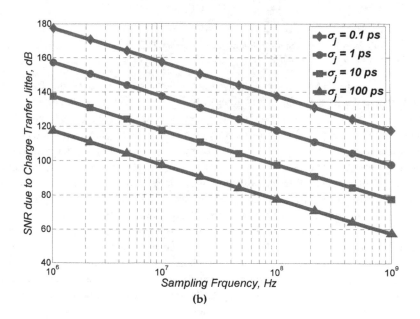

(b)

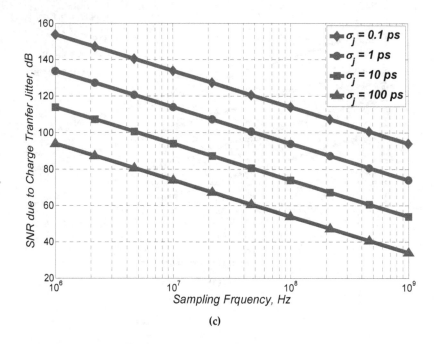

(c)

Figure 7. SNR variation with the input frequency due to charge transfer jitter for different rms jitter values. (a) $\tau = 0.05\,T_s$. (b) $\tau = 0.1\,T_s$. (c) $\tau = 0.2\,T_s$.

The plots in Figure 7 show the limitation on the achievable SNR vs. the signal frequency due to charge transfer jitter for different values of the rms jitter σ_j. Typical values of $\alpha = 0.5$ and $\beta = 1$ have been considered. The results are provided for $\tau = 0.05\,T_s, 0.1\,T_s$, and $0.2\,T_s$. As can be seen from the plots in Figure 7, for a given clock frequency, the SNR limitation due to charge transfer jitter is much more relaxed compared to the aperture jitter error (Figure 5). This result was expected because from equation (11), the effect of the jitter induced noise is reduced by an exponential factor indicating that charge transfer error in SC circuits should be less critical. This also can also be explained intuitively by noting that for the exponentially-decaying waveform in Figure 8, the amplitude of the pulse is rather low at the end of the clock-cycle and hence the amount of charge that varies over one clock period due to jitter is significantly reduced. However, for a given rms jitter and sampling frequency, the SNR limitation due to charge transfer jitter degrades as the discharging time-constant τ increases. This is because the value of the charge transfer current at the end of the clock-cycle (discharge phase) is varying exponentially with τ, thus for a given timing error Δt, the error in the amount of charge transferred is higher.

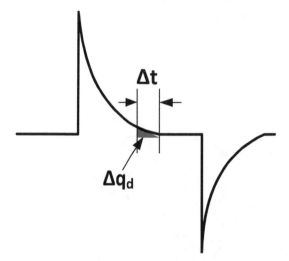

Figure 8. Jitter-tolerant exponentially-decaying waveform.

2.3. Pulse-width jitter

Continuous-time current-steering DAC, shown in Figure 9(a), is used to convert digital signals into CT analog pulses. Clock-jitter in the sampling-clock of a CT DAC modulates the pulse-width of the waveform at the DAC output. Called pulse-width jitter (PWJ), this problem generally shows up in circuits whose operation is based on current-switching, e.g. current-steering DACs, charge sampling circuits, and charge pumps. In systems using CT DACs (e.g. audio transmitters and CT $\Delta\Sigma$ modulators), the DAC is loaded by a CT filter stage that integrates the output current pulse from the DAC. The error in the amount of integrated charges is directly proportional to the timing error Δt in the pulse-width, as illustrated by the time-domain waveform in Figure 9(b). If the clock-jitter causes timing errors Δt with variance σ_j^2 and the switched-current levels are $\pm I_S$, the variance of the charge transferred per clock-cycle T_s is

$$\sigma_e^2 = \sigma_j^2 \, I_S{}^2. \tag{12}$$

For a sinusoidal signal, the maximum signal power in terms of the integrated charge signal per clock-cycle is given by

$$\sigma_{signal}^2 = \frac{I_S{}^2 \, T_s{}^2}{2}. \tag{13}$$

Thus, the maximum SNR against PWJ is given by

$$SNR|_{Due\ to\ pulse-width\ jitter} = 10\,Log\left(\frac{T_s{}^2}{2\,\sigma_j^2}\right), \tag{14}$$

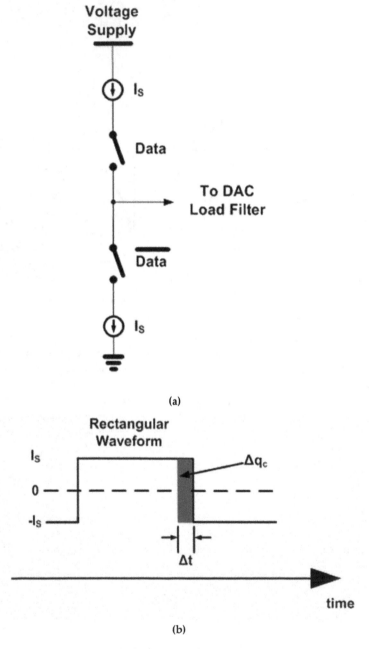

Figure 9. Pulse-width jitter in switched-current circuits.

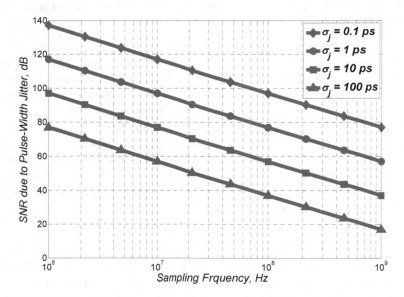

Figure 10. SNR variation with the input frequency due to pulse-width jitter for different rms jitter values.

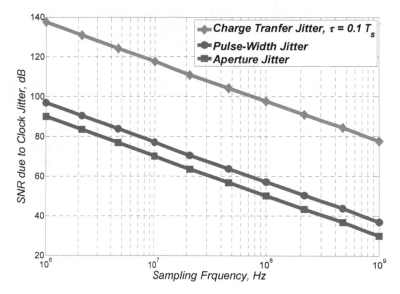

Figure 11. SNR variation with the sampling frequency due to different types of jitter induced errors for a rms jitter of 10 ps.

Thus, the SNR degradation by PWJ is less than that of the aperture jitter by a factor of $2\pi^2$. The plots in Figure 10 show the limitation on the achievable SNR vs. the signal frequency due to PWJ problem for different values of the rms jitter σ_j.

Figure 11 provides a comparative insight about the SNR limitation imposed by each one of the clock-jitter induced problems discussed above. It is worth noting that these plots are for Nyquist-rate sampling; however the foregoing analysis and results can be easily extended to include the effect of oversampling in oversampled circuits. As can be observed from the plots in Figure 11, for a given sampling frequency, the maximum limitation on the achievable SNR is caused by aperture jitter. However, the charge transfer jitter limits the SNR at very high frequencies; for example for an SNR of 80 dB, the charge transfer jitter starts to limit the achievable SNR at sampling frequency $F_s \geq 1\ GHz$ for $\tau = 0.1\ T_s$, and as mentioned before more robustness to charge transfer jitter at high frequencies can be obtained by reducing the discharging time-constant τ.

3. Sensitivity of $\Delta\Sigma$ modulators to clock-jitter

The purpose of this section is to address the effects of clock-jitter in the two main classes of $\Delta\Sigma$ modulators, shown in Figure 12, and provide a comparison between them in terms of sensitivity to clock-jitter. In order to determine the performance sensitivity to clock-jitter in DT and CT modulators, the critical sources of jitter induced errors in the loop should be identified in each one. The most critical clock-jitter errors in a $\Delta\Sigma$ modulator are those generated at the modulator input and in the feedback path through the outermost DAC feeding the first stage in the loop filter (recall that errors generated at inner nodes in the loop are suppressed by the previous stages of the loop filter).

The feedback signal is carrying a digital data (coming from the loop quantizer) and hence it is robust to aperture jitter[2]. However, depending on the type of the adopted feedback DAC, the feedback signal in a $\Delta\Sigma$ loop can suffer one of the other two kinds of jitter induced errors (namely, charge transfer jitter and PWJ). The effect of feedback jitter can be further discussed in the frequency domain with the aid of Figure 13 as follows. Recall that the modulator feedback signal includes the in-band desired signal (input signal) and the high-pass shaped noise. Since the sampling process ideally is a multiplication in time, the spectra of the analog input signal and the clock signal convolve. Thus, the error generated by DAC clock PN has two main components, as illustrated by Figure 13. First, the clock PN components close to the clock frequency modulates the in-band desired signal resulting in signal side-bands in the same manner like the PN of an upfront sampler [5]. Second, the wideband clock PN, modulates the high-pass shaped noise components and the modulation products fall over the desired band and hence elevate the in-band noise level.

---

[2] Since the digital data coming in the feedback is usually sampled at the middle of the clock-cycle, sampled signal in the feedback can suffer aperture jitter only if the clock-jitter is $\geq T_s/2$.

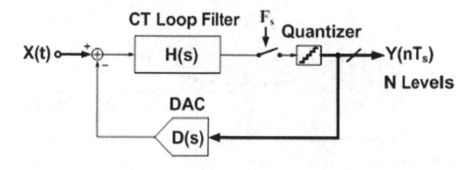

(a)

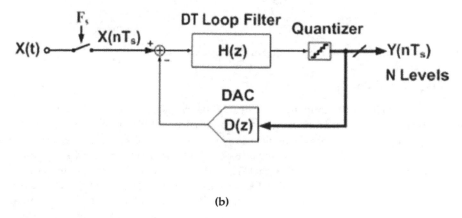

(b)

Figure 12. $\Delta\Sigma$ Modulators. (a) Continuous-Time. (b) Discrete-Time.

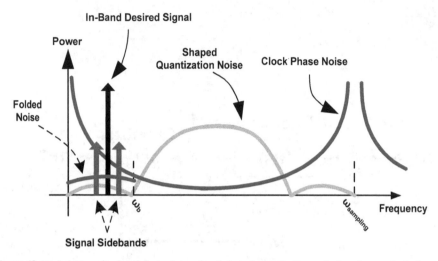

Figure 13. Modulation of in-band desired signal and shaped quantization noise by phase-noise in the DAC sampling clock.

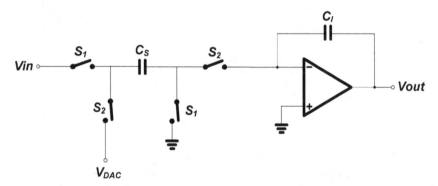

Figure 14. Non-inverting switched-capacitor discrete-time integrator.

3.1. DT ΔΣ modulators

In DT ΔΣ modulators, the sampling takes place at the modulator input. The SC integrator in Figure 14 is commonly used as an input stage for DT loop filters in ΔΣ modulators. The sampling aperture jitter errors due to the sampling switch (S_1) will be added to the signal at the input and hence will directly appear at the modulator output without any suppression. As mentioned earlier, the feedback signal (V_{DAC}) doesn't experience aperture jitter because the feedback signal is DT and also it has discrete amplitude levels. Thus, timing errors cannot result in a sampled value that is different from the original feedback one. Timing errors at switch S_2 cause charge transfer jitter errors being added at the input stage. However, the charge transfer jitter errors at S_2 are very small owing to the high robustness of the exponentially-decaying waveform to clock-jitter and moreover R_{ON} of the switches are usually very small resulting in a small time-constant τ which gives more jitter robustness to the waveform (recall the analysis given in the previous section).

According to the above discussion, the jitter induced noise in DT $\Delta\Sigma$ modulators is mainly dominated by the aperture error at S_1. At a given sampling speed, the only way to improve the performance of DT $\Delta\Sigma$ modulators is to improve the jitter performance of the clock generator which translates into significant increase in the total power consumption in case of $\Delta\Sigma$ ADCs targeting high resolution. On the other hand, for a given rms jitter, if the sampling frequency is reduced for the sake of improving tolerance to jitter errors, then to achieve high resolution at the resulting low OSR, the filter order and/or the quantizer levels need to be increased. This translates into significant power penalty too. Moreover, this approach wouldn't work for state-of-the-art wireless standards with continuously increasing channel bandwidths.

3.2. CT $\Delta\Sigma$ modulators

In CT $\Delta\Sigma$ modulators, sampling occurs after the loop filter and hence sampling errors including aperture jitter are highly suppressed when they appear at the output because this is the point of maximum attenuation in the loop. However, CT $\Delta\Sigma$ implementations suffer from jitter errors added to the feedback signal. Particularly, in a CT $\Delta\Sigma$ modulator the DAC converts the quantizer output DT signal into CT pulses. The waveform coming from the CT DAC is fed to the loop filter to be integrated in the CT integrator stages. Thus, PWJ in the DAC waveform causes uncertainty in the integrated values at the outputs of the loop filter integrators. Rectangular waveform DACs are commonly used in CT $\Delta\Sigma$ structures due to their simple implementation and the relatively relaxed slew-rate (SR) requirement they offer for the loop filter amplifiers. Return-to-zero (RZ) DACs are the most sensitive to feedback PWJ because the random variations are affecting the rising and falling edges of the waveform at every clock-cycle. The jitter sensitivity can be slightly reduced by using a NRZ DAC because in this case, the clock-jitter will be effective only during the clock edges at which data is changing. The equivalent input-referred errors induced by clock jitter in RZ and NRZ waveforms for a certain sequence of data are illustrated in Figure 15.

As mentioned earlier, clock-jitter errors added in the feedback path are the most critical because they entail random phase-modulation that folds back high-pass shaped noise components over the desired channel. For typical wideband CT $\Delta\Sigma$ modulators with NRZ current steering DACs in the feedback, the error induced by the PWJ in the DAC waveform can be up to 30% - 40% of the noise budget [3, 4, 6].

Convenience for low power implementations: CT $\Delta\Sigma$ modulators have gained significant attention in low power and high speed applications because they can operate at higher speed or lower power consumption compared to DT counterparts. Recall the relaxed gain bandwidth (GBW) product requirements they add on the loop filter amplifiers compared to DT implementations in which the loop filter is processing a DT signal and hence a GBW requirement on the amplifier is typically in the range of five times the sampling frequency.

Moreover, sensitivity of CT ΔΣ modulators to DAC clock-jitter can be minimized by processing the DAC pulse or modifying its shape so as to alleviate the error caused by the DAC clock jitter [7]. That is, the achievable SNR of a CT ΔΣ modulator can be improved against clock-jitter without having to improve the jitter performance of the clock generator or to reduce the sampling speed and increase the order of the loop filter or the quantizer resolution. This definitely translates into power savings because it avoids increasing the complexity of the clock generator or the ΔΣ modulator and hence avoiding extra power penalties[3].

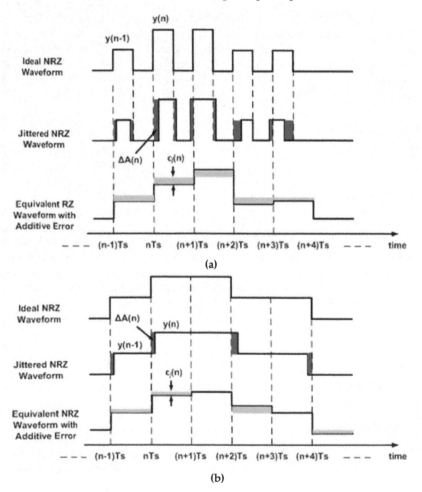

Figure 15. Equivalent input referred error induced by pulse-width jitter [7]. (a) RZ DAC. (b) NRZ DAC.

---

[3] This is provided that the solution adopted to improve the DAC tolerance to clock jitter errors is not adding high power overhead and thus not increasing the total power consumption.

4. Analysis of jitter effects in CT $\Delta\Sigma$ modulators

This section provides detailed analysis for the effects of DAC clock-jitter on the performance of CT $\Delta\Sigma$ modulators for the most commonly used DAC types.

4.1. Return-to-zero DAC waveforms

Return-to-zero DAC waveforms are known to be robust to even-order nonlinearities resulting from mismatch between rise and fall times, as well as less sensitive to excess loop delay in the quantizer compared to NRZ waveforms [3]. However, as mentioned in previous section, they are the most sensitive to PWJ because the additive jitter induced errors are linearly proportional to the random timing errors at the rise and fall edges every clock-cycle, as illustrated in Figure 15(a). The equivalent error induced by PWJ in a RZ DAC waveform is given by

$$\epsilon_j(n) = \frac{\Delta A(n)}{T_s} = y(n)\frac{T_s}{T_C}\frac{(\Delta t_r(n)+\Delta t_f(n))}{T_s}, \tag{15}$$

where $\Delta A(n)$ is the area difference resulting from the error in the total integrated charge per one clock period T_s between the ideal and the jittered waveforms, $y(n)$ is the modulator output at the nth clock cycle, T_C is the duty-cycle of the RZ pulse, and $\Delta t_r(n)$ and $\Delta t_f(n)$ are the random timing errors in the rise and fall edges, respectively, of the nth DAC pulse. The amplitude of the DAC pulse varies inversely proportional with the pulse duty-cycle so that to supply a constant amount of charge (determined by Full-Scale (FS) voltage level of the quantizer) to the loop filter per clock-cycle. Following the procedure in [7], for a single tone $V_{sig} \cdot sin(\omega_{sig}t)$ at the input of the $\Delta\Sigma$ modulator, the integrated in-band jitter-induced noise power (IBJN) for a RZ DAC is given by

$$IBJN|_{RZ} = \frac{2}{OSR}\left(\frac{\sigma_j}{T_C}\right)^2\left[\frac{V_{sig}^2}{2} + \frac{\Delta^2}{12}\cdot\frac{1}{2\pi}\int_{-\pi}^{\pi}|NTF(e^{j\omega})|^2\,d\omega\right]. \tag{16}$$

where σ_j is the rms jitter in the DAC sampling-clock, OSR is the oversampling ratio of the modulator, Δ is the quantization step of the loop quantizer, and NTF is the noise transfer-function of the modulator. From equation (16), the expressions for the IBJN due to input signal and shaped quantization noise can be written as follows

$$IBJN|_{RZ,due\ to\ input\ signal} = \frac{V_{sig}^2}{OSR}\left(\frac{\sigma_j}{T_C}\right)^2. \tag{17}$$

$$IBJN|_{RZ,due\ to\ shaped\ noise} = \frac{1}{OSR}\left(\frac{\sigma_j}{T_C}\right)^2\frac{\Delta^2}{12\pi}\int_{-\pi}^{\pi}|NTF(e^{j\omega})|^2\,d\omega. \tag{18}$$

From the expression in (16), it is evident that the IBJN decreases proportionally with the OSR and the duty cycle of the DAC pulse. Particularly, 1) as the OSR increases, the power spectral density (PSD) of the PWJ induced errors is reduced and hence the resulting integrated in-band noise is decreased accordingly, 2) the additive error in the amount of integrated charge in the loop filter varies linearly with the PWJ at the rise and fall edges by a factor roughly equal to the pulse amplitude (Figure 15(a)), which is inversely proportional to T_C. The IBJN due to in-band signal component, given in (17), causes sidebands of the input signal to appear in the desired band. Also, from (18), PWJ randomly modulating shaped noise results in noise folding back over the desired band and hence elevating the in-band noise level. In (16) and (18), the effect of the quantizer resolution is implicitly included in Δ^2.

4.2. Non-return-to-zero DAC waveforms

Non-return-to-zero DACs are known to be highly sensitive to excess loop delay and also they result in even-order nonlinearities due to mismatch between rise and fall times, in contrast to RZ DAC waveforms. However, they are commonly used in CT $\Delta\Sigma$ modulators due to their simple implementation, relaxed SR requirement on the integrating amplifiers, and lower sensitivity to clock-jitter compared to RZ DACs. As illustrated by Fig. 15(b), in NRZ waveforms the clock-jitter will be effective only during the clock edges at which data is changing. Equivalent error induced by clock-jitter in a NRZ waveform is given by

$$\epsilon_j(n) = \frac{\Delta A(n)}{T_s} = (y(n) - y(n-1))\frac{\Delta t(n)}{T_s}, \tag{19}$$

where $\Delta t(n)$ is the random timing error in the clock edge of the nth clock-cycle. From [7], for a single tone $V_{sig} \cdot sin(\omega_{sig}t)$ at the input of the $\Delta\Sigma$ modulator, the total IBJN for a NRZ DAC is given by

$$IBJN|_{NRZ} = 4 \cdot OSR \cdot BW^2 \cdot \sigma_j^2 \cdot \left[\frac{\pi^2}{2}\left(\frac{V_{sig}^2}{OSR_{sig}^2}\right) + \frac{\Delta^2 \cdot \sigma_{NTF,RMS}^2}{12}\right]$$

$$\leq 2\pi^2 \frac{V_{sig}^2 \cdot BW^2 \cdot \sigma_j^2}{OSR} + \frac{OSR \cdot BW^2 \cdot \Delta^2 \cdot \sigma_{NTF,RMS}^2 \cdot \sigma_j^2}{3}. \tag{20}$$

where BW is the input signal bandwidth, OSR_{sig} is the ratio of the sampling frequency to double the input signal frequency, and $\sigma_{NTF,RMS}^2 = \frac{1}{\pi}\int_{-\pi}^{\pi}\left[\left|NTF(e^{j\omega})\right|^2 \cdot (1 - \cos\omega)\right] d\omega$. Thus, the expressions for the IBJN due to input signal and shaped quantization noise can be written as follows

$$IBJN|_{NRZ,due\ to\ signal} \leq 2\pi^2 \frac{V_{sig}^2 \cdot BW^2 \cdot \sigma_j^2}{OSR}. \tag{21}$$

$$IBJN|_{NRZ,due\ to\ shaped\ noise} = \frac{OSR \cdot BW^2 \cdot \Delta^2 \cdot \sigma_{NTF,RMS}^2 \cdot \sigma_j^2}{3}. \tag{22}$$

From the expression in (21), the IBJN due to signal is inversely proportional with the OSR because, intuitively, as the OSR increases, less signal-related transitions will occur at the modulator output and hence less additive jitter noise will be generated. This note is applicable only to transitions at the modulator output in the frequency range of the input signal. For example, in case of DC inputs, the modulator output will exhibit limit cycles and yields discrete tones at the output spectrum [8]; however, these transitions at the output waveform are due to the shaped quantization noise and not the input signal. On the other hand, from (22), the IBJN due to shaped noise increases proportionally with the OSR because a higher OSR means more OOB shaped noise components will be modulated and fold back over the desired channel by the PN components at their respective frequencies. Therefore, the OSR needs to be optimized for better robustness to PWJ according to the contribution of each component (in-band signal and shaped noise). Also, the IBJN due to shaped noise is proportional to $\sigma_{NTF,RMS}{}^2$, and thus to minimize the PWJ, the aggressiveness of the NTF needs to be relaxed. This gives a trade-off between quantization noise suppression and sensitivity to PWJ and hence a compromise is needed.

4.3. Switched-capacitor-resistor DACs with exponentially-decaying waveforms

A commonly used solution to alleviate DAC sensitivity to PWJ is the switched-capacitor-resistor (SCR) DAC with exponentially-decaying waveform, shown in Figure 16. The exponentially-decaying waveform (Figure 8) of the SCR DAC makes the amount of charge transferred to the loop per clock-cycle less dependent on the exact timing of the DAC clock-edges [4, 9].

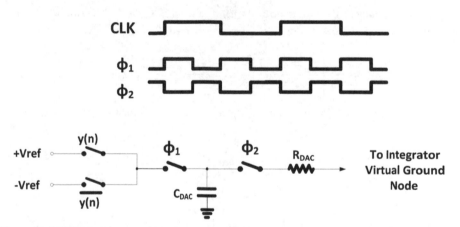

Figure 16. SCR DAC.

For a given clock-cycle n, the instantaneous exponentially-decaying current $I_n(t)$ resulting from the charge transfer is given by equation (4). Recall that the feedback value is sampled on C_{DAC} during the first clock half-cycle (when ϕ_1 is high) and then the sampled voltage is transferred to loop filter during the second clock half-cycle (when ϕ_2 is high). For a total integrated charge of $k_{DAC} \cdot y(n) \cdot T_S$ to be delivered by the SCR DAC during ϕ_1 of clock-cycle n,

$$k_{DAC} \cdot y(n) \cdot T_S = \int_{\alpha T_S}^{\beta T_S} I_P \ e^{\frac{-(\beta-\alpha)T_s}{\tau}} \ dt = \tau \, I_P \left(1 - e^{\frac{-(\beta-\alpha)T_s}{\tau}}\right). \tag{23}$$

where k_{DAC} is the feedback DAC gain coefficient. Therefore,

$$I_P = \frac{k_{DAC} \cdot y(n) \cdot T_S}{\tau \left(1 - e^{\frac{-(\beta - \alpha)T_S}{\tau}}\right)}. \tag{24}$$

However, in presence of timing error $\Delta t(n)$ in the pulse-width of the discharge phase $\emptyset_2$ in the nth clock cycle, the equivalent input-referred additive error in the integrated charge is given by

$$\epsilon_j(n) = \frac{1}{T_S} \frac{k_{DAC} \cdot y(n) \cdot T_S}{\tau \left(1 - e^{\frac{-(\beta - \alpha)T_S}{\tau}}\right)} \int_{\beta T_S}^{\beta T_S + \Delta t(n)} e^{\frac{-(t - \alpha)T_S}{\tau}} dt$$

$$= \frac{k_{DAC} \cdot y(n)}{\left(1 - e^{\frac{-(\beta - \alpha)T_S}{\tau}}\right)} e^{\frac{-(\beta - \alpha)T_S}{\tau}} \left[1 - e^{-\frac{\Delta t(n)}{\tau}}\right], \tag{25}$$

which for $\Delta t(n) \ll \tau$ can be approximated by

$$\epsilon_j(n) \approx \frac{k_{DAC} \cdot y(n)}{\tau \left(1 - e^{\frac{-(\beta - \alpha)T_S}{\tau}}\right)} e^{\frac{-(\beta - \alpha)T_S}{\tau}} \Delta t(n). \tag{26}$$

If σ_j^2 is the variance of the timing error $\Delta t(n)$, then for a single tone $V_{sig} \cdot sin(\omega_{sig}t)$ at the input of the $\Delta\Sigma$ modulator, the power of the input-referred IBJN is given by

$$IBJN|_{SCR} = \frac{1}{OSR} \cdot \left[\frac{e^{\frac{-(\beta - \alpha)T_S}{\tau}}}{\tau \left(1 - e^{\frac{-(\beta - \alpha)T_S}{\tau}}\right)}\right]^2 \cdot \sigma_j^2 \cdot \left[\frac{V_{sig}^2}{2} + \frac{\Delta^2}{12} \cdot \frac{1}{2\pi} \int_{-\pi}^{\pi} |NTF(e^{j\omega})|^2 \, d\omega\right]. \tag{27}$$

The expressions for the IBJN due to input signal and shaped quantization noise are given by

$$IBJN|_{SCR,due\ to\ input\ signal} = \frac{1}{OSR} \cdot \left[\frac{e^{\frac{-(\beta - \alpha)T_S}{\tau}}}{\tau \left(1 - e^{\frac{-(\beta - \alpha)T_S}{\tau}}\right)}\right]^2 \cdot \sigma_j^2 \cdot \frac{V_{sig}^2}{2}. \tag{28}$$

$$IBJN|_{SCR,due\ to\ shaped\ noise} = \frac{1}{OSR} \cdot \left[\frac{e^{\frac{-(\beta - \alpha)T_S}{\tau}}}{\tau \left(1 - e^{\frac{-(\beta - \alpha)T_S}{\tau}}\right)}\right]^2 \cdot \sigma_j^2 \cdot \frac{\Delta^2}{12} \cdot \frac{1}{2\pi} \int_{-\pi}^{\pi} |NTF(e^{j\omega})|^2 \, d\omega. \tag{29}$$

As expected, the sensitivity of SCR DACs to PWJ, given by (27)-(29) is the same as the RZ DAC case (16)-(18) but exponentially reduced. However, the increased peak current of the SCR DAC, given by (28), adds higher requirements on the SR and the GBW of the loop filter integrator [4, 10]. Moreover, CT $\Delta\Sigma$ modulators using SCR DACs have poor inherent anti-aliasing compared to those using current-steering DACs [11] due to the loading of the SCR DAC on the integrating amplifier input nodes. The hybrid SI-SCR DAC solution in [12] provides suppression to PWJ noise equivalent to that offered by SCR DACs without adding extra requirements on the SR or GBW of the integrating amplifier.

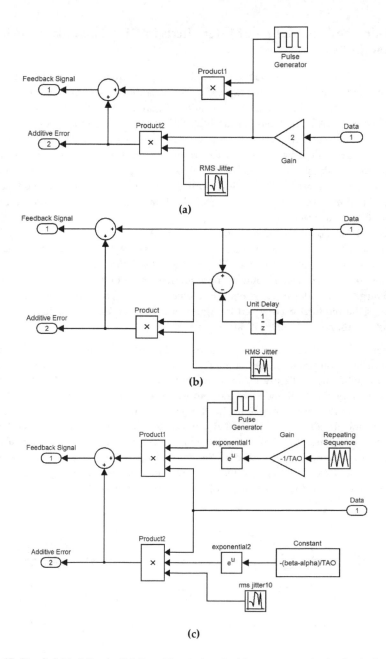

Figure 17. Simulink Modeling for DACs and jitter induced additive errors in the feedback of a CT ΔΣ modulator. (a) RZ DAC. (b) NRZ DAC. (c) SCR DAC.

5. Modeling and simulation of Jitter effects in CT $\Delta\Sigma$ modulators using Matlab/Simulink

In this section, Matlab/Simulink models for the jitter induced errors in different DAC types are shown. The models are based on the expressions of the additive jitter errors developed in the previous section and will be verified by simulations. Figure 17 shows the Simulink models for RZ, NRZ and SCR DACs, including the additive jitter errors based on the expressions in (15), (19), and (25), respectively. Note that these additive errors in the feedback should be multiplied by the gain coefficient of their respective feedback path. These models are examined through simulations in Matlab/Simulink to verify their accuracy and compliance with the developed analysis. The feed-forward third-order single-bit CT $\Delta\Sigma$ modulator in Figure 18 is used as a test vehicle for the system-level simulations. The modulator operates at an OSR of 100 with a target ENOB of 13 bits over a baseband channel bandwidth of 1.92 MHz for the WCDMA standard. The noise budgeting for the ADC to achieve the required ENOB is given in Table 1. Table 2 lists the specifications and summary of the achievable performance of the modulator when an SCR DAC model is used with DAC time-constant $\tau = 0.1\,T_S$. Recall that an SCR DAC is a convenient option to provide robustness to clock-jitter and maintain the low percentage of the jitter induced noise in the noise budget. The dynamic-range (DR) and PSD plots of the modulator are given in Figure 19 and Figure 20. The maximum signal-to-noise-plus-distortion ratio (SNDR) is calculated as 80dB.

To examine the sensitivity of the modulator to clock-jitter for different DAC types by simulations, the appropriate model for the feedback DAC including the additive jitter errors is chosen from the ones in Figure 17, according to the adopted DAC type (RZ, NRZ, or SCR), and is added to the Simulink model of the complete modulator. The plots in Figure 21 imply that for sufficiently large rms jitter in the DAC sampling-clock, the IBJN increases significantly and dominate the total in-band noise (IBN). For the SCR DAC, it can be seen from the plots in Figure 21(c) that the robustness to clock-jitter degrades proportionally with the DAC time-constant τ, as discussed earlier in the analysis. To compare the robustness to clock-jitter in the three DAC types, IBJN plots are combined together in Figure 22, and it is evident that the SCR DAC is the most tolerant to DAC jitter while RZ DAC is the most sensitive.

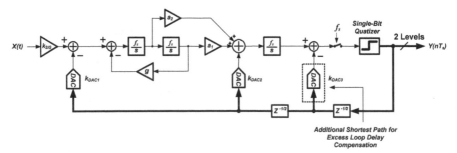

Figure 18. Adopted modified feed-forward CT single-bit $\Delta\Sigma$ modulator.

Noise/Distortion Source	Noise Budget	Signal-to-Noise-Ratio (SNR)
Quantization Noise	10%	90 dB
Thermal Noise	50%	83 dB
Jitter Induced Noise	10%	90 dB
Nonlinearity induced Distortion	20%	87 dB
Others	10%	90 dB

Table 1. Modulator noise budget

Property	Value
Sampling Frequency	384 MHz, RMS Jitter 10 ps
Signal Bandwidth	1.92 MHz
Oversampling Ratio (OSR)	100
ENOB	13
Peak SNDR	80 dB
Dynamic Range	84 dB
SFDR	83 dB

Table 2. Modulator specifications and performance summary

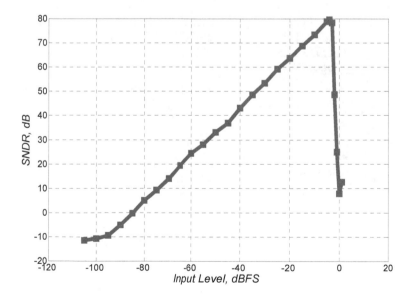

Figure 19. Dynamic-range of the adopted $\Delta\Sigma$ modulator.

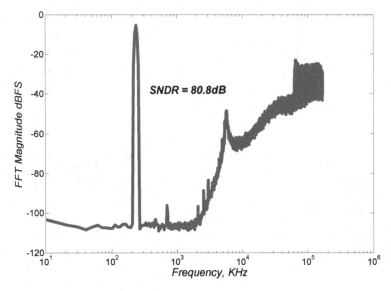

Figure 20. PSD at the modulator output calculated using 32768 FFT points with 16 averages.
Signal Amplitude = −4 dBFS, Signal Frequency = 270 KHz.

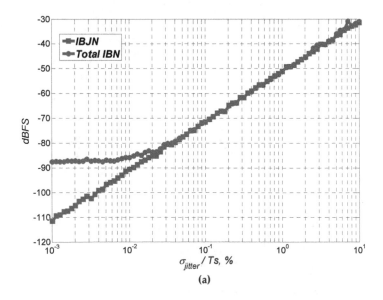

(a)

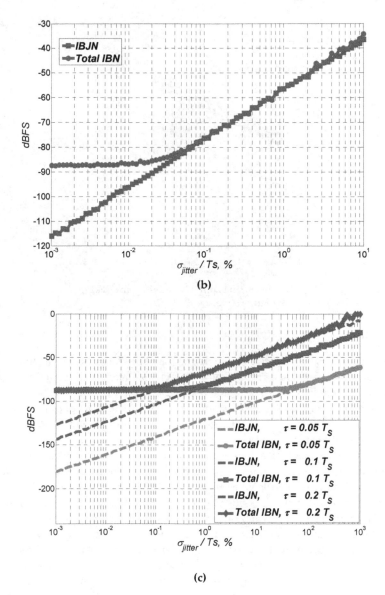

(b)

(c)

Figure 21. Sensitivity plots of the $\Delta\Sigma$ modulator in Figure 18 to clock-jitter in the DAC.
Signal Amplitude $= -4\ dBFS$, *Signal Frequency* $= 1.9\ MHz$. (a) RZ DAC. (b) NRZ DAC.
(c) SCR DAC.

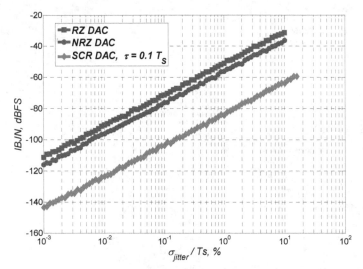

Figure 22. IBJN plots for the $\Delta\Sigma$ modulator in Figure 18 using different DAC types.
Signal Amplitude = −4 dBFS, Signal Frequency = 1.9 MHz.

6. Conclusion

In this chapter, the effects of clock-jitter in the sampling-clocks of $\Delta\Sigma$ modulators are analyzed and studied in details. The critical sources of jitter induced errors in a $\Delta\Sigma$ loop are discussed for $\Delta\Sigma$ modulators with DT and CT loop filters. The comparison between DT and CT modulators showed that CT architectures are more sensitive to clock-jitter than DT counterparts due to PWJ in the feedback signal caused by clock-jitter in the DAC sampling-clock. In essence, PWJ in the feedback waveform entails random phase-modulation that folds back high-pass shaped noise components over the desired channel bandwidth. Thus, a detailed analysis for the sensitivities of various signal waveforms provided by different types of CT DACs to clock-jitter is given thereafter. Also, efficient Matlab/Simulink models for additive errors induced by clock-jitter in the feedback DACs are shown so that to help designers characterize the sensitivities of various types of CT $\Delta\Sigma$ architectures to clock-jitter and obtain the specification requirement on the rms jitter of the sampling-clock for a given target performance. Furthermore, modeling of jitter induced errors is beneficial for system-level simulations adopted in the process of developing efficient solutions and modulator or DAC architectures that can remedy the effects of clock-jitter on the $\Delta\Sigma$ modulator performance. The robustness of these models is verified by CT simulations in Matlab/Simulink and simulations results show good agreement with the theoretical expectations.

Author details

Ramy Saad, Sebastian Hoyos, and Samuel Palermo
Department of Electrical and Computer Engineering, Texas A&M University,
College Station, Texas, USA

Acknowledgement

The authors would like to thank Semiconductor Research Corporation (SRC) for funding their research work in this topic under Grant 1836.013. Also, thanks should be expressed to the reviewers for their valuable feedback and helpful comments about the material given in this chapter.

7. References

[1] Murmann B. "ADC Performance Survey 1997-2012" [Online]. Available: http://www.stanford.edu/~murmann/adcsurvey.html.

[2] International Technology Roadmap for Semiconductors 2007. Radio Frequency and Analog/Mixed-Signal Technologies for Wireless Communities. Available: http://public.itrs.net.

[3] Cherry J. A. and Snelgrove W. M. (2000) Continuous-Time Delta-Sigma Modulators for High-Speed A/D Conversion. Norwell, MA: Kluwer Academic.

[4] Ortmanns M., Gerfers F., Manoli Y. (2005) A continuous-time Sigma Delta modulator with reduced sensitivity to clock jitter through SCR feedback. IEEE Trans. Circuits Syst. I. 52: 875–884.

[5] Mitteregger G., Ebner C., Mechnig S., Blon T., Holuigue C., Romani E. (2006) A 20-mW 640-MHz CMOS Continuous-Time $\Sigma\Delta$ ADC With 20-MHz Signal Bandwidth, 80-dB Dynamic Range and 12-bit ENOB. IEEE Journal of Solid-State Circuits. 41: 2641–2649.

[6] Chen X., Wang Y., Fujimoto Y., Lo Re P., Kanazawa Y., Steensgard J., Temes G. (2007) A 18mW CT $\Delta\Sigma$ Modulator with 25MHz Bandwidth for Next Generation Wireless Applications. Proc. IEEE Custom Integrated Circuits Conf. (CICC). 73–76.

[7] Chen X. (2007) A Wideband low-power continuous-time Delta-Sigma modulator for next generation wireless applications. Ph.D. dissertation, Sch. Elect. Eng. Comp. Sci., Oregon State Univ., Corvallis, OR.

[8] Gray R. (1989) Spectral analysis of quantization noise in a single-loop sigma-delta modulator with dc input. IEEE Transactions on Communications. 37: 588-599.

[9] Anderson M., Sundström L. (2007) A 312 MHz CT $\Delta\Sigma$ modulator using SC feedback with reduced peak current. Proc. 33rd European Solid-State Circuits Conf., ESSIRC 2007, München, Germany: 240–243.

[10] Anderson M., Sundström L. (2009) Design and Measurement of a CT $\Sigma\Delta$ ADC With Switched-Capacitor Switched-Resistor Feedback. IEEE Journal of Solid-State Circuits. 44: 473–483.

[11] Pavan S. (2011) Alias Rejection of Continuous-Time $\Delta\Sigma$ Modulators with Switched-Capacitor Feedback DACs. IEEE Trans. Circuits Syst. 58: 309–318.

[12] Saad R., Hoyos S. (2011) Feed-Forward Spectral Shaping Technique for Clock-Jitter Induced Errors in Digital-to-Analog Converters. IET Electronics Letters, 47: 171–172.

Chapter 3

Image Reconstruction Methods for MATLAB Users – A Moore-Penrose Inverse Approach

S. Chountasis, V.N. Katsikis and D. Pappas

Additional information is available at the end of the chapter

1. Introduction

In the last decades the Moore-Penrose pseudoinverse has found a wide range of applications in many areas of Science and became a useful tool for different scientists dealing with optimization problems, data analysis, solutions of linear integral equations, etc. At first we will present a review of some of the basic results on the so-called Moore-Penrose pseudoinverse of matrices, a concept that generalizes the usual notion of inverse of a square matrix, but that is also applicable to singular square matrices or even to non-square matrices.

The notion of the generalized inverse of a (square or rectangular) matrix was first introduced by H. Moore in 1920, and again by R. Penrose in 1955, who was apparently unaware of Moore's work. These two definitions are equivalent, (as it was pointed by Rao in 1956) and since then, the generalized inverse of a matrix is also called the Moore-Penrose inverse.

Let A be a $r \times m$ real matrix. Equations of the form $Ax = b, A \in \mathbb{R}^{r \times m}, b \in \mathbb{R}^r$ occur in many pure and applied problems. It is known that when T is singular, then its unique generalized inverse $A^\dagger$ (known as the Moore-Penrose inverse) is defined. In the case when A is a real $r \times m$ matrix, Penrose showed that there is a unique matrix satisfying the four Penrose equations, called the generalized inverse of A, noted by $A^\dagger$.

An important question for applications is to find a general and algorithmically simple way to compute $A^\dagger$. There are several methods for computing the Moore-Penrose inverse matrix (cf. [2]). The most common approach uses the Singular Values Decomposition (SVD). This method is very accurate but also time-intensive since it requires a large amount of computational resources, especially in the case of large matrices. Therefore, many other methods can be used for the numerical computation of various types of generalized inverses, see [16]; [25]; [30]. For more on the Moore-Penrose inverse, generalized inverses in general and their applications, there are many excellent texbooks on this subject, see [2]; [30]; [4].

The Moore-Penrose pseudoinverse is a useful concept in dealing with optimization problems, as the determination of a Şleast squaresŤ solution of linear systems. A typical application of the Moore-Penrose inverse is its use in Image and signal Processing and Image restoration.

The field of image restoration has seen a tremendous growth in interest over the last two decades, see [1]; [5]; [6]; [14]; [28]; [29]. The recovery of an original image from degraded observations is of crucial importance and finds application in several scientific areas including medical imaging and diagnosis, military surveillance, satellite and astronomical imaging, and remote sensing. A number of various algorithms have been proposed and intensively studied for achieving a fast recovered and high resolution reconstructed images, see [10]; [15]; [22].

The presented method in this article is based on the use of the Moore-Penrose generalized inverse of a matrix and provides us a fast computational algorithm for a fast and accurate digital image restoration. This article is an extension of the work presented in [7]; [8].

2. Theoretical background

2.1. The Moore-Penrose inverse

We shall denote by $\mathbb{R}^{r \times m}$ the algebra of all $r \times m$ real matrices. For $T \in \mathbb{R}^{r \times m}$, $R(T)$ will denote the range of T and $N(T)$ the kernel of T. The generalized inverse $T^\dagger$ is the unique matrix that satisfies the following four Penrose equations:

$$TT^\dagger = (TT^\dagger)^*, \qquad T^\dagger T = (T^\dagger T)^*, \qquad TT^\dagger T = T, \qquad T^\dagger TT^\dagger = T^\dagger,$$

where T^* denotes the transpose matrix of T.

Let us consider the equation $Tx = b$, $T \in \mathbb{R}^{r \times m}$, $b \in \mathbb{R}^r$, where T is singular. If T is an arbitrary matrix, then there may be none, one or an infinite number of solutions, depending on whether $b \in R(T)$ or not, and on the rank of T. But if $b \notin R(T)$, then the equation has no solution. Therefore, another point of view of this problem is the following: instead of trying to solve the equation $\|Tx - b\| = 0$, we are looking for a minimal norm vector u that minimizes the norm $\|Tu - b\|$. Note that this vector u is unique. So, in this case we consider the equation $Tx = P_{R(T)}b$, where $P_{R(T)}$ is the orthogonal projection on $\mathcal{R}(T)$. Since we are interested in the distance between Tx and b, it is natural to make use of $\|T\|_2$ norm.

The following two propositions can be found in [12].

Proposition 0.1. *Let $T \in \mathbb{R}^{r \times m}$ and $b \in \mathbb{R}^r, b \notin R(T)$. Then, for $u \in \mathbb{R}^m$, the following are equivalent:*

(i) $Tu = P_{R(T)}b$

(ii) $\|Tu - b\| \leq \| Tx - b\|, \forall x \in \mathbb{R}^m$

(iii) $T^*Tu = T^*b$

Let $\mathbb{B} = \{u \in \mathbb{R}^m | T^*Tu = T^*b\}$. This set of solutions is closed and convex; it therefore has a unique vector u_0 with minimal norm. In fact, $\mathbb{B}$ is an affine manifold; it is of the form $u_0 + \mathcal{N}(T)$. In the literature (c.f. [12]), $\mathbb{B}$ is known as the set of the least square solutions.

Proposition 0.2. *Let $T \in \mathbb{R}^{r \times m}$ and $b \in \mathbb{R}^r, b \notin R(T)$, and the equation $Tx = b$. Then, if $T^\dagger$ is the generalized inverse of T, we have that $T^\dagger b = u$, where u is the minimal norm solution defined above.*

We shall make use of this property for the construction of an alternative method in image processing inverse problems.

2.2. Image restoration problems

The general pointwise definition of the transform $\tau(u,v)$ that is used in order to convert an $r \times r$ pixel image $s(x,y)$ from the spatial domain to some other domain in which the image exhibits more readily reducible features is given in the following equation:

$$\tau(u,v) = \frac{1}{r} \sum_{x=1}^{r} \sum_{y=1}^{r} s(x,y)g(x,y,u,v) \tag{1}$$

where u and v are the coordinates in the transform domain and $g(x,y,u,v)$ denote the general basis function used by the transform. Similarly, the inverse transform is given as:

$$s(x,y) = \frac{1}{r} \sum_{u=1}^{r} \sum_{v=1}^{r} \tau(u,v)h(x,y,u,v) \tag{2}$$

where $h(x,y,u,v)$ represents the inverse of the basis function $g(x,y,u,v)$.

The two dimensional version of the function $g(x,y,u,v)$ in Equation (1) can typically be derived as a series of one dimensional functions. Such functions are referred to as being 'separable', we can derive the separable two dimensional functions as follows: The transform been performed across x

$$\tau'(u,y) = \frac{1}{\sqrt{r}} \sum_{x=1}^{r} s(x,y)g(x,u) \tag{3}$$

Moreover we transform across y:

$$\tau(u,v) = \frac{1}{\sqrt{r}} \sum_{y=1}^{r} \tau'(u,y)g(y,u) \tag{4}$$

and using Equation (3) we have

$$\tau(u,v) = \frac{1}{r} \sum_{x=1}^{r} \sum_{y=1}^{r} s(x,y)g(x,u)g(y,u) \tag{5}$$

We can use an identical approach in order to write Equation (1) and its inverse (Equation 2) in matrix form , using the standard orthonormal basis:

$$T = GSG^T, \quad S = HTH^T \tag{6}$$

in which T, S, G and H are the matrix equivalents of τ, s, g and h respectively. This is due to our use of orthogonal basis functions, meaning the basis function is its own inverse. Therefore, it is easy to see that the complete process to perform the transform, and then invert it is thus:

$$S = HGSG^T H^T \tag{7}$$

In order for the transform to be reversible we need H to be the inverse of G and H^T to be the inverse of G^T, i.e. , $HG = G^T H^T = I$.

Given that G is orthogonal it is trivial to show that this is satisfied when $H = G^T$. Given H is merely the transpose of G the inverse function for $g(x,y,u,v)h(x,y,u,v)$ is also separable.

In the scientific area of image processing the analytical form of a linear degraded image is given by the following integral equation :

$$x_{out}(i,j) = \int \int_D x_{in}(u,v)h(i,j;u,v)dudv$$

where $x_{in}(u,v)$ is the original image, $x_{out}(i,j)$ represents the measured data from where the original image will be reconstructed and $h(i,j;u,v)$ is a known Point Spread Function (PSF). The PSF depends on the measurement imaging system and is defined as the output of the system for an input point source.

A digital image described in a two dimensional discrete space is derived from an analogue image $x_{in}(u,v)$ in a two dimensional continuous space through a sampling process that is frequently referred to as digitization. The two dimensional continuous image is divided into r rows and m columns. The intersection of a row and a column is termed a pixel. The discrete model for the above linear degradation of an image can be formed by the following summation

$$x_{out}(i,j) = \sum_{u=1}^{r} \sum_{v=1}^{m} x_{in}(u,v)h(i,j;u,v) \tag{8}$$

where $i = 1,2,\ldots,r$ and $j = 1,2,\ldots,m$.

In this work we adopt the use of a shift invariant model for the blurring process as in [11]. Therefore, the analytically expression for the degraded system is given by a two dimensional (horizontal and vertical) convolution i.e.,

$$x_{out}(i,j) = \sum_{u=1}^{r} \sum_{v=1}^{m} x_{in}(u,v)h(i-u,j-v) = x_{in}(i,j) ** h(i,j) \tag{9}$$

where $**$ indicates two dimensional convolution.

In the formulation of equation (8) the noise can also be simulated by rewriting the equation as

$$x_{out}(i,j) = \sum_{u=1}^{r} \sum_{v=1}^{m} x_{in}(u,v)h(i,j;u,v) + n(i,j) = x_{in}(i,j) ** h(i,j) + n(i,j) \tag{10}$$

where $n(i,j)$ is an additive noise introduced by the system.

However, in this work the noise is image related which means that the noise has been added to the image.

2.3. The Fourier Transform, the Haar basis and the moments in image reconstruction problems

Moments are particularly popular due to their compact description, their capability to select differing levels of detail and their known performance attributes (see [3]; [9];[17]; [18]; [19]; [20]; [26]; [27]; [28]. It is a well-recognised property of moments that they can be used to reconstruct the original function, i.e., none of the original image information is lost in the projection of the image on to the moment basis functions, assuming an infinite number of moments are calculated. Another property for the reconstruction of a band-limited image using its moments is that while derivatives give information on the high frequencies of a signal, moments provide information on its low frequencies. It is known that the higher order moments capture increasingly higher frequencies within a function and in the case of an image the higher frequencies represent the detail of the image. This is also consistent with work on other types of reconstruction, such as eigenanalysis where it has been found that increasing numbers of eigenvectors are required to capture image detail ([23],) and again exceed the number required for recognition. Describing images with moments instead of other more commonly used image features means that global properties of the image are used rather than local properties. Moments provide information on its low frequency of an image. Applying the Fourier coefficients a low pass approximation of the original image is obtained. It is well known that any image can be reconstructed from its moments in the least-squares sense. Discrete orthogonal moments provide a more accurate description of image features by evaluating the moment components directly in the image coordinate space.

The reconstruction of an image from its moments is not necessarily unique. Thus, all possible methods must impose extra constraints in order to its moments uniquely solve the reconstruction problem.

The most common reconstruction method of an image from some of its moments is based on the least squares approximation of the image using orthogonal polynomials ([19]; [21]). In this paper the constraint that introduced is related to the bandwidth of the image and provides a more general reconstruction method. We must keep in mind that this constraint is a global, for a local one a joint bilinear distribution such as Wigner or wavelet must be used.

2.3.1. The Fourier Basis

In view of the importance of the frequency domain, the Fourier Transform (FT) has become one of the most widely used signal analysis tool across many disciplines of science and engineering. The FT is generated by projecting the signal on to a set of basis functions, each of which is a sinusoid with a unique frequency. The FT of a time signal $s(t)$ is given by

$$\tilde{s}(\omega) = \frac{1}{\sqrt{2\pi}} \int_{-\infty}^{+\infty} s(t) exp(-i\omega t) dt$$

where $\omega = 2\pi f$ is the angular frequency. Since the set of exponentials forms an orthogonal basis the signal can be reconstructed from the projection values

$$s(t) = \frac{1}{\sqrt{2\pi}} \int_{-\infty}^{+\infty} \tilde{s}(\omega) exp(i\omega t) d\omega$$

Following the property of the FT that the convolution in the spatial domain is translated into simple algebraic product in the spectral domain Equation (8) can be written in the form

$$\tilde{x}_{out} = \tilde{x}_{in}\tilde{H} \tag{11}$$

In a discrete Fourier domain the two-dimensional Fourier coefficients are defined as

$$F(m,n) = \frac{1}{\sqrt{XY}} \sum_{x=1}^{X} \sum_{y=1}^{Y} S_{XY} exp(-2\pi i(\frac{(x-1)(m-1)}{X} + \frac{(y-1)(n-1)}{Y})) \tag{12}$$

rearranging the above equation leads to

$$F(m,n) = \frac{1}{\sqrt{XY}} \sum_{x=1}^{X} exp(-2\pi i \frac{(x-1)(m-1)}{X}) \sum_{y=1}^{Y} S_{XY} exp(-2\pi i \frac{(y-1)(n-1)}{Y}))$$

thus, $F(m,n)$ can be written in matrix form as:

$$F(m,n) = K_S(x,m) S_{XY} K_S(y,n)^*$$

where $K_S(y,n)^*$ denotes the conjugate transpose of the forward kernel $K_S(y,n)$.

Using the same principles but writing Equation (12) in a form where the increasing indexes correspond to higher frequency coefficients we obtain

$$F(m,n) = \frac{1}{\sqrt{XY}} \sum_{x=1}^{X} \sum_{y=1}^{Y} S_{XY} \cdot exp[-2\pi i(\frac{(x-1)(m-\frac{(k-1)}{2}-1)}{X} + \frac{(y-\frac{(l-1)}{2}-1)(n-1)}{Y})]$$

 The Fourier coefficients can be seen as the projection coefficients of the image S_{XY} onto a set of complex exponential basis functions that lead to the basis matrix:

$$B_{kl}(m,n) = \frac{1}{\sqrt{k}} exp[-2\pi i \frac{(m-1)(n-\frac{(l-1)}{2}-1)}{k}]$$

The approximation of an image S_{XY} in the least square sense, can be expressed in terms of the projection matrix P_{kl} :

$$P_{kl} = (B_{Xk})^T S_{XY} B_{Yl}$$

as

$$S'_{XY} = B_{Xk}(B_{Xk}^T B_{Xk}^T)^{-1} P_{kl}(B_{Yl}^T B_{Yl})^{-1} B_{Yl}^T$$
$$= (B_{Xk})^- P_{kl}(B_{Yl})^\dagger$$

where $()^T$ and $()^{-1}$ denote the transpose and the inverse of the given matrix. The operations $()^-$ and $()^\dagger$ stand for the left and right inverses, both are equal to the Moore-Penrose inverse, and are unique. Among the multiple inverse solutions it chooses the one with minimum norm. When considering image reconstruction from moments, the number of moments required for accurate reconstruction will be related to the frequencies present within the original image. For a given image size it would appear that there should be a finite limit to the frequencies that are present in the image and for a binary image that limiting frequency will be relatively low. As the higher order moments approach this frequency the reconstruction will become more accurate.

2.3.2. The Haar basis

The reconstruction of an image from its moments is not necessarily unique. Thus, all possible methods must impose extra constraints in order to its moments uniquely solve the reconstruction problem. In this method the constraint that introduced is related to the number of coefficients and the spatial resolution of the image. The Haar basis is unique among the functions we have examined as it actually defines what is referred to as a 'wavelet'. Wavelet functions are a class of functions in which a 'mother' function is translated and scaled to produce the full set of values required for the full basis set. Limiting the resolution of an image means eliminating those regions of smaller size than a given one. The Haar coefficients are obtained from the projection of the image onto the discrete Haar functions $B_{k,l}(m)$ for k a power of 2, and are defined as

$$B_{k,l}(m) = \frac{1}{\sqrt{k}},$$

in the case $l = 1$, and for $l > 1$

$$B_{k,l}(m) = \begin{cases} +\sqrt{\frac{q}{k}}, & \text{if} \quad p \leq m < p + \frac{k}{2q} \\ -\sqrt{\frac{q}{k}}, & \text{if} \quad p + \frac{k}{2q} \leq m \leq p + \frac{k}{q} \\ 0, & \text{otherwise} \end{cases}$$

with $q = 2^{[log_2(l-1)]}$ and $p = \frac{k(l-1-q)}{q} + 1$, where [.] stands for the function fix(x), which rounds the elements of x to the nearest integer towards zero.

3. Restoration of a blurry image in the spatial domain

This work introduces a new technique for the removal of blur in an image caused by the uniform linear motion. The method assumes that the linear motion corresponds to a discrete number of pixels and is aligned with the horizontal or vertical sampling.

Given x_{out}, then x_{in} is the deterministic original image that has to be recovered. The relation between these two components in matrix structure is the following :

$$Hx_{in} = x_{out}, \tag{13}$$

where H represents a two dimensional $(r \times m)$ priori knowledge matrix or it can be estimated from the degraded X-ray image using its Fourier spectrum ([24]) . The vector x_{out}, is of r entries, while the vector x_{in} is of $m(= r + n - 1)$ entries, where $m > r$ and n is the length of the blurring process in pixels. The problem consists of solving the underdetermined system of equations (Eq. 13).

However, since there is an infinite number of exact solutions for x_{in} that satisfy the equation $Hx_{in} = x_{out}$, an additional criterion that finds a sharp restored vector is required. Our work provides a new criterion for restoration of a blurred image including a fast computational method in order to calculate the Moore-Penrose inverse of full rank $r \times m$ matrices. The method retains a restored signal whose norm is smaller than any other solution. The computational load for the method is compared with the already known methods.

The criterion for restoration of a blurred image that we are using is the minimum distance of the measured data, i.e.,

$$\min(\|x_{in}^* - x_{out}\|),$$

where x_{in}^* are the first r elements of the unknown image x_{in} that has to be recovered subject to the constraint $\|Hx_{in} - x_{out}\| = 0$. In fact, zero is not always attained, but following Proposition 0.1(ii) the norm is minimized.

In general, the PSF varies independently with respect to both (horizontal and vertical) directions, because the degradation of a PSF may depend on its location in the image. An example of this kind of behavior is an optical system that suffers strong geometric aberrations. However, in most of the studies, the PSF is accurately written as a function of the horizontal and vertical displacements independently of the location within the field of view.

3.1. The generalized inverse approach

A blurred image that has been degraded by a uniform linear motion in the horizontal direction, usually results of camera panning or fast object motion can be expressed as follows, as desribed in Eq. (13):

$$\begin{bmatrix} k_1 & \dots & k_n & 0 & 0 & 0 & 0 \\ 0 & k_1 & \dots & k_n & 0 & 0 & 0 \\ 0 & 0 & k_1 & \dots & k_n & 0 & 0 \\ \vdots & \vdots & \vdots & \vdots & \vdots & \vdots & \vdots \\ 0 & 0 & 0 & \dots & k_1 & \dots & k_n \end{bmatrix} \cdot \begin{bmatrix} x_{in\_1} \\ x_{in\_2} \\ x_{in\_3} \\ \vdots \\ x_{in\_m} \end{bmatrix} = \begin{bmatrix} x_{out\_1} \\ x_{out\_2} \\ x_{out\_3} \\ \vdots \\ x_{out\_r} \end{bmatrix} \quad (14)$$

where the index n indicates the linear motion blur in pixels. The element $k_1, \dots, k_n$ of the matrix are defined as: $k_l = 1/n \quad (1 \le l \le n)$.

Equation (3) can also be written in the pointwise form for $i = 1, \dots, r$,

$$x_{out}(i) = \frac{1}{n} \sum_{h=0}^{n-1} x_{in}(i+h)$$

that describes an underdetermined system of r simultaneous equations and $m = r + n - 1$ unknowns. The objective is to calculate the original column per column data of the image.

For this reason, given each column $[x_{out\_1}, x_{out\_2}, x_{out\_3}, \dots x_{out\_r}]^T$ of a degraded blurred image x_{out}, Eq. (3) results the corresponding column

$[x_{in\_1}, x_{in\_2}, x_{in\_3}, \dots, x_{in\_m}]^T$ of the original image.

As we have seen, the matrix H is a $r \times m$ matrix, and the rank of H is less or equal to m. Therefore, the linear system of equations is underdetermined. The proper generalized inverse for this case is a left inverse, which is also called a $\{1,2,4\}$ inverse, in the sense that it needs to satisfy only the three of the four Penrose equations. A left inverse gives the minimum norm solution of this underdetermined linear system, for every $x_{out} \in \mathcal{R}(H)$. The Moore-Penrose Inverse is clearly suitable for our case, since we can have a minimum norm solution for every $x_{out} \in \mathcal{R}(H)$, and a minimal norm least squares solution for every $x_{out} \notin \mathcal{R}(H)$.

The proposed algorithm has been tested on a simulated blurred image produced by applying the matrix H on the original image. This can be represented as

$$x_{out}(i,j) = \frac{1}{n} \sum_{h=0}^{n-1} x_{in}(i,j+h)$$

where $i = 1,\ldots,r$ $j = 1,\ldots,m$ for $m = r+n-1$, and n is the linear motion blur in pixels.

Following the above, and the analysis given in Section 3, there is an infinite number of exact solutions for x_{in} that satisfy the equation $Hx_{in} = x_{out}$, but from proposition 2.2, only one of them minimizes the norm $\|Hx_{in} - x_{out}\|$.

We shall denote this unique vector by $\hat{x}_{in}$. So, $\hat{x}_{in}$ can be easily found from the equation :

$$\hat{x}_{in} = H^\dagger x_{out}$$

The following section presents results that highlight the performance of the generalized inverse.

4. Experimental results

In this section we apply the proposed method on an boat picture and present the numerical results.

The numerical tasks have been performed using Matlab programming language. Specifically, the Matlab 7.4 (R2007b) environment was used on an Intel(R) Pentium(R) Dual CPU T2310 @ 1.46 GHz 1.47 GHz 32-bit system with 2 GB of RAM memory running on the Windows Vista Home Premium Operating System.

4.1. Recovery from a degraded image

Figure 1(a) provides the original boat picture. In Figure 1(b), we present the degraded boat picture where the length of the blurring process is equal to $n = 60$. Finally, in Figure 1(c) we present the reconstructed image using the Moore- Penrose inverse approach. As we can see, it is clearly seen that the details of the original image have been recovered.

The Improvement in Signal to Noise Ratio (ISNR) has been chosen in order to present the reconstructed images obtained by the proposed algorithm. It provides a criterion that has been used extensively for the purpose of objectively testing the performance of image processing algorithms expressed as:

$$ISNR = 10\log_{10} \left\{ \frac{\sum_{i,j}[x_{in}(i,j) - x_{out}(i,j)]^2}{\sum_{i,j}[x_{in}(i,j) - \hat{x}_{in}(i,j)]^2} \right\},$$

Figure 1. (a) Original Image (b) Blurred image for a length of the blurring process n = 60 (c) Restoration of a simulated degraded image with a length of the blurring process n = 60.

where x_{in} and x_{out} represent the original deterministic image and degraded image respectively, and $\hat{x}_{in}$ is the corresponding restored image. Figure 2(a) shows the corresponding ISNR values. for increasing the number of pixels in the blurring process $n = 1, \ldots, 60$.

The second set of tests aimed at accenting the reconstruction error between the original image x_{in} and the reconstructed image $\hat{x}_{in}$ for various values of linear motion blur, n. The calculated quantity is the normalized reconstruction error given by

$$E = \frac{1}{\sqrt{\sum_{i=1}^{r} \sum_{j=1}^{m} [x_{in}(i,j)]^2}} \sqrt{\sum_{i=1}^{r} \sum_{j=1}^{m} [x_{in}(i,j) - \hat{x}_{in}(i,j)]^2}$$

using the generalized inverse reconstructed method.

Figure 2(b) shows the reconstruction error by increasing the number of pixels in the blurring process $n = 1, \ldots, 60$.

4.2. Recovery from a degraded and noisy image

Noise may be introduced into an image in a number of different ways. In Equation (10) the noise has been introduced in an additive way. Here, we simulate a noise model where a number of pixels are corrupted and randomly take on a value of white and black (*salt and pepper* noise) with noise density equal to 0.02. The image that we receive from a faulty transmission line can contain this form of corruption. In Figure 3(b), we present the original boat image while a motion blurred and a salt and pepper noise has been added to it.

Image processing and analysis are based on filtering the content of the images in a certain way. The filtering process is basically an algorithm that modifies a pixel value, given the original value of the pixel and the values that surrounding it. Accordingly, Figure 4(a) provides a graphical representation for the ISNR of the reconstructed and filtered image for different values of n. Moreover, Figure 4(b) shows the reconstruction error by increasing the number of pixels in the blurring process $n = 1, \ldots, 60$.

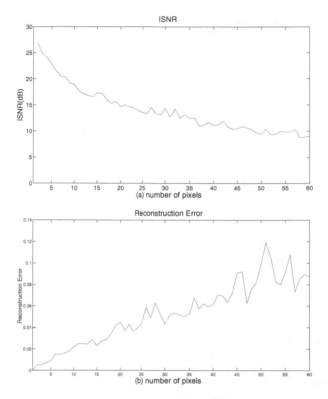

Figure 2. (a) ISNR and (b) Reconstruction Error calculations vs number of pixels in the blurring process ($n = 1, \ldots, 60$).

Figure 3. (a) Noisy Image (b) Blurred and noisy (salt and pepper) image for length of the blurring process n = 60 (c) Restoration of a simulated degraded (n = 60) and noisy (salt and pepper) image.

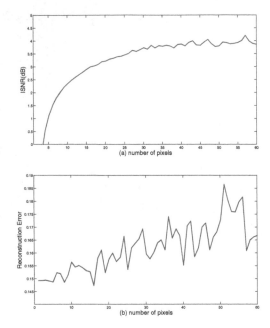

Figure 4. (a) ISNR and (b) Reconstruction Error calculations for a noisy and blurred image vs number of pixels in the blurring process ($n = 1, \ldots, 60$).

5. Deblurring in the spatial and spectral domain: Application of the Haar and Fourier moments on image reconstruction.

As mentioned before, images can be viewed as non-stationary two-dimensional signals with edges, textures, and deterministic objects at different locations. Although non-stationary signals are, in general, characterized by their local features rather than their global ones, it is possible to recover images by introducing global constrains on either its spatial or spectral resolution. The objective is to calculate the inverse matrix of the blurring kernel H and then applied back (simple multiplication in the spectral domain) to the degraded blurred image xout. Figure 5 shows the spectral representation of the degraded image obtained using Equation (11).

In order to obtain back the original image, Equation (13) is solved in the Fourier space

$$\tilde{x}_{in} = \tilde{x}_{out}\tilde{H}^{\dagger}$$

The reconstructed image is the inverse Fourier transform of $\tilde{x}_{in}$. By using our method not only we have the advantage of fast recovery but also provide us with an operator $\tilde{H}^{\dagger}$ that exists even for not full rank non square matrices. In this section the whole process of deblurring and restoring the original image is done in the spatial domain by using the Haar basis moments and in the spectral domain by applied the Fourier basis moments on the image. It provides us the ability of fast recovering and algorithmic simplicity. The former, obtained by using directly the original image and analysed that on its moments. The method is robust in the presence of noise, as can be seen on the results. In the latter, From the reconstruction point of view the basis matrix is applied to both original image and blurring kernel transforming these into spectral domain. After the inversion of the blurring kernel, its product with the degraded image is applied to inverted basis functions for the reconstruction of the original image. The method provides almost the same robustness for the case of degradation and noise presence as for the spatial moment analysis case.

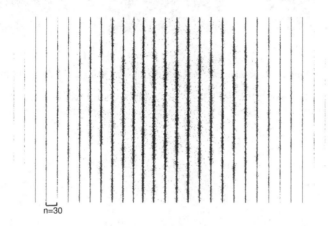

n=30

Figure 5. Spectral representations of the degraded image for n=30.

Figures $6(a), 6(b)$ and $6(c)$ present the reconstructed image using the Fourier basis,for the cases of $k = l = 30, k = l = 100$ and $k = l = 450$, respectively.

Figure 6. Fourier based moment reconstructed images for (a) k = l = 30 (b) k = l = 100 and (c) k = l = 450.

From the reconstruction point of view the basis matrix is applied to both original image and blurring kernel transforming these into spectral domain. After the inversion of the blurring kernel, its product with the degraded image is applied to inverted basis functions for the reconstruction of the original image.

Figures $7(a), 7(b)$ and $7(c)$ present the reconstructed image using the Haar basis,for the cases of $k = l = 30, k = l = 100$ and $k = l = 450$, respectively.

Figure 7. Haar based moment reconstructed images for (a) k = l = 30 (b) k = l = 100 and (c) k = l = 450.

Figures 8(a) and 8(b) show the ISNR and the Reconstruction Error accordingly, for various lengths of the blurring processes. Graphical representations on these Figures correspond to

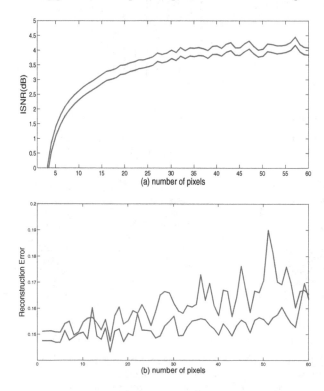

Figure 8. (a) ISNR and (b) Reconstruction Error calculations for a noisy and blurred image vs number of pixels in the blurring process ($n = 1, \ldots, 60$). The blue and red lines indicate the usage of Fourier and Haar based moment analysis of the image, respectively.

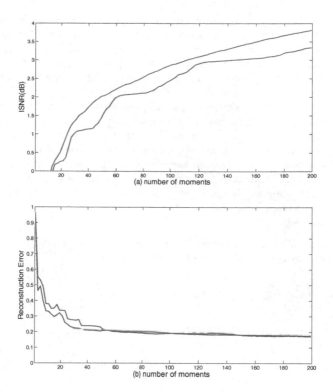

Figure 9. (a) ISNR and (b) Reconstruction Error calculations for a noisy and blurred image vs number of moments ($k = l = 1, \ldots, 200$). The blue and red lines indicate the usage of Fourier and Haar based moment analysis of the image, respectively.

moment values $k = l = 450$ (blue line for the Fourier moment and red line for the Haar moment case). The image is corrupted with white and black (salt and pepper) noise with noise density equal to 0.02. After the moment analysis took place a low pass rotationally symmetric Gaussian filter of standard deviation equal to 45 were applied. Finally, on Figures 9(a) and 9(b) we present the ISNR and the Reconstruction Error respectively, for a number of moments, $k = l = 1, \ldots, 200$ and keeping the number of blurring process at a high level equal to $n = 60$. Similarly, to the previous cases the value of the black and white noise density is equal to the 0.02 and a low-pass Gaussian filter was used for the filtering process.

6. Conclusions

In this study, we introduced a novel computational method based on the calculation of the Moore-Penrose inverse of full rank $r \times m$ matrix, with particular focus on problems arising in image processing. We are motivated by the problem of restoring blurry and noisy images via well developed mathematical methods and techniques based on the inverse procedures in order to obtain an approximation of the original image. By using the proposed algorithm, the resolution of the reconstructed image remains at a very high level, although the main advantage of the method was found on the computational load that has been decreased considerably compared to the other methods and techniques. The efficiency of the generalized inverse is evidenced by the presented simulation results. In this chapter the results presented were demonstrated in the spatial and spectral domain of the image. Orthogonal moments have demonstrated significant energy compaction properties that are desirable in the field of image processing, especially in feature and object recognition. The advantage of representing and recovered any image by choosing a few Haar coefficients (spatial domain) or Fourier coefficients (spectral domain), is the faster transmission of the image as well as the increased robustness when the image is subject to various attacks that can be introduced during the transmission of the data, including additive noise. The results of this work are well established by simulating data. Besides digital image restoration, our work on generalized inverse matrices may also find applications in other scientific fields where a fast computation of the inverse data is needed.

The proposed method can be used in any kind of matrix so the dimensions and the nature of the image do not play any role in this application

Author details

S. Chountasis
Hellenic Transmission System Operator, Greece

V. Katsikis
Technological Education Institute of Piraeus, Petrou Ralli & Thivon 250, 12244 Aigaleo, Athens, Greece

D. Pappas
Department of Statistics, Athens University of Economics and Business, Greece

Appendix

In this section we provide the interested readers with the Matlab codes used in this article.

The following Matlab functions where used to calculate the Fourier and the Haar basis coefficients, and the blurring matrix of the images used.

Function that calculates the Fourier Basis Coefficients (FBC) of an image.

```
%*************************%
%    General   Information.   %
%*************************%
% Synopsis:
% FB= FBC (b_r,b_c)
%Input:
%    b_r :   rows of FB,
%    b_c :  columns of FB
```

```
%
%Output: FB: Fourier base


function FB= FBC (b_r,b_c)

FB=zeros(b_r,b_c); i=(b_c-1)/2;
  for j=1:b_c
    l=(j-i-1);
    for k=1:b_r
      FB(k,j)=exp(-j*2*pi*((k-1)*l)/b_r);
    end
  end
FB=(1/sqrt(b_r))*FB;
```

Function that calculates the Haar Basis Coefficients (HBC) of an image.

```
%***************************%
%   General   Information.    %
%***************************%
% Synopsis:
% HB=HBC(h_r,h_c)
%Input:
%   h_r : rows of HB,
%   h_c : columns of HB
%
%Output: HB: Haar base matrix

function HB=HBC(h_r,h_c)

 if (fix(log2(h_r))~=log2(h_r))
    error('The number of rows must be power of 2');
 end
  HB=zeros(h_r,h_c);
  for i=1:h_r
    HB(i,1)=1;
  end
   for l=2:h_c
    k=2^fix(log2(l-1));
    length=h_r/k;
    start=((l-1)-k)*length+1;
    middle=start+length/2-1;
    last=start+length-1;
    v=sqrt(k);
```

```
   for j=start:middle
     HB(j,l)=v;
   end
    for j=middle+1:last
      HB(j,l)=-v;
    end
   end
 HB=(1/sqrt(h_r))*HB;
```

Function that calculates the blurring matrix of an image.

```
%***************************%
%    General   Information.    %
%***************************%
% Synopsis:
% H = buildH(Fo,h)
%Input:
%   Fo : original image,
%   h : array of blurring process
%
%Output: H: blurring Matrix

function H = buildH(Fo,h)

n = length(h);
N=size(Fo,2);
M=N + n - 1;
H=zeros(N,M);
for j =1:N
H(j,j:j+n-1) = h;
end
```

7. References

[1] Banham M. R. & Katsaggelos A. K., (1997) "Digital Image Restoration" *IEEE Signal Processing Magazine*, 14, 24-41.
[2] Ben-Israel A. & Grenville T. N. E (2002) *Generalized Inverses: Theory and Applications*, Springer-Verlag, Berlin.
[3] Bovik A. (2009) *The essential guide to the image processing*, Academic Press.
[4] Campbell S. L. & Meyer C. D. (1977) *Generalized inverses of Linear Transformations*, Dover Publ. New York.
[5] Castleman K. R. (1996), Digital Processing, Eglewood Cliffs, NJ: Prentice - Hall.
[6] Chantas J., Galatsanos N. P. & Woods N. (2007), Super Resolution Based on Fast Registration and Maximum A Posteriori Reconstruction, *IEEE Trans. on Image Pro-*

cessing, 16, 1821-1830.

[7] Chountasis S.,Katsikis V. N., D. Pappas D. (2009) *Applications of the Moore-Penrose inverse in digital image restoration*, *Mathematical Problems in Engineering*, Volume 2009, Article ID 170724, 12 pages doi:10.1155/2009/170724.

[8] Chountasis S., Katsikis V. N. & D. Pappas D.(2010) *Digital Image Reconstruction in the Spectral Domain Utilizing the Moore-Penrose Inverse*, *Math. Probl. Eng.*, Volume 2010, Article ID 750352, 14 pages doi:10.1155/2010/750352.

[9] Dudani S.A., Breeding K.J. & McGhee R.B. (1977) Aircraft identification by moment invariants, *IEEE* Trans. on Computers C-26 (1), 39-46.

[10] El-Sayed Wahed M.(2007) Image Enhancement Using Second Generation Wavelet Super Resolution, *International Journal of Physical Sciences*, 2 (6), 149-158.

[11] Gonzalez R., P. Wintz (1987) Digital Processing, U.S.A., 2nd Ed. Addison - Wesley Publishing Co.

[12] Groetsch C.(1977), Generalized inverses of linear operators, Marcel Dekker.

[13] Hansen P. C., Nagy J. G. & O'Leary D. P. (2006) *Deblurring images: matrices, spectra, and filtering, SIAM, Philadelphia.*

[14] Hillebrand M. & Muller C. H. (2007) Outlier robust corner-preserving methods for reconstructing noisy images, *The Annals of Statistics.* 35, 132-165.

[15] Katsaggelos A. K., Biemond J., Mersereau R.M.& Schafer R. W. (1985), A General Formulation of Constrained Iterative Restoration Algorithms, *IEEE Proc. ICASSP*, Tampa, FL, 700-703.

[16] Katsikis V. N., Pappas D. & Petralias A.,(2011) *An improved method for the computation of the Moore-Penrose inverse matrix, Appl. Math. Comput.* **217**, 9828-9834.

[17] Martincz J., Porta J.M. & Thomas F.,(2006) *A* Matrix-Based Approach to the Image Moment Problem, Journal of Mathematical Imaging and Vision, 26 , 1-2, 105-113.

[18] Milanfar P., Karl W.C. & Willsky A.S. (1996) *A* moment-based variational approach to tomographic reconstruction *IEEE* Trans. on Image Processing 5 (3), 459-470.

[19] Mukundan R., Ong S. H. & Lee P. A. (2001) Image analysis by Tchebychef moments. *IEEE* Trans. on Image Processing, 10(9) 1357-1364.

[20] Nguyen T.B. and Oommen B.J. (1997) Moment-Preserving piecewise linear approximations of signals and images. *IEEE* Trans. on Pattern Analysis and Machine Intelligence, 19 (1) 84-91.

[21] Pawlak M.(1992) On the reconstruction aspects of moment descriptors, *IEEE* Trans. on Information Theory, 38, 1698Ű1708.

[22] Schafer R. W., Mersereau R. M. & Richards M.A. (1981) "Constrained Iterative Restoration Algorithms," *Proc. IEEE*, 69, 432-450, .

[23] Schuurman D.C. , Capson D.W. (2002) Video-rate eigenspace methods for position tracking and remote monitoring. Fifth IEEE Southwest Symposium on Image Analysis and Interpretation, 45-49.

[24] Sondhi, M. (1972) Restoration: The Removal of Spatially Invariant Degradations, Proc. IEEE, 60, no. 7, 842-853.

[25] Stanimirović I.P. & Tasić M.B.,(2011) Computation of generalized inverses by using the LDL^* decomposition, *Appl. Math. Lett.*, doi:10.1016/j.aml.2011.09.051.

[26] Teague M.R., (1980)Image analysis via the general theory of moments. Journal of the Optical Society of America, vol.70 (8), 920-930.

[27] Teh C. H., Chin, R. T. (1988) On image analysis by the methods of moments. *IEEE* Trans. Pattern Anal. Machine Intell, 10, 496-513.

[28] Trussell H.J. & S. Fogel,(1992) Identification and Restoration of Spatially Variant Motion Blurs in Sequential Images, *IEEE* Trans. Image Proc., 1, 123-126.

[29] Tull D. L & Katsaggelos A.K.,(1996) Iterative Restoration of Fast Moving Objects in Dynamic Images Sequences, *Optical Engineering*, 35(12), 3460-3469.

[30] Wang G., Wei Y. & Qiao S. (2004) *Generalized Inverses: Theory and Computations*, Science Press, Beijing/New York.

Chapter 4

Matlab-Based Algorithm for Real Time Analysis of Multiexponential Transient Signals

Momoh-Jimoh E. Salami, Ismaila B. Tijani,
Abdussamad U. Jibia and Za'im Bin Ismail

Additional information is available at the end of the chapter

1. Introduction

Multiexponential transient signals are particularly important due to their occurrences in many natural phenomena and human applications. For instance, it is important in the study of nuclear magnetic resonance (NMR) in medical diagnosis (Cohn-Sfetcu et al., 1975)), relaxation kinetics of cooperative conformational changes in biopolymers (Provencher, 1976), solving system identification problems in control and communication engineering (Prost and Guotte, 1982), fluorescence decay of proteins (Karrakchou et al., 1992), fluorescence decay analysis (Lakowicz, 1999). Several research work have been reported on the analysis of multicomponent transient signals following the pioneer work of Prony in 1795 (Prony, 1975) and Gardner et al. in 1959 (Gardner, 1979). Detailed review of several techniques for multicomponent transient signals' analysis was recently reported in (Jibia, 2010).

Generally, a multiexponential transient signal is represented by a linear combination of exponentials of the form

$$S(\tau) = \sum_{k}^{M} A_k \exp(-\lambda_k \tau) + n(\tau) \qquad (1)$$

where M is the number of components, A_k and λ_k respectively represent the amplitude and real-valued decay rate constants of the kth component and $n(\tau)$ is the additive white Gaussian noise with variance σ_n^2. The exponentials in equation (1) are assumed to be separable and unrelated. That is, none of the components is produced from the decay of another component. Therefore, in determination of the signal parameters, M, A_k and λ_k from equation (1), it is not sufficient that equation (1) approximates data accurately; it is also important that these parameters are accurately estimated.

There are many problems associated with the analysis of transient signals of the form given in equation (1) due to the nonorthogonal nature of the exponential function. These problems include incorrect detection of the peaks, poor resolution of the estimated decay and inaccurate results for contaminated or closely-related decay rate data as reported in (Salami et.al., 1985). These problems become increasingly difficult when the level of noise is high. Although Gardner transform eliminated the nonorthogonality problem, it introduced error ripples due to short data record and nonstationarity of the preprocessed data. Apart from these problems, analysis of multiexponential signal is computationally intensive and requires efficient tools for its development and implementation in real-time.

To overcome these problems, modification of Gardner transform has been proposed recently with Multiple Signal Classification (MUSIC) superposition modeling technique (Jibia et al., 2008); with minimum norm modeling technique (Jibia and Salami, 2007), with homomorphic deconvolution, with eigenvalues decomposition techniques, and the Singular Value Decomposition (SVD) based-Autoregressive Moving Average (ARMA) modeling techniques (Salami and Sidek, 2000; Jibia, 2009). As reported in (Jibia, 2009), performance comparison of these four modeling techniques has been investigated. Though, all the four techniques were able to provide satisfactory performances at medium and high signal-to-noise ratio (SNR), the SVD-ARMA was reported to have the highest resolution, especially at low SNR.

Hence, the development of SVD-ARMA based algorithm for multiexponential signal analysis using MATLAB software package is examined in this chapter.

MATLAB provides computational efficient platform for the analysis and simulation of complex models and algorithms. In addition, with the aid of inbuilt embedded MATLAB Simulink block, it offers a tool for the integration of developed algorithm/model in an embedded application with little programming efforts as compared to the use of other programming languages (Mathworks, 2008). This functionality is explored in integrating the developed MATLAB-based algorithm into National Instrument (NI) Labview embedded programming tool. Hence, an integrated MATLAB-Labview software interface is proposed for real-time deployment of the algorithm. To this end, the analytical strength of MATLAB together with simplicity and user-friendly benefits of the National Instrument (NI), Labview design platforms are explored in developing an efficient, user-friendly algorithm for the real-time analysis of multiexponential transient signal.

The rest of the chapter is organized as follows. Section 2 provides brief review of techniques for multiexponential signal analysis. The MATLAB algorithm development for the signal analysis is presented in section 3. The development of an integrated MATLAB-Labview real-time software interface is then examined in section 4. Section 5 presents sample real-time data collection together with results and analysis. The chapter is concluded in section 6 with recommendation for future study.

2. Techniques of multiexponential transient signal analysis

Several techniques have been reported for the analysis of transient multiexponential signal. They are classified as: (i) time domain or frequency domain, and (ii) parametric or nonparametric techniques. The main objective of these techniques in analyzing the multiexponentially decaying signals is to estimate the signal parameters as accurately as possible and to get better display of the signal spectra. Time-domain techniques constitute the oldest methods of multiexponential signal analysis prior to the advent of Gardner transformation technique (Gardner et al, 1959; Salami, 1985). Gardner transformation is one of the most important methods of the transient signal analysis based on spectral analysis. Generally, spectral analysis involves transformation of a time-domain signal to a frequency domain so that certain features of the signals that characterized them are easily discerned such as its decay constant, λ_k and amplitude, A_k. In other words, it is the process of obtaining the frequency content (spectrum) of a signal (Proakis and Manolakis 1996). The spectral analysis approach is further categorized into nonparametric and parametric techniques. Nonparametric technique is a frequency-domain technique that obtains the signal spectra directly from the deconvolved data, while the parametric technique obtains the signal spectra indirectly by determining a finite set of parameters that defines a closed form mathematical model for the deconvolved data. Therefore the techniques of multiexponential transient signal analysis are sub-divided into time-domain, nonparametric frequency domain and parametric frequency domain techniques as shown in Figure 1 with their associated methods.

Among the earliest time-domain technique is the peeling technique. However, this technique produces poor results when $S(\tau)$ contains more than two components. Other time-domain techniques such as Prony's method and its variants produce better performance than the peeling technique, however they are very sensitive to noise (Smyth, 2002; Salami, 1995). The nonlinear least squares technique (Smyth, 2002) is computationally inefficient and the solution sometimes fails to converge, which means that the estimate of the signal parameters cannot be accurately obtained.

The nonparametric techniques of spectral analysis are introduced to overcome some limitations of the time-domain techniques. The Gardner transformation technique produces error ripples which obscure the real peaks of the spectrum due to the cutoff points. This technique is good in analyzing signal with high SNR. The fast Fourier transform (FFT) technique, which is an improvement over the original Gardner transformation produces improved resolution. However, the problem of error ripples still exists. The extension of this technique involving the use of digital signal processing and Gaussian filtering is sensitive to noise and its data range has to be limited to get accurate estimates of the signal parameters. Whilst the modified FFT technique is better than the previous methods, it often fails to estimate λ_k correctly especially when the peaks are closely related. The differential technique (Swingler, 1977) provides some improvements over the existing techniques such as better resolution display but it is not suitable for analyzing noisy signal. Furthermore, modifying the FFT technique by incorporating integration procedure (Balcou,1981) does not produce better results as compared to the previous digital technique and the modified FFT technique. Moreover, this technique is still affected by error ripples.

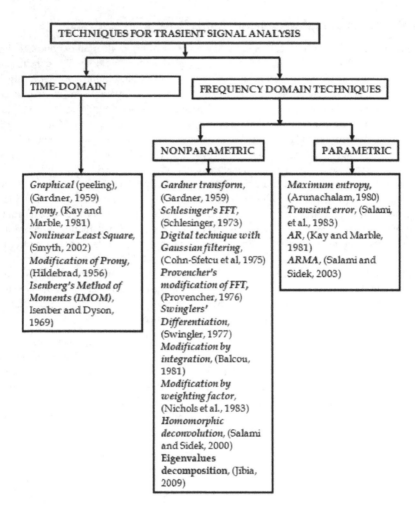

Figure 1. Overview of Techniques for Multiexponential signal analysis

Parametric techniques such as Autoregressive (AR), Moving Average (MA) and ARMA models are introduced to the analysis of multiexponential signals to alleviate the drawbacks of the nonparametric techniques. The AR modeling technique requires less computation than the ARMA modeling technique as its model parameters are relatively easy to estimate. However, it is sensitive to noise due to the assumed all-pole model. On the other hand, MA parameters are difficult to estimate and the resultant spectral estimates have poor resolution. Although, the ARMA modeling technique is much better in estimating noisy signal than the AR modeling technique, it requires a lot of computation. A detailed review of these techniques can be obtained in (Jibia, 2009; Salam and Sidek, 2000).

3. MATLAB-based Algorithm development

The systematic process involved in the development of the MATLAB-based SVD-ARMA algorithm for multiexponential transient signal analysis suitable for real-time application is discussed in this section. Apart from performance evaluation and signal generation, the algorithm consists of five major steps: obtaining convolution integral of the exponential signal using modified Gardner transformation; signal interpolation using spline technique; generation of deconvolved data; SVD-ARMA modeling of the deconvolved data; and power spectrum computation to finally estimate the transient signal parameters. A brief summary of the steps involved are as shown in Figure 2, and briefly highlighted as follows:

Step 1. Signal generation

Generate the required signal, $S(\tau)$ from MATLAB or from the fluorescence substances. For simulation data, MATLAB inbuilt function is used to generate the white Gaussian noise and the DC offset.

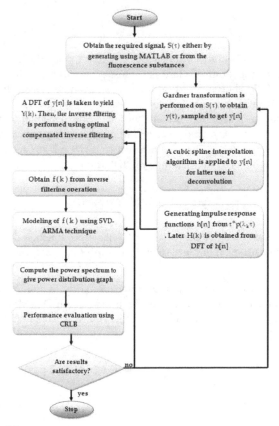

Figure 2. Flowchart of the MATLAB-based algorithm for Multicomponent transient signal analysis

Step 2. Signal preprocessing via Gardner transformation:

This involves the conversion of the measured or generated signal $S(\tau)$ and $p(\tau)$ to y(t) and h(t) respectively using modified Gardner transformation (Salami and Sidek, 2003). This yields a convolution integral as subsequently described.

In general, equation (1) is expressed as

$$S(\tau) = \sum_{k=1}^{M} A_k p(\lambda_k \tau) + n(\tau), \tag{2}$$

where the basis function, $p(\tau) = \exp(-\tau)$. This equation can also be expressed as

$$S(\tau) = \int_0^\infty g(\lambda) p(\lambda \tau) d\lambda + n(\tau), \tag{3}$$

where $g(\lambda) = \sum_{k=1}^{M} A_k \delta(\lambda - \lambda_k)$.

Both sides of equation (3) are multiplied by τ^α in the modified Gardner transformation instead of only τ in the original Gardner transformation. The value of the modifying parameter, α is carefully chosen based on the criteria given by Salami (1995) to avoid poor estimation of the signal parameters because α modifies the amplitude of the signal. Salami (1995) suggested to use $0 < \alpha \leq 1$ in the analysis of multiexponential signals. According to Salami (1985), the choice of α can lead to improved signal parameters estimation as it produces noise reduction effect. The nonlinear transformation $\lambda = e^{-\tau}$ and $\tau = e^t$ are applied to equation (3), resulting in a convolution integral of the form

$$y(t) = \int_{-\infty}^\infty x(\lambda) h(t - \lambda) d\lambda + v(t), \tag{4}$$

where the output function, $y(t) = \exp(\alpha t) S\{\exp(t)\}$, the input function, $x(t) = \exp\{(\alpha-1)t\}g(e^{-t})$, the impulse response function of the system, $h(t) = \exp(\alpha t)p(e^t)$ and the additive noise, $v(t) = \exp(\alpha t)n(e^t)$.

The discrete impulse response function, $h[n]$ is obtained by sampling $\tau^\alpha p(\lambda_k \tau)$ at $1/\Delta t$ Hz. Later, $H(k)$ is obtained from the discrete Fourier transform (DFT) of $h[n]$. Next, equation (4) is converted into a discrete-time convolution. This is done by sampling $y(t)$ at a rate of $1/\Delta t$ Hz to obtain

$$y[n] = \sum_{m=-n_{min}}^{n_{max}} x[m]h[n-m] + v[n], \tag{5}$$

where the total number of samples, N equals $n_{max} - n_{min} + 1$, both n_{max} and n_{min} represent respectively the upper and lower data cut-off points. The criteria for the selection of these sampling conditions have been thoroughly discussed by Salami (1987) and Sen (1995) and these are not discussed further here. Equation (5) forms the basis of estimating the signal parameters since ideally $x(n)$ can be recovered from the observed data by deconvolution. It is necessary to interpolate the discrete time convolution of $y[n]$ since the log samples, $\tau_n = \exp(n\Delta t)$ are not equally spaced.

Step 3. Cubic spline Interpolation

The discrete-time signal y[n] obtained in (5) consists of non-equally spaced samples which would be difficult to digitally process. A cubic interpolation is therefore applied to y[n] using MATLAB function 'spline' to obtain equally spaced samples of y[n].

Step 4. Generation of deconvolved data

In this stage, deconvolved data is generated from y[n] using optimally compensated inverse filtering due to its ability to handle noisy signal when compared to conventional inverse filtering (Salami,1995).

Conventionally, this is done by taking the DFT of equation (5) to produce:

$$Y(k) = X(k)H(k) + V(k) \tag{6}$$

The deconvolved data, $\hat{X}(k)$ can be obtained by computing $Y(k)/H(k)$, that is

$$\hat{X}(k) = \frac{Y(k)}{H(k)} = X(k) + \frac{V(k)}{H(k)} \quad for \ 0 \leq k \leq N-1 \tag{7}$$

where $Y(k)$, $X(k)$, $H(k)$ and $V(k)$ represent the discrete Fourier transform of $y(n)$, $x(n)$, $h(n)$ and $v(n)$ respectively. This inverse filtering operation is called the conventional inverse filtering. It yields deconvolved data with decreasing SNR for increasing values of k. Therefore, the accuracy of $\hat{X}(k)$ deteriorates when the noise variance level is high.

To overcome this problem, an optimally compensated inverse filtering is introduced. In this approach, $H(k)$ is modified by adding an optimally selected value, μ into it. This procedure is done according to Riad and Stafford (1980) by initially designing a transfer function, $H_T(k)$ that yields a better $\hat{X}(k)$ in equation (7), where $H_T(k)$ is given by:

$$H_T(k) = \frac{H^*(k)}{\left[|H(k)|^2 + \mu\right]}, \tag{8}$$

where * denotes the complex conjugate. Substituting equation (8) into equation (7) yields

$$\hat{X}(k) = \frac{Y(k)H^*(k)}{\left[|H(k)|^2 + \mu\right]}, \tag{9}$$

which is referred to as the optimally compensated inverse filtering. It is noted that a small value of μ has a very little effect in the range of frequency when $|H(k)|^2$ is significantly larger than μ. However, if $|H(k)|^2$ is very small, the effect of μ on the deconvolved data is quite substantial, that is μ tends to make $\hat{X}(k)$ less noisy. Therefore, μ puts limit on the noise amplification because the denominator becomes lower bounded according to Dabóczi and Kollár (1996). The parameter μ is carefully selected according to the SNR of the data to obtain good results. The choice of the optimum value of μ according to Salami and Sidek (2001) is best determined by experimental testing.

Equation (9) shows one-parameter compensation procedure, however, multi-parameter compensation is considered in this study. Thus, a regularization operator L(k) is introduced into (8), that is

$$F(k) = \frac{H^*(k)}{\left[|H(k)|^2 + \alpha|L(k)|^2\right]} \qquad (10)$$

where α is the controlling parameter and the regularization operator, $L(k)$ is the discrete Fourier transform of the second order backward difference sequence. $|L(k)|^2$ is given as

$$|L(k)|^2 = 16\sin^4\left(\frac{\pi k}{N}\right), \qquad (11)$$

where N is the number of samples. Using both the second and fourth order backward difference operations in equation (10) yield

$$F(k) = \frac{H^*(k)}{\left[|H(k)|^2 + \mu + \alpha|L(k)|^2 + \beta|L(k)|^4\right]} \qquad (12)$$

where $|L(k)|^4$ denotes the fourth order backward difference operator and μ, α and β are the varied compensation parameters to improve the SNR of the deconvolved data.

Unwanted high frequency noise can still be introduced by this optimally compensated inverse filtering which can make some portion of $X(k)$ unusable. Therefore, a good portion of $\hat{X}(k)$ denoted as $f(k)$, is given as

$$f(k) = \sum_{i=1}^{M} B_i \exp(j2\pi k\Delta f \ln \lambda_i) + V(k), \qquad (13)$$

where $1 \le k \le 2N_d+1$, $B_i = A_i / \lambda_i^\alpha$, $N_d \le (N/2)-1$, N_d is the number of useful deconvolved data points, N is the number of data samples and $V(k)$ is the noise samples of the deconvolved data. Equation (13) is interpreted as a sum of complex exponential signals. The number of deconvolved data points, N_d is carefully selected to produce good results from $f(k)$.

Step 5. Signal parameters estimation using SVD-ARMA modeling

SVD-ARMA algorithm is applied to f(k) to estimate the signal parameters M and λ_k as it provides consistent and accurate estimates of AR parameters with minimal numerical problem which is necessary for real-time application. In addition, it is a powerful computational procedure for matrix analysis especially for solving over determined system of equations. The detailed mathematical analysis of this algorithm is reported in (Salami, 1985).

Generally, the ARMA model assumes that $f(k)$ satisfies the linear difference equation (Salami 1985)

$$f(k) = -\sum_{i=1}^{p} a(i)f(k-i) + \sum_{i=1}^{q} b(i)V(k-i) \tag{14}$$

where V(k) is the input driving sequence, $f(k)$ is the output sequence, $a[i]$ and $b[i]$ are the model coefficients with AR and MA model order of p and q respectively. Usually, the white Gaussian noise becomes the input driving sequence in the analysis of exponentially decaying transient signals.

One of the most effective procedures for estimating these model parameters is by solving a modified Yule-Walker equation (Kay and Marple 1981). This procedure is subsequently discussed.

Equation (14) is multiplied by $f^*(k-m)$ and taking the expectation yields:

$$R_{ff}(k) = -\sum_{n=1}^{p} a[n]R_{ff}(k-n) + \sum_{n=0}^{q} b[n]h(k-m), \tag{15}$$

where $R_{ff}(k)$ is the autocorrelation function of $f(k)$ and $h(k)$ is the impulse response function of the ARMA model. Next, considering the AR portion of equation (15) leads to the modified Yule-Walker equation

$$R_{ff}(k) + \sum_{n=1}^{p} a[n]R_{ff}(k-n) = 0; k \geq q+1. \tag{16}$$

Equation (16) may not hold exactly in practice because both p and q are unknown prior to analysis and $R_{ff}(k)$ has to be estimated from noisy data. This problem is solved by using an SVD algorithm. This algorithm is used by first expressing equation (16) in matrix form as **Ra** = **e** with **R** having elements $r(i,l) = R_{ff}(q_e+1+i-l)$, where $1 \leq i \leq r$; $1 \leq l \leq p_e + 1$. Note that both p_e and q_e are the guess values of the AR and MA model order respectively, **a** is a $p_e \times 1$ and **e** is a $r \times 1$ error vector with $r > p_e$. The SVD algorithm is applied to **R** to produce

$$\mathbf{R} = \mathbf{U\Sigma V}^T = \sum_{n=1}^{p_e} \sigma_n u_n v_n^H \tag{17}$$

where the $r \times (p_e+1)$ unitary matrix $\mathbf{U} = [u_1\ u_2\ ...\ u_{p_e+1}]$, $(p_e+1) \times (p_e+1)$ unitary matrix $\mathbf{V} = [v_1\ v_2\ ...\ v_{p_e+1}]$ and Σ is a diagonal matrix with diagonal elements $(\sigma_1, \sigma_2\ ...\ \sigma_{p_e+1})$. These diagonal elements are called singular values and are arranged so that $\sigma_1 > \sigma_2 > ... > \sigma_{p_e+1} > 0$. Only the first M singular values will be nonzero so that $\sigma_{M+1} = \sigma_{M+2} = \ldots = \sigma_{p_e+1} = 0$. However, $\sigma_{M+1} \neq \sigma_{M+2} \neq \ldots \neq \sigma_{p_e+1} \neq 0$ due to noise contamination. The problem is solved by constructing a lower rank matrix $\mathbf{R_L}$ from $\mathbf{R}$ using the first M singular values, that is

$$\mathbf{R_L} = \mathbf{U_M \Sigma_M V_M}^H = \sum_{n=1}^{M} \sigma_n u_n v_n^H, \tag{18}$$

where $\mathbf{U_M}$, $\mathbf{\Sigma_M}$ and $\mathbf{V_M}$ are the truncated version of $\mathbf{U}$, $\mathbf{\Sigma}$ and $\mathbf{V}$ respectively. The AR coefficients are then estimated from the relation $\mathbf{a} = -\mathbf{R_L}^{\#}\mathbf{r}$, where $\mathbf{r}$ corresponds to the first column of $\mathbf{R_L}$ and $\mathbf{R_L}^{\#}$ is given as

$$\mathbf{R_L}^{\#} = \sum_{n=1}^{M} \sigma_n^{-1} u_n^H v_n. \tag{19}$$

The estimated AR coefficients are then used to generate the residual error sequences:

$$\beta(k) = \sum_{l=0}^{p_e} \sum_{m=0}^{p_e} a[l]a^*[m]R_{ff}(k+m-l) \tag{20}$$

from which the actual MA parameters are obtained directly from equation (20). However, MA spectra can be obtained from the DFT of the error sequences, $\beta(k)$. An exponential window is applied to $\beta(k)$ to ensure that the MA spectra derived from the error sequences are positive definite. Next, the ARMA spectrum is computed from

$$S_f(z) = \frac{\sum_{k=-p_e}^{p_e} \beta(k)z^{-k}}{|A(z)|^2} \tag{21}$$

and the desired power distribution of $x(t)$, denoted as $P_x(t)$ is obtained by evaluating $S_f(z)$ on the unit circle $z = \exp\left\{2\pi j \dfrac{t}{N\Delta t}\right\}$, that is:

$$P_x(t) = S_f(z)\Big|_{z=\exp\left\{\frac{j2\pi t}{N\Delta t}\right\}} = \sum_{k=1}^{M} B_k^2 \delta(t - \ln \lambda_k). \tag{22}$$

Eventually, M and $\ln \lambda_k$ are obtained from $P_x(t)$.

Step 6. Graphical presentation of output

Power distribution graph has been used to display the results of multiexponential signal analysis. This is computed from the power spectrum of the resulting output signal from SVD-ARMA modeling method as shown in equation (21).

Step 7. Performance evaluation

The efficiency of the algorithm with SVD-ARMA modeling technique in estimating λ_k correctly is determined by the Cramer-Rao lower bound (CRLB) expressed as:

$$\text{CRLB}(\lambda_k) = \frac{6(1 + 0.7(\lambda_k N)^{3/2})^2}{N^3 SNR}, \tag{23}$$

where N is the number of data points, the CRB(λ_k) is the CRLB for estimating λ_k and SNR equals to A_k^2 divided by the variance of the white Gaussian noise.

The Cramer-Rao lower bound will determine whether the estimator is efficient by comparing the variance of the estimator, $var(\lambda_k)$ with the Cramer-Rao lower bound. Variance that approaches the CRLB is said to be optimal according to Kay and Marple (1981) and Sha'ameri (2000). Consequently, the closer the variance of the estimator is to the CRLB, the better is the estimator.

A MATLAB-mfile code has been written to implement the steps 1 to 6 described above, details of this have been thoroughly discussed in (Jibia, 2009).

4. Integrated MATLAB-labview for real-time implementation

This section discusses the development of proposed integrated Labview-MATLAB software interface for real-time (RT) implementation of the algorithm for multicomponent signal analysis as described in section 3. Real-time signal analysis is required for most practical applications of multicomponent signal analysis. In this study, reference is made to the application to fluorescence signal analysis. A typical multicomponent signal analyzer comprises optical sensor which is part of the spectrofluorometer system, signal conditioning/data acquisition system, embedded processor that runs the algorithm in real-time, and display/storage devices as shown in Figure 3. National Instrument (NI) real-time hardware and software are considered for the development of this system due to its ease of implementation.

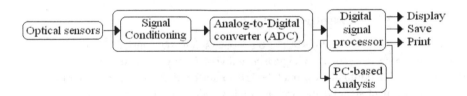

Figure 3. Block diagram of the multicomponent signal analyzer prototype.

4.1. Labview real-time module and target

The Labview real-time module (RT-software) together with NI sbRIO-9642 (RT-hardware) has been adopted in this study. The Labview Real-Time software module allows for the creation of reliable, real-time applications which are easily downloaded onto the target hardware from Labview GUI programming tool.

The NI sbRIO-9642 is identical in architecture to CompactRIO system, only in a single circuit board. Single-Board RIO hardware features a real-time processor and programmable FPGA just as with CompactRIO, and has several inputs and outputs (I/O) modules as shown in Figure 4.

System development involves graphical programming with Labview on the host Window computer, which is then downloaded and run on real-time hardware target. Since the algorithm has been developed with MATLAB scripts, an integrated approach was adopted in the programme development as subsequently described.

Figure 4. NI sbRIO-9642 for real-time hardware target

4.2. MATLAB-labview software integration

The developed algorithm with MATLAB scripts was integrated inside Labview for real-time embedded set-up as shown in Figure 5. Labview front-panel and block diagrams were developed with inbuilt Labview math Scripts to run the MATLAB algorithm for the analysis of multicomponent signals. The use of Labview allows for ease of programming, and real-time deployment using the Labview real-time module described in section 4.1. Also, it provides a user friendly software interface for real-time processing of the fluorescence signals.

As shown in Figure 5, the sampled data produced by the spectrofluorometer system are pre-processed by the NI-DAQ Cards. These signals are then read by the embedded real-time software, analyze the signals and display the results in a user friendly manner. The user is prompted to enter the number of samples to be analyzed from the front-panel using the developed SVD-ARMA algorithm.

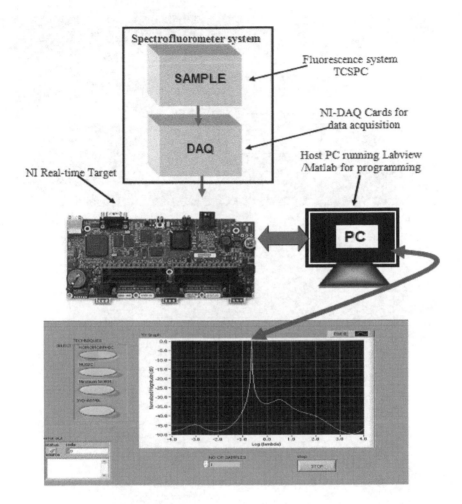

Figure 5. Block Diagram of the real-time set-up

Generally, the developed algorithm with MATLAB scripts was integrated inside Labview for real-time embedded set-up as follows:

i. Pre-simulation of the MATLAB algorithm inside embedded MATLAB Simulink block: this requires re-structuring of the codes to be compatible for embedded Simulink implementation, and hence deployment inside Labview MathScript. Figure 7 shows the MATLAB Simulink blocks configuration with embedded MATLAB function together with cross-section of the algorithm. The DATA with time vector is prepared inside the workspace and linked to the model input. Figure 10 (a-f) shows the simulation results with experimental data described in section 5.

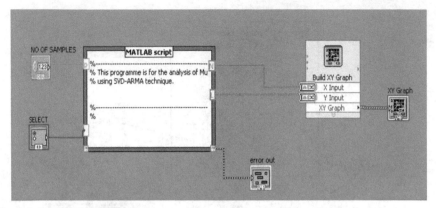

Figure 6. Lab view Block Diagram

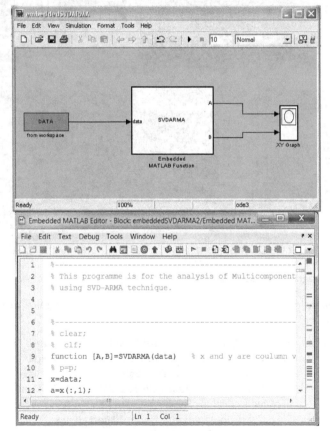

Figure 7. Embedded MATLAB set-up for algorithm simulation

ii.   Labview programming: Development of Labview front-panel and block diagram is as shown in Figure 4. In the block diagram programming, the Labview MathScript node is employed to integrate the MATLAB codes in the overall Labview programme. The script (Figure 8) invokes the MATLAB software script server to execute scripts written in the MATLAB language syntax

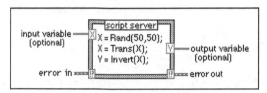

Figure 8. NI Labview MATLAB script nodes

iii. The integrated software interface is evaluated with the real-time fluorescence data collected from a spectrofluorometer.

5. Sample collection, results and discussion

Due to unavailability of spectrofluorometer system that can be directly linked with the set-up, sampled data collected from fluorescence decay experiment conducted using Spectramax Germini XS system were used to test the performance of the integrated system. The schematic diagram of the spectrofluorometer operation is shown in Figure 9, and itemized as follows:

Step 1.   The excitation light source is the xenon flash lamp.

Step 2.   The light passes through the excitation cutoff wheel. This wheel reduces the amount of stray light into the movable grating.

Step 3.   The movable grating selects the desired excitation wavelength. Then, this excitation light enters a 1.0 mm diameter fiber.

Step 4.   This 1.0 mm diameter fiber focuses the excitation light before entering the sample in the micro-plate well. This focusing prevents part of the light from striking adjacent wells.

Step 5.   The light enters the wheel and if fluorescent molecules are present, the two mirrors focus the light from the well into a 4.0 mm optical bundles.

Step 6.   The movable, focusing grating allows light of chosen emission wavelength to enter the emission cutoff wheel.

Step 7.   This emission cutoff wheel will further filter the light before the light enters the photomultiplier tube.

Step 8.   The photomultiplier tube detects the emitted light and passes a signal to the instrument's electronics which then send the signal to the data acquisition system inside the spectrofluorometer.

Three intrinsic fluorophores (Acridine Orange; Fluorescein Sodium and Quinine) were used in the experiment. The details of the substances are given in Table 1.

	Acridine Orange	Fluorescein Sodium	Quinine
Molecular formula	$C_{17}H_{12}ClN_3$	$C_{20}H_{10}Na_2O_5$	$C_{20}H_{24}N_2O_2$
Manufacturer	Merck	Merck	Merck
Molecular weight	301.8g/mol	376.28	324.43
Purity by HPLC	99.1%	Extra pure	Extra pure
Form	Solid	Solid	Powder,
Colour	Orange red	Reddish brown	White
Solubility in water	28g/l	500g/l	0.5g/l
Solutility in ethanol	Soluble	140g/l	1200g/l

Table 1. Characteristics of the fluorophores samples

The simulation results for Acridine orange, Fluorescein Sodium, Quinine, Quinine plus Arcridine, Fluorescein Sodium plus Acridine orange, and Fluorescein Sodium plus Acridine orange plus Quinin in water are shown in Figure 10 (a-f) respectively.

Figure 11 to Figure 13 show the sample of results obtained from the integrated MATLAB-Labview real-time software which has been developed. Both results of simulation and real-time software interface yield accurate estimates of the fluorescence data as shown in Figure 10-Figure 13, and presented in Table 2. The singular values for each of the samples combination are given in Table 3. The results indicate accurate determination of the constituent samples

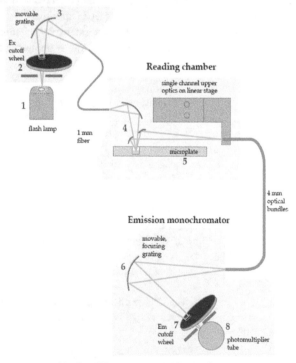

Figure 9. Schematic diagram of the SPECTRAMAX Gemini Spectrofluorometer operation (SPECTRAmax®)

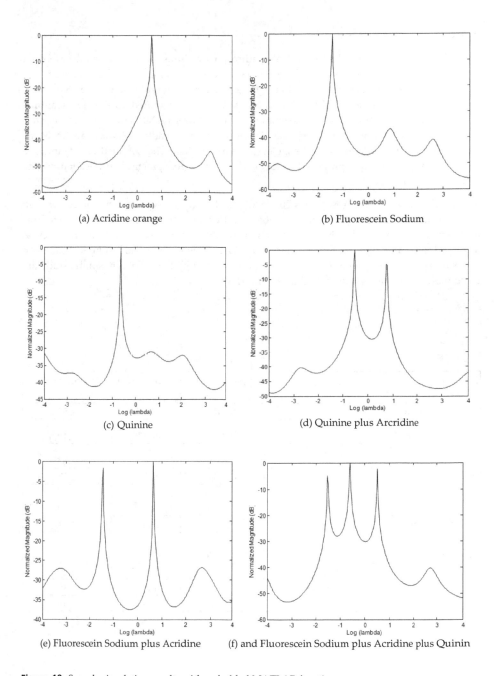

(a) Acridine orange

(b) Fluorescein Sodium

(c) Quinine

(d) Quinine plus Arcridine

(e) Fluorescein Sodium plus Acridine

(f) and Fluorescein Sodium plus Acridine plus Quinin

Figure 10. Sample simulation results with embedded MATLAB function

6. Conclusion/Future study

The development of MATLAB-based algorithm for real-time analysis of multicomponent transient signal analysis based on SVD-ARMA modeling technique has been presented in this chapter. To enhance real-time interface and rapid prototyping on target hardware, complementary benefits of MATLAB and Labview were explored to develop real-time software interface downloadable into single board computer by NI Labview. In the absence of the spectrofluorometer system, the developed user friendly software for real-time deployment was validated with the collected real-time data. The obtained results indicate the effectiveness of the proposed integrated software for practical application of the proposed algorithm.

Future direction of this research will be directed towards development of customized spectrofluorometer sub-system that can be directly integrated to the overall system. This will eventually facilitate direct application of the developed algorithm in practical applications involving transient signal analysis. Also, other algorithms based on homomorphic and eigenvalues decomposition developed by the authors in similar study are to be made available as option on the user interface.

Mixture	Expected value	SVD-ARMA	Percentage error
Acridine orange	0.5978	0.625	4.55
Fluorescein Sodium	-1.4584	-1.438	1.40
Quinine	-0.6419	-0.625	2.63
AcridineOrange +	0.6539	0.6563	0.37
Fluorescein Sodium	-1.4584	-1.438	1.40
AcridineOrange	0.7750	0.761	1.81
+Quinine	-0.5539	-0.5313	4.08
	0.5105	0.5325	4.31
Acridine Orange + Fluorescein Sodium	-0.6152	-0.5938	3.48
+Quinine	-1.5260	-1.533	0.46

Table 2. Estimated Log of decay rates and percentage error from fluorescence decay experiment ($In\lambda$)

Singular values for Acridine Orange +Fluorescein Sodium (MPD)	Singular values for Acridine orange and Quinine (MPD)	Singular values for Acridine Orange +Fluorescein Sodium + Quinine (MPD)
1.4539e+005	1.784e+005	1.9659e+005
1742.9	14341	15247
1.8877e-011	2.7015e-011	1753.9
5.8244e-012	6.348e-012	3.4341e-011
5.2379e-012	6.0042e-012	8.2283e-012
4.9242e-012	5.6011e-012	7.3577e-012
4.5305e-012	4.9272e-012	6.899e-012
4.267e-012	4.8779e-012	6.5831e-012
3.891e-012	4.6323e-012	5.6838e-012
3.5599e-012	4.0781e-012	5.3607e-012
3.1474e-012	3.8214e-012	5.0667e-012
3.0647e-012	3.73e-012	4.5693e-012
2.6685e-012	3.4865e-012	4.1823e-012
2.4369e-012	3.3531e-012	3.859e-012
2.1072e-012	2.9901e-012	3.6511e-012
1.8205e-012	2.4538e-012	3.1307e-012
1.7258e-012	2.1495e-012	3.0133e-012
1.5546e-012	1.6585e-012	2.4723e-012
1.3322e-012	1.5298e-012	1.9237e-012
1.1956e-012	1.3568e-012	1.8882e-012

Table 3. Singular values for SVD-ARMA using experimental data

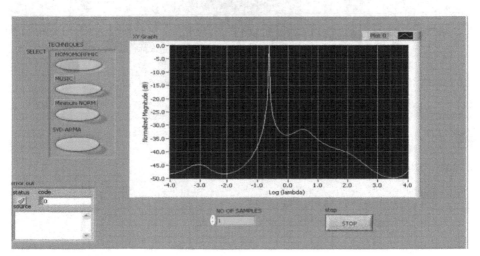

Figure 11. Power distributions for Quinine in water

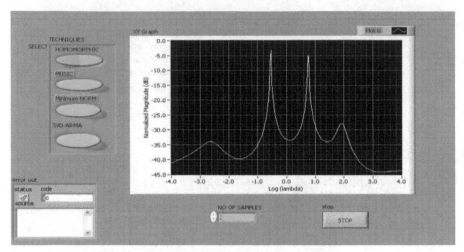

Figure 12. Power distribution Quinine plus Arcridine Sodium in water

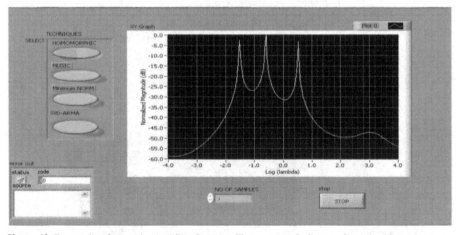

Figure 13. Power distribution for Acridine Orange + Fluorescein + Sodium and quinine in water

Author details

Momoh-Jimoh E. Salami, Ismaila B. Tijani and Za'im Bin Ismail
Intelligent Mechatronics Research Unit, Department of Mechatronics, International Islamic University Malaysia, Gombak, Malaysia

Abdussamad U. Jibia
Department of Electrical/Electronic Engineering, Bayero University Kano, Kano, Nigeria

7. References

Abdulsammad Jibia,2010."Real Time Analysis of Multicomponent Transient Signal using a Combination of Parametric and Deconvolution Techniques", A PhD thesis submitted to Department of ECE, IIUM, Malaysia.

Arunachalam, V. (1980). Multicomponent Signal Analysis. PhD dissertation, Dept. of Electrical Engineering, The University of Calgary, Alberta, Canada.

Balcou, Y. (1981). Comments on a numerical method allowing an improved analysis of multiexponential decay curves. *International journal of modelling and simulation. 1* (1), 47-51.

Cohn-Sfetcu, S., Smith, M.R., Nichols, S.T. & Henry, D.L. 1975. A digital technique for analyzing a class of multicomponent signals. *Processings of the IEEE.* 63(10): 1460-1467.

Embedded MATLAB User guide, 2008. Ww.mathworks.com, accessed date: Jan., 2011

Gardner, D.G., Gardner, J.C. & Meinke, W.W. 1959. Method for the analysis of multicomponent exponential decay curves. *The journal of chemical physics.* 31(4): 978-986.

Gutierrez-Osuna, R., Gutierrez-Galvez, A., & Powar, N. (2003). Transient response analysis for temperature-modulated hemoresistors. *Sensors and Actuators Journal B (Chemical), 93* (1-3), 57-66.

Hildebrad, F.B., (1956). *Introduction to numerical analysis.* New York: McGraw-Hill.

Istratov, A. A., & Vyvenko, O. F. (1999). Exponential Analysis in Physical Phenomena. *Rev. Sci. Instruments, 70* (2), 1233-1257.

Isernberg, I., & Dyson, R. D. (1969). The analysis of fluorescence decay by a method of moments. *The Biophysical Journal, 9* (11), 1337-1350.

Jibia, A.U., Salami, M.J.E., & Khalifa, O.O. (2009). Multiexponential Data Analysis Using Gardner Transform . (a draft ISI review journal paper)

Jibia, A.U. & Salami, M.J.E. (2007). Performance Evaluation of MUSIC and Minimum Norm Eigenvector Algorithms in Resolving Noisy Multiexponential Signals. *Proceedings of World Academy of Science, Eng. and Tech* Vol. 26, Bangok, Thailand. 24-28.

Karrakchou, M., Vidal, J., Vesin, J.M., Feihl, F., Perret, C. & Kunt, M. 1992. Parameter estimation of decaying exponentials by projection on the parameter space. *Elsevier Publishers B.V.* 27: 99-107.

Kay, S.M. &Marple, S.L. (1981). Spectrum analysis – A modern perspective. Labview usr manual,2010. www.ni.com/pdf/manuals. accessed Jan., 2011

Lakowicz, J.R. 1999. *Principles of fluorescence spectroscopy.* 2nd Ed. New York: Kluwer Academic/Plenum Publishers.

Nichols, S.T., Smith, M.R. & Salami, M.J.E. (1983). *High Resolution Estimates in Multicomponent Signal Analysis* (Technical Report). Alberta: Dept. of Electrical Enginering, University of Calgary.

Provencher, S.W. 1976. A Fourier method for the analysis of exponential decay curves. *Biophysical journal.* 16: 27-39.

Prost, R. & Goutte, R. 1982. Kernel splitting method in support constrained deconvolution for super-resolution. Institut National des Science, France.

Prony, R. (1795). Essai Experimentals et Analytique. *J. ecole* Polytech., Paris, 1, 24- 76.

Proakis, J.G. & Manolakis, D.G. (2007). *Digital signal processing: Principles, algorithms, and applications*. New Jersey: Prentice-Hall.

Prony, R. (1795). Essai Experimentals et Analytique. *J. ecole Polytech., Paris*, 1, 24-76.

Provencher, S.W. (1976). A Fourier method for the analysis of exponential decay curves. *Biophysical journal*, 16, 27-39.

Salami, M.J.E. (1985).Application of ARMA models in multicomponent signal analysis. Ph.D. Dissertation, Dept. of Electrical Engineering, University of Calgary, Calgary, Canada

Salami, M.J.E. (1995). Performance evaluation of the data preprocessing techniques used in multiexponential signal analysis. *AMSE Press. 33* (2), 23-38.

Salami, M.J.E. (1999). Analysis of multicomponent transient signal using eigen-decomposition based methods.*Proc. Intern. Wireless and Telecom. Symp.,3* (5), 214-217.

Salami, M.J.E., & Bulale, Y.I. (2000). Analysis of multicomponent transient signals: A MATLAB approach. 4th International Wireless and Telecommunications Symposium/Exhibition, 253-256.*Proceedings of the IEEE, 69* (11), 1380-1419.

Salami M.J.E. & Ismail Z. (2003). Analysis of multiexponential transient signals using interpolation-based deconvolution and parametric modeling techniques. *IEEE International conference on Industrial Technology*, 1, 271-276.

Salami M.J.E. and Sidek S.N. (2000). Performance evaluation of the deconvolution techniques used in analyzing multicomponent transient signals. *Proc. IEEE Region 10 International Conference on Intelligent System and Technologies for the New Millennium (TENCON 2000)*, 1, 487-492.

Sarkar, T.K., Weiner, D.D. & Jain V.K. (1981). Some mathematical considerations in dealing with the inverse problem. *IEEE transactions on antennas and propagation, 29* (2), 373-379.

Schlesinger, J. (1973). Fit to experimental data with exponential functions using the fast Fourier transform. *Nuclear instruments and methods.* 106, 503-508.

Sen, R. 1995. On the identification of exponentially decaying signals. *IEEE Transaction Signal Processing.* 43(8): 1936-1945.

Smyth, G.K. (2002). Nonlinear regression. *Encyclopedia of environmetrics.* 3, 1405-1411.

SPECTRAmax® GEMINI XS product literature. http://www.biocompare.com/Product-Reviews/41142-Molecular-Devices-8217-SPECTRAmax-GEMINI-XS-Microplate-Spectrofluorometer/ accessed on December, 2008.

Swingler, D.N. (1999). Approximations to the Cramer-Rao lower bound for a single damped exponential signal. . *Signal Processing, 75* (2), 197-200.

Trench, W.F. (1964). An algorithm for the inversion of finite Toeplitz matrices. *J. SIAM, 12* (3), 515-522.

Ulrych, T.J. (1971). Application of homomorphic deconvolution to seismology. *Geophysics, 4* (36), 650-660.

Chapter 5

Digital FIR Hilbert Transformers: Fundamentals and Efficient Design Methods

David Ernesto Troncoso Romero and Gordana Jovanovic Dolecek

Additional information is available at the end of the chapter

1. Introduction

Digital Hilbert transformers are a special class of digital filter whose characteristic is to introduce a $\pi/2$ radians phase shift of the input signal. In the ideal Hilbert transformer all the positive frequency components are shifted by $-\pi/2$ radians and all the negative frequency components are shifted by $\pi/2$ radians. However, these ideal systems cannot be realized since the impulse response is non-causal. Nevertheless, Hilbert transformers can be designed either as Finite Impulse Response (FIR) or as Infinite Impulse Response (IIR) digital filters [1], [2], and they are used in a wide number of Digital Signal Processing (DSP) applications, such as digital communication systems, radar systems, medical imaging and mechanical vibration analysis, among others [3]-[5].

IIR Hilbert transformers perform a phase approximation. This means that the phase response of the system is approximated to the desired values in a given range of frequencies. The magnitude response allows passing all the frequencies, with the magnitude obtained around the desired value within a given tolerance [6], [7]. On the other hand, FIR Hilbert transformers perform a magnitude approximation. In this case the system magnitude response is approximated to the desired values in a given range of frequencies. The advantage is that their phase response is always maintained in the desired value over the complete range of frequencies [8].

Whereas IIR Hilbert transformers can present instability and they are sensitive to the rounding in their coefficients, FIR filters can have exact linear phase and their stability is guaranteed. Moreover, FIR filters are less sensitive to the coefficients rounding and their phase response is not affected by this rounding. Because of this, FIR Hilbert transformers are often preferred [8]-[15]. Nevertheless, the main drawback of FIR filters is a higher complexity compared with the corresponding IIR filters. Multipliers, the most costly elements in DSP implementations, are required in an amount linearly related with the length of the filter. A linear phase FIR Hilbert transformer, which has an anti-symmetrical impulse response, can be designed with either an odd length (Type III symmetry) or an even length (Type IV symmetry). The number of multipliers m is given in terms of the filter length L as $m \approx C \cdot L$, where $C = 0.25$ for a filter with Type III symmetry or $C = 0.5$ for a filter with Type IV symmetry.

The design of optimum equiripple FIR Hilbert transformers is usually performed by Parks-McClellan algorithm. Using the MATLAB Signal Processing Toolbox, this becomes a straightforward procedure through the function firpm. However, for small transition bandwidth and small ripples the resulting filter requires a very high length. This complexity increases with more stringent specifications, i.e., narrower transition bandwidths and also smaller pass-band ripples. Therefore, different techniques have been developed in the last 2 decades for efficient design of Hilbert transformers, where the highly stringent specifications are met with an as low as possible required complexity. The most representative methods are [9]-[15], which are based in very efficient schemes to reduce complexity in FIR filters.

Methods [9] and [10] are based on the Frequency Response Masking (FRM) technique proposed in [16]. In [9], the design is based on reducing the complexity of a half-band filter. Then, the Hilbert transformer is derived from this half-band filter. In [10], a frequency response corrector subfilter is introduced, and all subfilters are designed simultaneously under the same framework. The method [11] is based on wide bandwidth and linear phase FIR filters with Piecewise Polynomial-Sinusoidal (PPS) impulse response. These methods offer a very high reduction in the required number of multiplier coefficients compared to the direct design based on Parks-McClellan algorithm. An important characteristic is that they are fully parallel approaches, which have the disadvantage of being area consuming since they do not directly take advantage of hardware multiplexing.

The Frequency Transformation (FT) method, proposed first in [17] and extended in [18], was modified to design FIR Hilbert transformers in [12] based on a tapped cascaded interconnection of repeated simple basic building blocks constituted by two identical subfilters. Taking advantage of the repetitive use of identical subfilters, the recent proposal [13] gives a simple and efficient method to design multiplierless Hilbert transformers, where a combination of the FT method with the Pipelining-Interleaving (PI) technique of [19] allows getting a time-multiplexed architecture which only requires three subfilters. In [14], an optimized design was developed to minimize the overall number of filter coefficients in a modified FT-PI-based structure derived from the one of [13], where only two subfilters are needed. Based on methods [13] and [14], a different architecture which just requires one subfilter was developed in [15].

In this chapter, fundamentals on digital FIR Hilbert transformers will be covered by reviewing the characteristics of analytic signals. The main connection existing between

Hilbert transformers and half-band filters will be highlighted but, at the same time, the complete introductory explanation will be kept as simple as possible. The methods to design low-complexity FIR filters, namely FRM [16], FT [17] and PPS [11], as well as the PI architecture [19], which are the cornerstone of the efficient techniques to design Hilbert transformers presented in [9]-[15], will be introduced in a simplified and concise way. With such background we will provide an extensive revision of the methods [9]-[15] to design low-complexity efficient FIR Hilbert transformers, including MATLAB routines for these methods.

2. Complex signals, analytic signals and Hilbert transformers

A real signal is a one-dimensional variation of real values over time. A *complex signal* is a two-dimensional signal whose value at some instant in time can be specified by a single complex number. The variation of the two parts of the complex numbers, namely the real part and the imaginary part, is the reason for referring to it as two-dimensional signal [20]. A real signal can be represented in a two-dimensional plot by presenting its variations against time. Similarly, a complex signal can be represented in a three-dimensional plot by considering time as a third dimension.

Real signals always have positive and negative frequency spectral components, and these components are generally real and imaginary. For any real signal, the positive and negative parts of its real spectral component always have even symmetry around the zero-frequency point, i.e., they are mirror images of each other. Conversely, the positive and negative parts of its imaginary spectral component are always anti-symmetric, i.e., they are always negatives of each other [1]. This conjugate symmetry is the invariant nature of real signals.

Complex signals, on the other hand, are not restricted to these spectral conjugate symmetry conditions. The special case of complex signals which do not have a negative part neither in their real nor in their imaginary spectral components are known as *analytic signals* or also as quadrature signals [2]. An example of analytic signal is the complex exponential signal $x_c(t)$, presented in Figure 1, and described by

$$x_c(t) = e^{j\omega_0 t} = x_r(t) + jx_i(t) = \cos(\omega_0 t) + j\sin(\omega_0 t). \tag{1}$$

The real part and the imaginary part of the analytic signal are related trough the *Hilbert transform*. In simple words, given an analytic signal, its imaginary part is the Hilbert transform of its real part. Figure 1 shows the complex signal $x_c(t)$, its real part $x_r(t)$ and its imaginary part, $x_i(t)$. Figure 2 presents the frequency spectral components of these signals. It can be seen that the real part $x_r(t)$ and the imaginary part $x_i(t)$, both real signals, preserve the spectral conjugate symmetry. The complex signal $x_c(t)$ does not have negative parts neither in its real spectral component nor in its imaginary spectral component. For this reason, analytic signals are also referred as one-side spectrum signals. Finally, Figure 3 shows the Hilbert transform relation between the real and imaginary parts of $x_c(t)$.

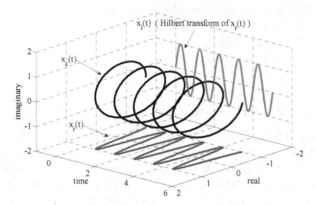

Figure 1. The Hilbert transform and the analytic signal of $x_r(t) = \cos(\omega_0 t)$, $\omega_0 = 2\pi$.

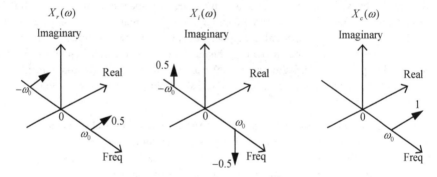

Figure 2. From left to right, frequency spectrum of $x_r(t)$, $x_i(t)$ and $x_c(t)$.

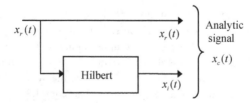

Figure 3. Hilbert transform relations between $x_r(t)$ and $x_i(t)$ to generate $x_c(t)$.

The motivation for creating analytic signals, or in other words, for eliminating the negative parts of the real and imaginary spectral components of real signals, is that these negative parts have in essence the same information than the positive parts due to the conjugate symmetry previously mentioned. The elimination of these negative parts reduces the required bandwidth for the processing. For the case of DSP applications, it is possible to form a complex sequence $x_c(n)$ given as follows,

$$x_c(n) = x_r(n) + jx_i(n), \tag{2}$$

with the special property that its frequency spectrum $X_c(e^{j\omega})$ is equal to that of a given real sequence $x(n)$ for the positive Nyquist interval and zero for the negative Nyquist interval, i.e.,

$$X_c(e^{j\omega}) = \begin{cases} X(e^{j\omega}) & \text{for } 0 \le \omega < \pi, \\ 0 & \text{for } -\pi \le \omega < 0. \end{cases} \tag{3}$$

Although analyticity has no formal meaning for sequences [2], the same terminology, i.e., analytic sequence, will be applied for complex sequences whose frequency spectrum is one-sided, like in (3).

If $X_r(e^{j\omega})$ and $X_i(e^{j\omega})$ respectively denote the frequency spectrums of $x_r(n)$ and $x_i(n)$, then

$$X_c(e^{j\omega}) = X_r(e^{j\omega}) + jX_i(e^{j\omega}). \tag{4}$$

The spectrums of $x_r(n)$ and $x_i(n)$ can be readily deduced as

$$X_r(e^{j\omega}) = \tfrac{1}{2}[X_c(e^{j\omega}) + X_c^*(e^{-j\omega})], \tag{5}$$

$$jX_i(e^{j\omega}) = \tfrac{1}{2}[X_c(e^{j\omega}) - X_c^*(e^{-j\omega})], \tag{6}$$

where $X_c^*(e^{j\omega})$ is the complex conjugate of $X_c(e^{j\omega})$. Note that (6) gives an expression for $jX_i(e^{j\omega})$, which is the frequency spectrum of the imaginary signal $jx_i(n)$. Also, note that $X_r(e^{j\omega})$ and $X_i(e^{j\omega})$ are both complex-valued functions in general. However, $X_r(e^{j\omega})$ is conjugate symmetric, i.e., $X_r(e^{j\omega}) = X_r^*(e^{-j\omega})$. Similarly, $jX_i(e^{j\omega})$ is conjugate anti-symmetric, i.e., $jX_i(e^{j\omega}) = -jX_i^*(e^{-j\omega})$. These relations are illustrated in Figure 4.

From (5) and (6) we obtain

$$X_c(e^{j\omega}) = 2X_r(e^{j\omega}) - X_c^*(e^{-j\omega}), \tag{7}$$

$$X_c(e^{j\omega}) = 2jX_i(e^{j\omega}) + X_c^*(e^{-j\omega}), \tag{8}$$

and since $X_c^*(e^{-j\omega}) = 0$ for $0 < \omega < \pi$ (see Figure 4b), eqs. (3), (7) and (8) give

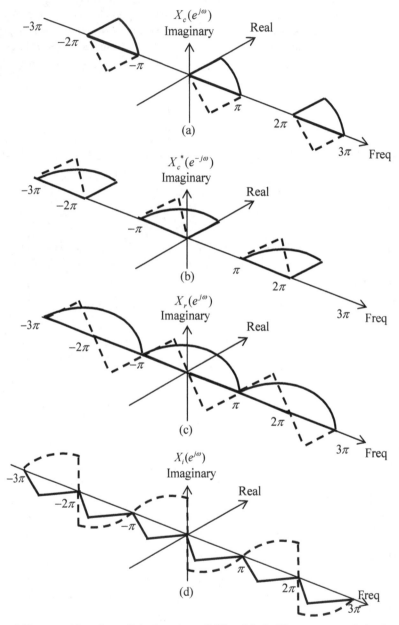

Figure 4. Decomposition of an unilateral spectrum. Solid and dashed lines are, respectively, the real and imaginary parts.

$$X_c(e^{j\omega}) = \begin{cases} 2X_r(e^{j\omega}) & \text{for } 0 \le \omega < \pi, \\ 0 & \text{for } -\pi \le \omega < 0. \end{cases} \tag{9}$$

$$X_c(e^{j\omega}) = \begin{cases} 2jX_i(e^{j\omega}) & \text{for } 0 \le \omega < \pi, \\ 0 & \text{for } -\pi \le \omega < 0. \end{cases} \tag{10}$$

Thus

$$X_i(e^{j\omega}) = -jX_r(e^{j\omega}) \quad \text{for } 0 \le \omega < \pi. \tag{11}$$

On the other hand, from (4), and since $X_c(e^{j\omega}) = 0$ for $-\pi \le \omega < 0$, we have

$$X_i(e^{j\omega}) = jX_r(e^{j\omega}) \quad \text{for } -\pi \le \omega < 0. \tag{12}$$

Therefore, (11) and (12) can be expressed as

$$X_i(e^{j\omega}) = \begin{cases} -jX_r(e^{j\omega}) & \text{for } 0 \le \omega < \pi, \\ jX_r(e^{j\omega}) & \text{for } -\pi \le \omega < 0, \end{cases} \tag{13}$$

or

$$X_i(e^{j\omega}) = H(e^{j\omega})X_r(e^{j\omega}), \tag{14}$$

where

$$H(e^{j\omega}) = \begin{cases} -j & \text{for } 0 \le \omega < \pi, \\ j & \text{for } -\pi \le \omega < 0. \end{cases} \tag{15}$$

According to (14), $x_i(n)$ can be obtained by processing $x_r(n)$ with a linear time-invariant discrete-time system whose frequency response $H(e^{j\omega})$ is given in (15). This frequency response has unity magnitude, a phase angle of $-\pi/2$ radians for $0 < \omega < \pi$, and a phase angle of $\pi/2$ radians for $-\pi < \omega < 0$. A system of this type is commonly referred to as *Hilbert transformer* or sometimes as 90-degree phase shifter.

The impulse response $h(n)$ of a Hilbert transformer is [2]

$$h(n) = \begin{cases} \dfrac{2}{n\pi}\sin^2\left(\dfrac{n\pi}{2}\right) & \text{for } n \ne 0, \\ 0 & \text{for } n = 0. \end{cases} \tag{16}$$

This impulse response is not absolutely summable and thus the frequency response of (15) is ideal. However, approximations to the ideal Hilbert transformer can be obtained with IIR or FIR systems. Thus, Hilbert transformers are considered a special class of filter.

IIR Hilbert transformers have phase error as well as magnitude error in approximating the ideal frequency response. Basically, these filters can be designed by using two all-pass systems whose phase responses differ by approximately $\pi/2$ over some well-defined portion of the band $0 < |\omega| < \pi$. By taking the outputs of the two all-pass filters as the real and imaginary parts of a complex signal it can be found that the spectrum of such signal nearly vanishes over much of the negative frequency interval. As such, the outputs of the two all-pass filters are quite nearly a Hilbert transformer.

FIR Hilbert transformers with constant group delay can be easily designed. The $\pi/2$ phase shift is realized exactly, with an additional linear phase component required for a causal FIR system. By evaluating (16) over some positive and negative values of n, it can be seen that the impulse response is anti-symmetric. Therefore, FIR Hilbert transformers are based on either Type III (i.e., anti-symmetric impulse response with odd length L) or Type IV (i.e., anti-symmetric impulse response with even length L) symmetry. Filters with Type III symmetry have amplitude equal to zero in $\omega = 0$ and $\omega = \pi$ and filters with Type IV symmetry have amplitude equal to zero only in $\omega = 0$. Thus, the FIR approximation is acceptable over a given range of frequencies (a pass-band region) which does not include these extremes.

The exactness of the phase of Type III and Type IV FIR systems is a compelling motivation for their use in approximating Hilbert transformers. Additionally, whereas IIR Hilbert transformers can present instability and they are sensitive to rounding error in their coefficients, FIR filters have guaranteed stability, are less sensitive to the coefficients rounding and their phase response is not affected by this rounding. Because of this, FIR Hilbert transformers are often preferred [8]-[15]. The rest of this chapter will be focused on the design of FIR Hilbert transformers.

2.1. Basic design of FIR Hilbert transformers with MATLAB

Since the phase requirement in FIR Hilbert transformers is accomplished, the design of a FIR Hilbert transformer consists on finding the impulse response $h(n)$, for $n = 0$ to $L-1$, which satisfies the following magnitude response specification,

$$(1-\delta) \le \left| H(e^{j\omega}) \right| \le (1-\delta) \quad \text{for } \omega_L \le \omega \le \omega_H, \tag{17}$$

where δ is the allowed pass-band ripple, ω_L is the lower pass-band edge and ω_H is given as $\omega_H = \pi - \omega_L$ if the desired Hilbert transformer is a Type III filter or $\omega_H = \pi$ if it is Type IV. The values ω_L and ω_H can be made to approach 0 and π, respectively, as closely as desired by increasing the length L of the filter. For Hilbert transformers, the value $\omega_L/2\pi$ is considered the transition band.

The design of optimum equiripple Type III and Type IV FIR linear phase Hilbert transformers is usually performed by Parks-McClellan algorithm. With the MATLAB Signal Processing Toolbox this becomes a straightforward procedure through the function `firpm`. The order of the filter, $L-1$, must be estimated in advance. A useful formula to estimate L, presented in [10], is

$$L \approx \varphi(\delta,\ \omega_L) = \left[0.002655\left(\log_{10}(\delta)\right)^3 + 0.031843\left(\log_{10}(\delta)\right)^2 - \dots \right.$$
$$\left. 0.554993\log_{10}(\delta) - 0.049788 \right] / \left(\tfrac{\omega_L}{2\pi}\right) + 1. \tag{18}$$

Example 1. The following code example illustrates the design of a Type III Hilbert transformer with δ= 0.01, ω_L= 0.1π and ω_H= π− ω_L= 0.9π using the MATLAB Signal Processing Toolbox. From (18), L is estimated as $L \approx 24.3266$. For convenience, we use $L = 4k+3$ with k integer and the closest value for L, higher than the estimated value, is chosen. In this case we use $L = 4*6+3 = 27$.

```
d = 0.01; w_L = 0.1*pi; w_H = 0.9*pi; L = 27;
h = firpm(L-1,[w_L/pi w_H/pi],[1 1],'hilbert');
[H w] = freqz(h,1);
figure; stem(0:length(h)-1, h,'fill')
figure; plot(w/pi, abs(H))
```

Figure 5a shows the impulse response and Figure 5b shows the magnitude response of the obtained Hilbert transformer.

As we mentioned earlier, the most expensive elements in digital filters are multipliers. For a Type III Hilbert transformer, the number of multipliers, m, is $(L+1)/4$ if $L = 4k+3$, or $(L-1)/4$ if $L = 4k+1$, with k integer. In this last case the impulse response values $h(0)$ and $h(L-1)$ are zero. For a Type IV Hilbert transformer, the number of multipliers is $L/2$. This number can be simplified as

$$m \approx C \cdot L, \tag{19}$$

where $C = 0.25$ for a Type III Hilbert transformer or $C = 0.5$ for a Type IV Hilbert transformer.

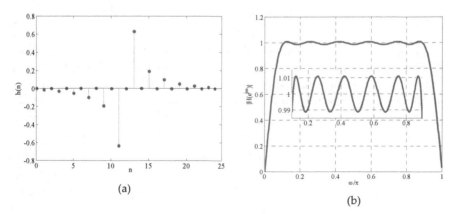

(a)

(b)

Figure 5. (a) Impulse response and (b) Magnitude response of a digital FIR Hilbert transformer.

It is worth highlighting the following point. A Type III Hilbert transformer can be derived from a Type IV Hilbert transformer by adding one zero-valued impulse response sample between each two impulse response samples of the Type IV Hilbert transformer. This is equivalent to replacing each z^{-1} in the transfer function of this filter by z^{-2}. The opposite procedure can be straightforwardly followed to derive a Type IV Hilbert transformer from a Type III Hilbert transformer.

From (18), it can be seen that the length L increases inversely proportional with the transition band $\omega_L/2\pi$. Hence, for cases with narrow transition band and small ripple the implementation cost becomes very high. As a simple example, the estimated length for a Hilbert transformer with $\delta = 0.001$ and $\omega_L = 0.001\pi$ is $L \approx 3661.2$. It implies approximately 915.3 multipliers, which is impractical. Therefore, the design of FIR Hilbert transformers with strict specifications requires specialized techniques to reduce the number of multipliers and the computational complexity of the filter. Before of the revision of these techniques, in the next section we will highlight the relation between Hilbert transformers and half-band filters because this relation is crucial for developing the specialized techniques to design low-complexity FIR Hilbert transformers.

3. The Hilbert transformer and its relation with the half-band filter

Half-band filters have their transfer function given by

$$H_{Hb}(z) = \sum_{n=0}^{2M} h_{Hb}(n)z^{-n},$$ (20)

where $h_{Hb}(n)$ is the impulse response, M is an odd integer and $2M$ is the filter order [21]. The coefficients are symmetric with respect to the central coefficient $h_{Hb}(M)$, namely, they accomplish the following relation,

$$h_{Hb}(2M - n) = h_{Hb}(n) \quad \text{for} \quad n = 0,1,...,2M.$$ (21)

The length of the filter, L, is an odd number given as $L = 2M + 1$ with $M = 1, 3, 5...$ etc. In a lineal phase half-band filter, almost a half of the coefficients are zero. Figure 6 shows the procedure to design a half-band filter. It starts with the transfer function of a Type II lineal phase filter, i.e., a filter with symmetric impulse response whose length is even. For this filter we have,

$$Q(z) = \sum_{n=0}^{M} q(n)z^{-n} \quad \text{for} \quad q(M - n) = q(n).$$ (22)

First, samples with value zero are introduced between the $q(n)$ impulse samples (see Figure 6a and 6c). This generates a transfer function with Type I symmetry, whose order is $2M$, given by

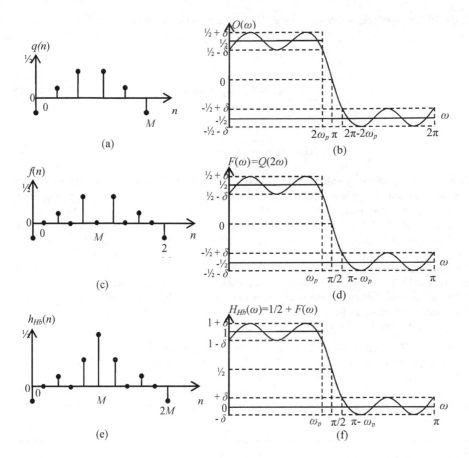

Figure 6. Low-pass half-band filter design. (a) Impulse response of a Type II filter with order M, $q(n)$. (b) Zero-phase frequency response of the Type II filter with order M, $Q(\omega)$. (c) Impulse response of a Type I filter with order $2M$, $f(n)$. (d) Zero-phase frequency response of the Type I filter with order $2M$, $F(\omega)$. (e) Impulse response of a half-band filter, $h_{Hb}(n)$. (f) Zero-phase frequency response of the half-band filter, $H_{Hb}(\omega)$.

$$F(z) = \sum_{n=0}^{2M} f(n)z^{-n} = Q(z^2) = \sum_{n=0}^{M} q(n)z^{-2n}. \tag{23}$$

Then, the zero-valued sample with index $n = M$ is replaced by the value $1/2$ (See Figure 6e). Thus we obtain

$$H_{Hb}(z) = \frac{1}{2}z^{-M} + F(z) = \frac{1}{2}z^{-M} + \sum_{n=0}^{M} q(n)z^{-2n}. \tag{24}$$

The coefficients of the half-band filter are obtained from (20) and (24) as

$$h_{Hb}(M) = \frac{1}{2}, \quad h_{Hb}(n) = q\left(\frac{n}{2}\right) \text{ for } n \text{ even,} \qquad (25)$$

$$h_{Hb}(n) = 0, \text{ for } n \text{ odd and } n \neq M, \qquad (26)$$

and the zero-phase frequency response of $H_{Hb}(z)$ is

$$H_{Hb}(\omega) = \frac{1}{2} + Q(2\omega) = \frac{1}{2} + F(\omega). \qquad (27)$$

Based on the previous relations, the design of a half-band low-pass filter with pass-band frequency ω_p and pass-band ripple δ can be carried out by designing the $Q(z)$ filter, such that its zero-phase frequency response, $Q(\omega)$, oscillates within $1/2 \pm \delta$ over the range of frequencies $[0, 2\omega_p]$ (See Figure 6b). Since $Q(z)$ has a Type II transfer function, it presents a fixed zero in $z = -1$ ($\omega = \pi$). Note from Figure 6b that $Q(\omega)$ oscillates within $-1/2 \pm \delta$ over the range of frequencies $[2\pi - 2\omega_p, 2\pi]$. The corresponding zero-phase frequency response of the filter $F(z)$, given as $F(\omega) = Q(2\omega)$, remains within $1/2 \pm \delta$ over the range of frequencies $[0, \omega_p]$ and within $-1/2 \pm \delta$ over the range of frequencies $[\pi - \omega_p, \pi]$ (See Figure 6d). Finally, $H_{Hb}(\omega)$ oscillates around 1 over the range of frequencies $[0, \omega_p]$ with tolerance δ and around 0 over the range of frequencies $[\pi - \omega_p, \pi]$ with the same tolerance δ (See Figure 6f). Note that, as a low-pass filter, the half-band filter has the relations $\omega_s = \pi - \omega_p$ and $\delta_p = \delta_s$.

Example 2. The following code example illustrates the design of a half-band filter with $\delta_p = \delta_s = 0.005$, $\omega_p = 0.4\pi$ and $\omega_s = \pi - \omega_p = 0.5\pi$ using the MATLAB Filter Design Toolbox. Eq. (18) can be applied to estimate the filter length L, by substituting $\omega_L = (\pi/2) - \omega_p$ and $\delta = 2\delta_p$. The length L is estimated as $L \approx 24.3266$. Since L must be represented as $L = 2M+1$ with M odd to avoid zero-valued impulse response samples in the left and right extremes of the impulse response, we use $L = 2*13 + 1 = 27$.

```
dp = 0.005;w_p = 0.4*pi;w_s = 0.5*pi; L = 27;
h_half = firhalfband(L-1, w_p/pi);
[H_half w] = freqz(h_half,1);
figure; stem(0:length(h_half)-1, h_half,'fill')
figure; plot(w/pi, abs(H_half))
```

3.1. Hilbert transformer derived from a half-band filter

A Hilbert transformer filter can be designed from a half-band filter. First, the sample with value 1/2, located in the index $n = M$, is replaced by the value 0 (See Figures 7a and 7d). Thus we obtain

$$\tilde{H}(z) = H_{Hb}(z) - \frac{1}{2}z^{-M}. \qquad (28)$$

The subtraction of this coefficient, drawn in Figure 7d, causes the zero-phase frequency response of the half-band filter to be shifted downwardly, as illustrated in Figure 7c. The filter $\tilde{H}(\omega)$ must be shifted by $\pi/2$ on the horizontal direction in the frequency domain. This is accomplished by multiplying the remaining coefficients, $\tilde{h}(n)$, by $(j)^{-n}$. The effect of this action produces a Hilbert transformer with odd length and a pass-band gain equal to 0.5. Therefore, a Hilbert transformer with unitary gain will be obtained by scaling all the coefficients by 2. This is illustrated in Figure 8. The transfer function of the Hilbert transformer given in terms of the transfer function of a half-band filter is

$$H(z) = 2\left[H_{Hb}(jz) - \frac{1}{2}(jz)^{-M} \right] = 2 \sum_{\substack{n=0 \\ n \neq M}}^{2M} h_{Hb}(n)(jz)^{-n}. \tag{29}$$

The impulse response of the Hilbert transformer is related with the impulse response of the half-band filter through the following expression,

$$h(n) = \begin{cases} 0; & n = 2k+1, \\ 2(-1)^{k-1}h_{Hb}(n); & n = 2k \quad \text{with} \quad k = 0,1,2,...,M. \end{cases} \tag{30}$$

It was mentioned earlier that the useful bandwidth in a Hilbert transformer is restricted to some range given as $0 < \omega_L \le \omega \le \omega_H < \pi$, where $\omega_H = \pi - \omega_L$. The relation of the low-pass edge frequency ω_L with the band-edge frequencies of the half-band filter, ω_p and ω_s, is given by

$$\omega_L = (\pi/2) - \omega_p, \tag{31}$$

$$\omega_L = \omega_s - (\pi/2), \tag{32}$$

where $\omega_s = \pi - \omega_p$.

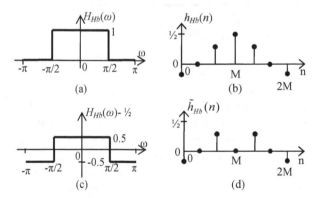

Figure 7. (a) Ideal zero-phase frequency response of the half-band filter $H_{Hb}(\omega)$. (b) Impulse response of the half-band filter $h_{Hb}(n)$. (c) Ideal zero-phase frequency response resulting of the subtraction of the central coefficient, located at $n = M$, $\tilde{H}(\omega) = H_{Hb}(\omega) - \frac{1}{2}$. (d) Impulse response, $\tilde{h}(n)$.

Hilbert transformers designed from half-band filters have odd length. In these cases, there is a coefficient of value zero between each coefficient of its impulse response. Thus, a Hilbert transformer with even length can be obtained by eliminating these zero-valued coefficients.

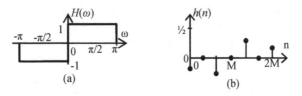

(a)   (b)

Figure 8. Hilbert transformer design, (a) Ideal zero-phase frequency response of the Hilbert transformer obtained from $H_{Hb}(\omega)$. (b) Impulse response $h(n)$.

Example 3. The following code example illustrates a simple way to obtain the impulse response of a Hilbert transformer from the impulse response of a half-band filter. If we consider that the code of Example 2 has been previously run, it can be assumed that h_half and L are already defined. The resulting Hilbert transformer coefficients in h are the same as the ones obtained in Example 1, since the half-band filter generated in Example 2 accomplish the relations $\omega_L = (\pi/2) - \omega_p$ and $\delta = 2\delta_p$ with regard to the specifications in Example 1.

```
index = [1:L];
middle_sample = [zeros(1,(L-1)/2) 1/2 zeros(1,(L-1)/2)];
m = (ones(1,L)*i).^(-(index-1));
h = 2*(h_half.*m - middle_sample.*m);
```

4. Efficient methods to design FIR filters

It is known that the complexity of FIR digital filters increases in an inverse proportion with the transition bandwidth. A simple example in Sub-section 2.1 was given for the case of a Hilbert transformer with small ripple and bandwidth. Several efficient techniques have been developed to efficiently design FIR filters with strict specifications, such that the resulting filter accomplishes the desired specification with a lower complexity than the direct design obtained with the Parks-McClellan algorithm. For Hilbert transformers, however, these methods have been specially adapted, since Hilbert transform filtering has special characteristics as we saw in Section 2. Prior to starting the review of the special methods to design FIR Hilbert transformers with low complexity, we will briefly introduce in this section the general techniques which are the origin of these methods. These techniques are Frequency-Response Masking (FRM), Frequency Transformation (FT) and Piecewise Polynomial Sinusoidal (PPS).

4.1. Frequency-Response Masking technique

The FRM technique, introduced in [16], uses the so-called expanded-by-M filters as basic building blocks, where the transfer functions have the form $G(z^M)$. In general, a filter $G(z)$ becomes expanded-by-M by replacing every of its elements z^{-1} by z^{-M} or, in other words, by inserting M–1 zero-valued impulse response samples between two of its original impulse response samples. The periodic frequency response of these filters has M periods in the frequency range $[0, 2\pi]$.

Figures 6a to 6d show how a filter $F(z) = Q(z^2)$ has a compressed-by-two frequency response in comparison with the original filter $Q(z)$, whose impulse response is depicted in Figure 6a. The zero-phase frequency response of $Q(z)$, presented in Figure 6b, shows a period that covers the frequency range $[0, 2\pi]$. On the other hand, the filter $F(z)$ has a very similar zero-phase frequency response, with the only difference that its period covers the frequency range $[0, \pi]$. The transition bandwidth of this expanded-by-2 filter $F(z)$ is a half of the transition bandwidth of the filter $Q(z)$. However, now this expanded filter has a replica of the frequency response of $Q(z)$ (which covers the range of frequency $[2\pi, 4\pi]$) over the range $[\pi, 2\pi]$. The number of multipliers of $F(z)$ is the same as the one of $Q(z)$. This can be seen in Figure 6c, where several impulse response samples are zero-valued.

The main idea of the FRM technique is using an expanded filter $G(z^M)$ and its complementary filter, $G_c(z^M)$, to form the transition band of a desired filter $H(z)$. Because of that, these filters are so-called band-edge shaping filters. The complementary filter is given as

$$G_c(z) = z^{-(L_G -1)/2} - G(z),$$ (33)

where L_G is the length of the filter $G(z)$. Since the frequency response of these filters is periodical, two non-periodic masking filters, $H_{Ma}(z)$ and $H_{Mc}(z)$, are respectively cascaded with $G(z^K)$ and $G_c(z^K)$ to eliminate the unwanted periodic replicas of frequency response. The overall filter formed with the FRM technique is given as

$$H(z) = G(z^M)H_{Ma}(z) + [z^{-M(L_G-1)/2} - G(z^M)]H_{Mc}(z) .$$ (34)

Extensive information about the basic FRM method can be found in [16] and [23].

4.2. Frequency Transformation technique

The FT technique, first studied in [22] and then generalized in [17], is based on the repetitive use of an identical simple subfilter $G(z)$. Let us consider $G(\omega)$ as the zero-phase frequency response of $G(z)$ and an amplitude change function $Q(x)$ given as

$$Q(x) = \sum_{k=0}^{M} q(k)x^k .$$ (35)

The function $Q(x)$ allows changing the values $x = G(\omega)$ to new values $y = Q(x)$. Basically, the new amplitude values $y = Q(x)$ must approximate the desired values $d = D(x)$ for $x \in X_p \cup X_s$, where X_p is the range of values $[x_{p,l}, x_{p,u}]$ and X_s is the range of values $[x_{s,l}, x_{s,u}]$, such that the zero-phase frequency response of the overall filter $H(z)$ achieves the desired values d with a maximum absolute pass-band deviation δ_p over the pass-band region Ω_p, as well as a maximum absolute stop-band deviation δ_s over the stop-band region Ω_s. This characteristic is reached if the following conditions are simultaneously met,

$$D(x) - \delta_p \leq Q(x) \leq D(x) + \delta_p, \text{ for } x_{p,l} \leq x \leq x_{p,u}, \tag{36}$$

$$D(x) - \delta_s \leq Q(x) \leq D(x) + \delta_s, \text{ for } x_{s,l} \leq x \leq x_{s,u}, \tag{37}$$

$$x_{p,l} \leq G(\omega) \leq x_{p,u}, \text{ for } \omega \in \Omega_p, \tag{38}$$

$$x_{s,l} \leq G(\omega) \leq x_{s,u}, \text{ for } \omega \in \Omega_s \tag{39}$$

Usually, $D(x) = 1$ for $x \in X_p$ and $D(x) = 0$ for $x \in X_s$. Basically, two problems can be solved from this approach:

Problem 1. Given M, the number of subfilters, find the optimal coefficients of $Q(x)$ and the optimal coefficients of $G(z)$ to meet the conditions (36) to (39) with the minimum length L_G (which must be odd).

Problem 2. Given the subfilter $G(z)$, find the optimal coefficients of $Q(x)$ to meet the conditions (36) to (39) with the minimum value M.

The overall filter formed with the FT technique is given as

$$H(z) = \sum_{k=0}^{M} q(k) z^{-(M-k)(L_G-1)/2} [G(z)]^k . \tag{40}$$

Detailed information about the FT method can be found in [16] and [23].

4.3. Piecewise Polynomial Sinusoidal technique

In the PPS technique, introduced in [24] for wide-band Type I filters, extended in [25] for Hilbert transformers and detailed in [11] for both cases, the idea is to divide the impulse response of a wideband filter into sub-responses and to generate each sub-response with polynomials with a given degree. For wideband linear-phase filters, the impulse response has a narrow main lobe and the side lobes have very rapid change in sign. Therefore, it is taken advantage of sinusoids in such a way that the polynomial pieces follow the polynomial-sinusoidal shapes to decrease the number of polynomial pieces and, as a consequence, to reduce the number of coefficients.

The overall transfer function $H(z)$ for a desired Type I filter with length $2N+1$ is constructed with M parallel branches connected and delayed with z^{-N_m} in order to keep the center of symmetry at the same location for all the sub-impulse responses. These sub-responses are modulated with a sinusoidal function and finally an arbitrary number of separately generated filter coefficients is added as follows,

$$H(z) = \sum_{m=1}^{M} z^{-N_m} H_m(z) + z^{-\hat{N}} \hat{H}(z), \tag{41}$$

where,

$$H_m(z) = h_m(N - N_m) z^{-(N-N_m)} + \sum_{n=0}^{(N-N_m)-1} h_m(n)[z^{-n} + z^{-(2(N-N_m)-n)}]. \tag{42}$$

The integers N_m in the delay terms z^{-N_m} satisfy $N_1 = 0$ and $N_{m+1} > N_m$ for $m = 1, 2, ..., M - 1$, and the order of $H_m(z)$ is $2(N - N_m)$. The impulse response is given as

$$h_m(n) = \sum_{r=0}^{L} a_m^{(L)}(r) n^r \times \sin[\omega_c(n - (N - N_m))]. \tag{43}$$

In addition, $z^{-\hat{N}}\hat{H}(z)$ is a conventional direct-form transfer function with non-zero impulse response coefficients $\hat{h}(n)$, with $n = N{-}c{+}1, N{-}c{+}2, ..., N{-}c{+}T$, where $c = \lceil T/2 \rceil$ and T is the number of additional coefficients at the center of the filter. Given the values N_m for $m = 1, 2, ..., M - 1, M$ and L, the objective is finding the polynomial coefficients such that the error with respect to a desired amplitude characteristic is minimized. An extensive explanation on this method can be reviewed in [11].

4.4. Pipelining-Interleaving architecture

The Pipelining-Interleaving (PI) technique developed in [19] provides efficient structures of FIR digital filters to avoid the repetitive use of an identical filter. Suppose that we have two sequences of independent signals, $x_1(n)$ and $x_2(n)$, that are filtered by two identical filters $H(z)$. Thus, two corresponding sequences of independent outputs, $y_1(n)$ and $y_2(n)$, are obtained. An alternative form for this purpose is the multirate implementation using $H(z^2)$ as shown in Figure 9. This structure uses a single filter to implement two identical filters. The clock rate for this implementation must be twice the data rate [19]. If only one sequence of input signal is filtered, it is possible to connect the first output sequence $y_1(n)$ to the second input $x_2(n)$. In this way, $H(z^2)$ is used to implement $H^2(z)$.

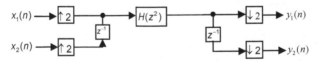

Figure 9. Filtering of two independent sequences using one filter.

The PI structure of the Figure 9 can be extended to implement the filtering of K different signals, each one filtered by an identical filter $H(z)$, with K being an arbitrary positive integer. From this, it is possible to implement the filtering of one signal with K identical filters in cascade. Figure 10a presents the general structure to filter a signal using one filter $H(z^K)$. Figure 10b shows the equivalent structure, which consists of the filtering of a signal by a cascade of K identical filters $H(z)$ [19].

In the structure shown in Figure 10a, the clock rate of $H(z^K)$ must be K times the data rate. Clearly, for high data rate applications, K must be chosen as a relatively small integer, otherwise a very high clock rate will be required. More details on this time-multiplexed architecture can be found in [19].

5. Efficient Methods to design FIR Hilbert transformers

It has been mentioned earlier that the design of low-complexity FIR Hilbert transformers with stringent specifications requires special efficient methods. In the following we will review the most representative and useful methods, which are based on the techniques revised in the previous section.

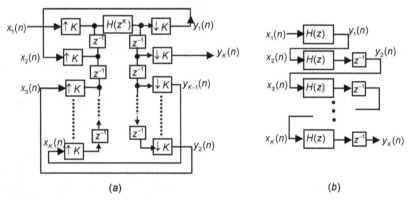

(a)   (b)

Figure 10. Filtering of a sequence with K identical cascaded filters, (a) PI architecture with only one filter, (b) equivalent single-rate structure.

5.1. Hilbert transformer design based on Frequency Response Masking

This method, proposed in [9], relies on the special case of FRM for the synthesis of a half-band filter $H_{Hb}(z)$ [26]. Consider a half-band filter $H_a(z)$ as a band-edge shaping filter whose transfer function is given by

$$H_a(z) = \tfrac{1}{2}z^{-2K+1} + A(z), \tag{44}$$

$$A(z) = \sum_{k=1}^{K} a(2k - 1 + 2K - 1)\left[z^{2k-1-2K+1} + z^{-2k+1-2K+1} \right], \tag{45}$$

where $L_a = 4K - 1$ is the length of $H_a(z)$, with K being an integer greater than zero, and $a(n)$ is the impulse response of $H_a(z)$. Replacing $G(z)$ by $H_a(z)$ in (34) we have

$$H_{Hb}(z) = H_a(z^M)H_{Ma}(z) + [z^{-M(2K-1)} - H_a(z^M)]H_{Mc}(z). \tag{46}$$

We can express the transfer function of the overall half-band filter as

$$H_{Hb}(z) = \left[\tfrac{1}{2} z^{-M(2K-1)} + A(z^M) \right] H_{Ma}(z) + \left[\tfrac{1}{2} z^{-M(2K-1)} - A(z^M) \right] H_{Mc}(z). \tag{47}$$

If M is odd, then either $[\tfrac{1}{2} z^{-M(2K-1)} + A(z^M)]$ or $[\tfrac{1}{2} z^{-M(2K-1)} - A(z^M)]$ has a transition band centered at $\pi/2$, just as desired for a half-band filter.

If M is given by the form

$$M = 4k+1, \quad \text{with } k = \{0,1,2,...\}, \tag{48}$$

then the pass-band of $H_{Ma}(z)$ is greater than the pass-band of $H_{Mc}(z)$. With ω_p and ω_s denoting the band-edge frequencies of $H_{Hb}(z)$, these values can be express as [26]

$$\omega_p = \frac{2\pi m + \theta}{M}, \qquad \omega_s = \frac{2\pi m + \phi}{M}, \tag{49}$$

where m is an integer less than M. The values m, θ and φ can be calculated as

$$m = \left\lfloor \frac{\omega_p M}{2\pi} \right\rfloor, \qquad \theta = \omega_p M - 2\pi m, \qquad \phi = \omega_s M - 2\pi m \tag{50}$$

where $\lfloor x \rfloor$ represents the integer part of x, whereas θ and φ are the pass-band and stop-band edges of $H_a(z)$. The pass-band and stop-band edge frequencies of the masking filter $H_{Ma}(z)$, θ_{Ma} and φ_{Ma}, as well as the pass-band and stop-band edge frequencies of the masking filter $H_{Mc}(z)$, θ_{Mc} and φ_{Mc}, are given by

$$\theta_{Ma} = \omega_p = \frac{2\pi m + \theta}{M}, \phi_{Ma} = \frac{2\pi(m+1) - \phi}{M}, \theta_{Mc} = \frac{2\pi m - \theta}{M}, \phi_{Mc} = \omega_s = \frac{2\pi m + \phi}{M} \tag{51}$$

If M is given by the form

$$M = 4k+3, \quad \text{con } k = \{0,1,2,...\}. \tag{52}$$

then the passband of $H_{Mc}(z)$ is greater than the pass-band of $H_{Ma}(z)$. In this case the frequencies ω_p and ω_s are given by

$$\omega_p = \frac{2\pi m - \phi}{M}, \; \omega_s = \frac{2\pi m - \theta}{M}, \tag{53}$$

To calculate m, θ and φ we use the following relations,

$$m = \left\lceil \frac{\omega_s M}{2\pi} \right\rceil, \theta = 2\pi m - \omega_s M, \phi = 2\pi m - \omega_p M, \tag{54}$$

where $\lceil x \rceil$ represents the rounding operation to the closest integer greater than x. The values, θ_{Ma}, φ_{Ma}, θ_{Mc} and φ_{Mc}, are given by

$$\theta_{Ma} = \frac{2\pi(m-1)+\phi}{M}, \, \phi_{Ma} = \omega_s = \frac{2\pi m - \theta}{M}, \, \theta_{Mc} = \omega_p = \frac{2\pi m - \phi}{M}, \, \phi_{Mc} = \frac{2\pi m + \theta}{M}. \quad (55)$$

If $H_{Ma}(z)$ is a Type I filter with length $L_{Ma} = 4k + 1$, where k is an integer, we can write

$$H_{Ma}(z) = h_{Ma}\left((L_{Ma}-1)/2\right) + \sum_{k=1}^{(L_{Ma}-1)/2} h_{Ma}\left(k+(L_{Ma}-1)/2\right)\left[z^{k-(L_{Ma}-1)/2} + z^{-k-(L_{Ma}-1)/2}\right]. \quad (56)$$

Now we define the transfer functions $B(z)$ and $C(z)$ as

$$B(z) = h_{Ma}\left(1+(L_{Ma}-1)/2\right)\left[z^{1-(L_{Ma}-1)/2} + z^{-1-(L_{Ma}-1)/2}\right] + \\ h_{Ma}\left(3+(L_{Ma}-1)/2\right)\left[z^{3-(L_{Ma}-1)/2} + z^{-3-(L_{Ma}-1)/2}\right] + \ldots \quad (57)$$

$$C(z) = h_{Ma}\left((L_{Ma}-1)/2\right) + \\ h_{Ma}\left(2+(L_{Ma}-1)/2\right)\left[z^{2-(L_{Ma}-1)/2} + z^{-2-(L_{Ma}-1)/2}\right] + \\ h_{Ma}\left(4+(L_{Ma}-1)/2\right)\left[z^{4-(L_{Ma}-1)/2} + z^{-4-(L_{Ma}-1)/2}\right] + \ldots \quad (58)$$

with $h_{Ma}(n)$ as coefficients of the filter $H_{Ma}(z)$. Replacing (57) and (58) in (56), we have

$$H_{Ma}(z) = B(z) + C(z). \quad (59)$$

In the half-band filter design, the masking filters are related by

$$H_{Mc}(z) = z^{-(L_{Ma}-1)/2} - H_{Ma}(-z). \quad (60)$$

From (59) and (60), and noting that $B(-z) = -B(z)$ and that $C(-z) = C(z)$, we have

$$H_{Mc}(z) = z^{-(L_{Ma}-1)/2} + B(z) - C(z). \quad (61)$$

Once known the transfer function of the masking filters from (59) and (61), the overall transfer function of the half-band filter can be obtained by substituting (59) and (61) in (47). Finally, we obtain

$$H_{Hb}(z) = \tfrac{1}{2}z^{-[M(2K-1)+(L_{Ma}-1)/2]} + z^{-M(2K-1)}B(z) + A(z^M)[2C(z) - z^{-(L_{Ma}-1)/2}]. \quad (62)$$

The half-band filter with desired deviation δ and pass-band edge frequency ω_p can be designed with the FRM technique by applying the following steps:

1. Get the optimal value of M, using the following approximation,

$$M_{opt} \approx \frac{1}{2}\sqrt{\frac{2\pi}{\omega_s - \omega_p}}. \quad (63)$$

Note that the obtained value must be rounded to an odd integer.

2. Find if M can be expressed either as in (48) or (52). Then obtain the pass-band and stop-band edge frequencies of the band-edge shaping filter $H_a(z)$, θ and φ, as well as the ones of the masking filter $H_{Ma}(z)$, θ_{Ma} and φ_{Ma}, using (50) and (51) if M is expressed as in (48), or (54) and (55) if M is expressed as in (52).Design these filters with a ripple approx. 15% less than the desired ripple.
3. Obtain $A(z)$ from $H_a(z)$ using (44) and (45). Then obtain $B(z)$ and $C(z)$ from $H_{Ma}(z)$ using (56), (57) and (58).
4. Synthesize the overall structure of (62) in terms of $A(z^M)$, $B(z)$ and $C(z)$.

A Hilbert transformer can be derived from a unity gain half-band filter by subtracting the constant ½ from its transfer function and then modulating the remaining coefficients by $e^{-j\pi n/2}$ (see section 3.1). The transfer function of the Hilbert transformer $H(z)$ is given by [9]

$$H(z) = 2(jz)^{-M(2K-1)} B(jz) + 2A\left((jz)^M\right)[2C(jz) - (jz)^{-(L_{Ma}-1)/2}]. \tag{64}$$

It is worth highlighting that the filter in (64) does not need complex-number arithmetic processing because of the following reasons. First, note that the filter $A(j^M z^M)$ has only real coefficients since the imaginary unit generated by $(jz)^{-n}$ with n odd is eliminated by zero-valued coefficients in these indexes n. Second, note that all the coefficients in $[2C(jz) - (jz)^{-(L_{Ma}-1)/2}]$ are real and all the coefficients in $B(jz)$ are imaginary when L_{Ma} is expressed as $4k+1$, with k integer. Third, the term $(jz)^{-M(2K-1)}$ is always imaginary, since its exponent is always odd. From these reasons, we have that if $B(jz)$ has imaginary coefficients, the term $(jz)^{-M(2K-1)}$ makes them real and the overall filter has real coefficients.

The Hilbert transformer from (64) can be seen as a parallel connection of two branches. In the first branch we have $H_b(z) = 2(jz)^{-M(2K-1)}B(jz)$ and in the second branch we have the cascade of $H_1(z^M)$ and $H_M(z)$, where $H_1(z^M) = 2A(j^M z^M)$ and $H_M(z) = [2C(jz) - (jz)^{-(L_{Ma}-1)/2}]$. This structure is presented in Figure 11. Let us review a different point of view of the FRM technique, presented in [10].

The filter $H_b(z)$ can be seen as a low-order Hilbert transformer, the filter $H_1(z^M)$ as a band-edge shaping filter and $H_M(z)$ as a masking filter. The basic filter $H_b(z)$ provides a low order approximation (with wide transition bandwidth) to the desired specification. The cascaded connection of $H_1(z^M)$ and $H_M(z)$ produces a correction term to the transfer function that decreases the transition bandwidth. The transfer function for the overall filter is given by

$$H(z) = H_1(z^M)H_M(z) + H_b(z). \tag{65}$$

Let the lengths of $H_b(z)$, $H_1(z)$ and $H_M(z)$ be L_b, L_1 and L_M, respectively. The length of $H_1(z^M)H_M(z)$ is $ML_1 + L_M - M$. The delay introduced by $H_b(z)$ and the delay introduced by $H_1(z^M)H_M(z)$ must be the same; otherwise, pure delays must be introduced into the shorter-delay branch to equalize them.

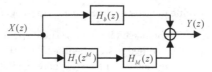

Figure 11. Structure for the synthesis of a Hilbert transformer using the FRM technique.

In order to avoid inserting half-sample delay in the implementation, the parities of L_b and of $(ML_1 + L_M - M)$ must be the same. Furthermore, $H_1(z^M)H_M(z)$ must have anti-symmetrical impulse response.

Consider the magnitude response of $H_b(z)$ as $|H_b(e^{j\omega})|$, as shown in Figure 12a, where L_b is even. The computational complexity of $H_b(z)$ is low since its transition band is wide. Now consider the magnitude response of a transition band correction filter, $|H_e(e^{j\omega})|$, as shown in Figure 12b. The Hilbert transformer with sharp transition bandwidth, as shown in Figure 12c, is obtained from the parallel connection of the correction filter with $H_b(z)$.

The objective is designing a correction filter with very low complexity using FRM technique. Consider the band-edge shaping filter $H_1(z)$ with magnitude response $|H_1(e^{j\omega})|$, as shown in Figure 12d. The complexity of $H_1(z)$ is low because it has a wide transition band. Replacing each delay of $H_1(z)$ by M delays, a magnitude response $|H_1(e^{jM\omega})|$ is obtained, as shown in Figure 12e. A masking filter $H_M(z)$, with magnitude response $|H_M(e^{j\omega})|$ shown in Figure 12f, is used to mask the unwanted pass-band of $|H_1(e^{jM\omega})|$. With this masking, the magnitude response $|H_e(e^{j\omega})|$, shown in Figure 12b, is produced. $H_M(z)$ has low complexity because its magnitude response has a wide transition band.

Since the length of $H_b(z)$ is even, the length of $H_1(z^M)$ $H_M(z)$, i.e., $MN_1 + N_M - M$, must also be even. If M is odd, N_1 and N_M must have different parities. By considering the gain of $|H_M(e^{j\omega})|$ in the vicinity of $\omega = 0$, it is clear that $H_M(z)$ has symmetrical impulse response. Thus, $H_1(z)$ must have anti-symmetrical impulse response to satisfy the condition that $H_1(z^M)$ $H_M(z)$ must have anti-symmetrical impulse response.

The band-edges of $H_b(z)$ and $H_M(z)$ are the same. Let the band-edge of $H_b(z)$ be θ_b and let the band-edge of $H_1(z)$ be θ_1. It can be seen from Figure 12 that the value θ_b satisfies $\theta_b \leq (2\pi - \theta_1)/M$. For an arbitrary value θ_1, it is possible to obtain θ_b if the appropriate value of M is known, which is obtained with the objective of minimizing the overall number of coefficients. Finally, the overall filter is designed with a joint simultaneous optimization of $H_1(z^M)$, $H_b(z)$ and $H_M(z)$. For the examples in [10], the algorithm in [27] was used.

In the following we present a simple example to design an efficient FIR Hilbert transformer with stringent specifications based on the FRM technique. The approach presented in this example follows the procedure based on the four steps to design a half-band filter in terms of filter $A(z)$, $B(z)$ and $C(z)$.

The Hilbert transformer is derived using (64). Since this approach does not require a simultaneous optimization for all the filters, it is simple and straightforward. Additionally, the sensitivity to the rounded coefficients is less since every filter is designed separately [28].

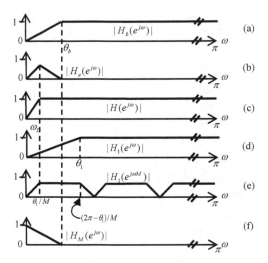

Figure 12. Magnitude responses of the subfilters for even length $H_b(z)$. Note that $\omega_L/2\pi$ is the desired transition bandwidth.

Example 4. The following code example illustrates the design of a Type III Hilbert transformer with $\delta= 0.0001$, $\omega_L= 0.00125\pi$ and $\omega_H= \pi- \omega_L= 0.99875\pi$ using the MATLAB Signal Processing Toolbox and the Filter Design Toolbox to generate the half-band filter. The conversion of filters with argument z into filters with argument jz is performed with the same principle illustrated in the code of example 3.

```
wL=0.00125*pi; wH=0.99875*pi; d=0.0001; % Hilbert transformer specification
wp=pi/2 - wL;  ws=pi/2 + wL;  %find the half-band band-edge frequencies
dp=d/2;         ds=d/2; %find the half-band ripple specification
%--------STEP 1. Optimum M----------
M = (1/2)*round(sqrt(2*pi/(ws-wp))); if mod(M,2)==0; M = M+1; end
%------------------------------------
%-------STEP 2. Band-edge-Shaping and Masking Filters--------------
if mod((M-1)/4,1)==0;
    m=floor(wp*M/(2*pi));  theta=(wp*M)-(2*pi*m);  phi=(ws*M)-(2*pi*m);
    theta_Ma=wp; phi_Ma=(2*pi*(m+1)-phi)/M; theta_Mc=((2*pi*m)-theta)/M;
    phi_Mc=ws;
else
    m=ceil(ws*M/(2*pi));  theta=(2*pi*m)-(ws*M);  phi=(2*pi*m)-(wp*M);
    theta_Ma=(2*pi*(m-1)+phi)/M;  phi_Ma=ws;  theta_Mc=wp;
    phi_Mc=((2*pi*m)+theta)/M;
```

```
end

La=firpmord([theta/pi  phi/pi],[1 0], [0.85*dp 0.85*ds]);

if mod(La,2)==0; La=La+1; end

if mod((La+1)/4,1)~=0; La=La+2; end

K=(La+1)/4;

[L_Ma,fo,ao,W]=firpmord([theta_Ma/pi  phi_Ma/pi],[1 0], [0.85*dp 0.85*ds]);

if mod(L_Ma,2)==0; L_Ma=L_Ma+1; end

if mod((L_Ma-1)/4,1)~=0; L_Ma=L_Ma+2; end

ha = firhalfband(La-1,theta/pi);

h_Ma = firpm(L_Ma-1,fo,ao,W);

%-------------------------------------------------------------------
%--------STEP 3. Filters A(z), B(z) and C(z)----------------------
a = ha - [zeros(1,2*K-1) 1/2 zeros(1,2*K-1)];

for i=1:L_Ma; if mod(i-1,2)==0; b(i)=0; c(i)=h_Ma(i); else b(i)=h_Ma(i);
c(i)=0; end

end

delay_b = [zeros(1,M*(2*K-1)) 1 zeros(1,M*(2*K-1))];

delay_c = [zeros(1,(L_Ma-1)/2) 1 zeros(1,(L_Ma-1)/2)];

%-------------------------------------------------------------------
%--------STEP 4. Form the Hilbert transformer (or half-band filter)-------
a_M = upsample(a,M); a_M = a_M(1:end-(M-1));

index_a_M = [1:length(a_M)];

m_a_M = (ones(1,length(a_M))*j).^(-(index_a_M-1));

index_b = [1:length(b)];

m_b = (ones(1,length(b))*j).^(-(index_b-1));

index_c = [1:length(c)];

m_c = (ones(1,length(c))*j).^(-(index_c-1));

index_delay_b = [1:length(delay_b)];

m_delay_b = (ones(1,length(delay_b))*j).^(-(index_delay_b-1));

index_delay_c = [1:length(delay_c)];

m_delay_c = (ones(1,length(delay_c))*j).^(-(index_delay_c-1));

h = 2*conv(delay_b.*m_delay_b, b.*m_b) +...
    2*conv(a_M.*m_a_M,(2*c.*m_c - delay_c.*m_delay_c));

[H w] = freqz(h,1,10000);

figure; plot(w/pi, abs(H))

%-------------------------------------------------------------
```

Figure 13 shows the magnitude response of the obtained Hilbert transformer. The overall structure requires 148 coefficients in total, i.e., 69 for $A(j^M z^M)$, 39 for $B(jz)$ and 40 for $C(jz)$. Clearly, the FRM-based design is a very efficient method comparing to a direct design, like the one presented in example 1, where the estimated length is 4017 and which would require approximately 1005 coefficients.

5.2. Hilbert transformer Design based on Frequency Transformation

The Frequency Transformation (FT) method, developed in [12] to design FIR Hilbert transformers, allows designing FIR Hilbert transformers using a tapped cascaded interconnection of repeated simple basic building blocks constituted by two identical subfilters. To this end, two simple filters are required, namely, a prototype filter and a subfilter. The number of times that the subfilter is used, as well as the coefficients used between each cascaded subfilter, depends on the prototype filter. Both, the prototype filter and the subfilter are Hilbert transformers. The former is always a Type IV filter whereas the latter can be a Type III or Type IV filter according to the type of the desired Hilbert transformer [12].

The prototype filter must be a Type IV FIR filter, i.e., with even length given as $L_P = 2N$ and anti-symmetric impulse response of the form $p(2N - 1 - n) = -p(n)$. Its frequency response is expressed as

$$P(e^{j\Omega}) = e^{-j((2N-1)\Omega/2 - \pi/2)}P(\Omega),\tag{66}$$

where $P(\Omega)$, the zero-phase term, is given by

$$P(\Omega) = j \cdot \sin\left(\tfrac{\Omega}{2}\right)\sum_{n=0}^{N-1}\tilde{d}(n)\cos\left(\Omega n\right),\tag{67}$$

and Ω denotes the frequency domain of the prototype filter. The coefficients $\tilde{d}(n)$ can be obtained directly from the impulse response $p(n)$ [1].

Using the equivalence $\cos(\Omega n) = T_n\{\cos(\Omega)\}$ [17], where $T_n\{x\}$ is the nth-degree Chebyshev polynomial defined with the following recursive formulas,

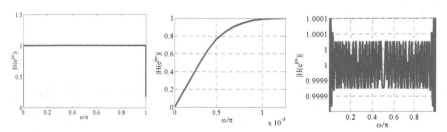

Figure 13. Magnitude responses of the FRM-based Hilbert transformer. From left to right: overall magnitude response, transition bandwidth detail and passband ripple detail.

$$T_0\{x\} = 1,\ T_1\{x\} = x \ \text{ and } \ T_n\{x\} = 2xT_{n-1}\{x\} - T_{n-2}\{x\}, \tag{68}$$

the zero-phase term can be rewritten as

$$P(\Omega) = j \cdot \sin\left(\tfrac{\Omega}{2}\right) \sum_{n=0}^{N-1} \alpha(n)\left[\cos(\Omega)\right]^n, \tag{69}$$

where $\alpha(n)$ are obtained from $\tilde{d}(n)$ using the coefficients of the Chebyshev polynomials. Based on the equivalence given as

$$\cos(2x) = 1 - 2\sin^2(x) = 1 + 2(j \cdot \sin x)^2, \tag{70}$$

the zero-phase term can be expressed by

$$P(\Omega) = j \cdot \sin\left(\tfrac{\Omega}{2}\right) \sum_{n=0}^{N-1} \alpha(n)\left[1 + 2\left(j \cdot \sin\left(\tfrac{\Omega}{2}\right)\right)^2\right]^n. \tag{71}$$

Consider the case of a Type III subfilter with odd length given as $L_G = 2M + 1$ and anti-symmetric impulse response of the form $g(2M - n) = -g(n)$. Its frequency response is expressed as

$$G(e^{j\omega}) = e^{-j(2M\omega/2)}G(\omega), \tag{72}$$

where $G(\omega)$ is the zero-phase term, given by

$$G(\omega) = j \cdot \sum_{n=1}^{M} c(n)\sin(\omega n). \tag{73}$$

The coefficients $c(n)$ can be obtained directly from $g(n)$ [1]. Note that the term $G(\omega)$ can be put in (71) by using the following expression,

$$j \cdot \sin\left(\tfrac{\Omega}{2}\right) = j \cdot \sum_{n=1}^{M} c(n)\sin(\omega n), \tag{74}$$

resulting in

$$H(\omega) = j \cdot \sum_{n=1}^{M} c(n)\sin(\omega n) \sum_{n=0}^{N-1} \alpha(n)\left[1 + 2\left(j \cdot \sum_{n=1}^{M} c(n)\sin(\omega n)\right)^2\right]^n, \tag{75}$$

where $H(\omega)$ is the zero-phase term of the overall filter. Therefore, the frequency transformation is obtained from (74) and is given by

$$\Omega = 2\sin^{-1}\left[\sum_{n=1}^{M} c(n)\sin(\omega n)\right]. \tag{76}$$

Equation (76) implies that the magnitude response of the prototype filter is preserved, but its frequency domain is changed by the subfilter.

The transfer function of the overall Hilbert transformer is given as

$$H(z) = G(z) \sum_{n=0}^{N-1} z^{-2M(N-1-n)} \alpha(n) \left[H_1(z) \right]^n, \ H_1(z) = z^{-2M} + 2G^2(z) \tag{77}$$

with $G(z)$ being the transfer function of the subfilter.

For a desired Hilbert transformer specification expressed as in (17), the magnitude response $|P(\Omega)|$ of the prototype filter must satisfy the following condition,

$$(1-\delta) \le |P(\Omega)| \le (1+\delta), \quad \text{for } \Omega_L \le \Omega \le \pi, \tag{78}$$

with Ω_L being the lower band-edge frequency of the prototype filter. The magnitude response of the subfilter, $|G(\omega)|$, must fulfill simultaneously

$$v_d - \delta_G \le |G_0(\omega)| \le 1, \quad \text{for } \omega_L \le \omega \le \pi - \omega_L, \tag{79}$$

$$v_d = \frac{1}{2} + \frac{1}{2}\sin\left(\frac{\Omega_L}{2}\right), \ \delta_G = \frac{1}{2} - \frac{1}{2}\sin\left(\frac{\Omega_L}{2}\right). \tag{80}$$

The design procedure proposed in [12] starts with an arbitrary prototype filter, and then the subfilter is designed accordingly.

Note that the complexity of the subfilter depends almost exclusively on its transition bandwidth, since its ripple specification is considerably relaxed. Similarly, the prototype filter is a low-complexity filter because, even though its ripple specification is strict, its transition bandwidth is relaxed. The relaxed ripple specification of the subfilter makes it suitable to be implemented as a simple, multiplierless system with rounded coefficients [13]. Additionally, it was observed in [13] that the repeated use of identical subfilters can be avoided by taking advantage of the PI technique, which has been introduced in sub-section 4.4. Therefore, a time-multiplexed design with lower area can be obtained.

Figure 14 presents the PI-based architecture proposed in [13]. This structure was straightforwardly derived from [19], where a similar example is given for the sharpening technique of [22]. Additionally, the design of the Hilbert transformer was made multiplierless by applying rounding to the coefficients of the prototype filter and the subfilter.

Instead of choosing an arbitrary prototype filter as in [12], a heuristic search was employed to select the prototype filter and the subfilter, such that the proposed architecture uses a number of coefficients less or equal to 0.25 times the estimated number of multipliers required in a direct design using the Parks-McClellan algorithm.

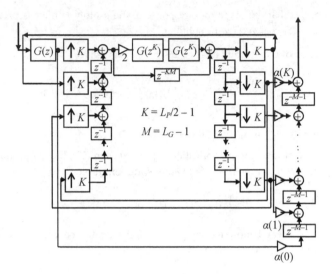

Figure 14. PI-based structure with three subfilters [13].

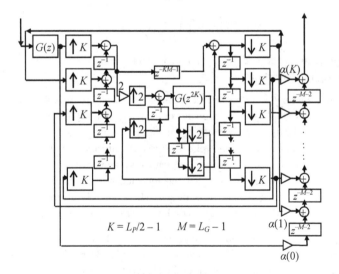

Figure 15. PI-based structure with two subfilters [14].

In [14] the authors observed that the cascaded interconnection of the two subfilters $G(z)$ required to build $H_1(z)$ can be decoupled and also implemented with the PI technique. Thus, the PI-based architecture shown in Figure 15, which only requires two subfilters, was obtained. The approach of PI-based architectures for FT designs was further developed in

[15], and a simple procedure to derive a PI-based structure from a FT-based design with identical subfilters was proposed. With this procedure, the architecture presented in Figure 16 was proposed for Hilbert transformers, where only a simple subfilter is required.

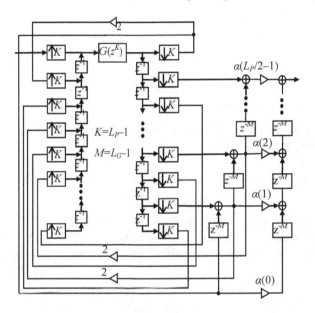

Figure 16. PI-based structure with one subfilter [15].

An important insight proposed in [14] was avoiding the arbitrary selection of the prototype filter as in [12] through the optimized search of the adequate prototype filter, such that a cost metric is minimized. Since multipliers are the most expensive elements in digital filters, reducing the overall number of coefficients is the goal. In general terms, this is equivalent to improve the original heuristic search proposed in [13]. From (78), (79) and (80) it can be observed that the prototype filter and the subfilter can be designed if the frequency Ω_L is known. The problem consists on finding the optimal frequency Ω_L.

Consider a function $\phi(\delta, \omega_L)$, which can estimate with an acceptable exactitude the length of a HT in terms of its ripple δ and its lower passband edge ω_L, such as the one presented in (18). We have, for the prototype filter and the subfilter,

$$L_G \approx \mathcal{L}_G = \phi(\delta_G / v_d, \omega_L), \tag{81}$$

$$L_P \approx \mathcal{L}_P = \phi(\delta, \Omega_L), \tag{82}$$

where $\mathcal{L}_G$ and $\mathcal{L}_P$ are the respective approximations to the lengths of the subfilter, L_G, and the prototype filter, L_P, whereas v_d and δ_G are given in (80). Clearly, $\mathcal{L}_G$ and $\mathcal{L}_P$ are given as functions of the ripple and transition band of the subfilter and of the prototype filter, respectively.

For the previously revised PI-based structures, it is always possible to express the overall number of multipliers m in terms of the numbers of multipliers of the prototype filter and the subfilter as,

$$m = f(m_G, m_P),\tag{83}$$

$$m_G \approx C \cdot L_G,\tag{84}$$

$$m_P = L_P / 2,\tag{85}$$

where m_P and m_G are taken from (19).

Substituting v_d and δ_G from (80) in (81), and using the approximations (81) and (82) respectively in (84) and (85) we have

$$m(\delta, \omega_L, \Omega_L) \approx f\left(C \cdot \phi\left(\frac{1-\sin(\Omega_L/2)}{1+\sin(\Omega_L/2)}, \omega_L\right), \tfrac{1}{2} \cdot \phi(\delta, \Omega_L)\right).\tag{86}$$

Note that, even though $m(\delta, \omega_L, \Omega_L)$ is a function of δ, ω_L and Ω_L, the values δ and ω_L are known a priori because they are given by the problem at hand (see (17)). Therefore, since the unique unknown is Ω_L, the approach consists in finding the optimum value Ω'_L for Ω_L, with $0 < \Omega_L < \pi$, such that $m(\delta, \omega_L, \Omega_L)$ is minimized. This optimization problem is given as

$$\min_{\Omega_L \in \mathbb{R}} m(\delta, \omega_L, \Omega_L)$$
$$\text{such that } 0 < \Omega_L < \pi,\tag{87}$$

where $m(\delta, \omega_L, \Omega_L)$ is given in (86). The result obtained from (86) is an estimation which depends on the exactitude of the function $\phi(\delta, \omega_L)$.

Equation (18) was utilized in [17] as the function $\phi(\delta, \omega_L)$. However, this function does not give good length estimation for filters with a huge ripple (like the subfilters in the FT method). Using the proposal from [29] as starting point, we have recently derived the following more accurate formula,

$$\phi(\delta, \omega_L) = \frac{1}{2} + \left[\frac{1.101\left[-\log_{10}(\delta)\right]^{1.1}}{\left(\frac{\omega_L}{2\pi}\right)} + 1\right]\left[\frac{2}{3\pi}\arctan\left\{\left[2.325\left[0.30103 - \log_{10}(\delta)\right]^{-0.445}\cdots\right.\right.\right.$$
$$\left.\left.\left.\left(\frac{\omega_L}{2\pi}\right)^{-1.39}\right]\left[\frac{1}{0.5 - \left(\frac{\omega_L}{2\pi}\right)}\right]\right\} + \frac{1}{6}\right].\tag{88}$$

Thus, the FT method consists on finding the optimum value Ω_L by solving (87). With this value, the prototype filter and the subfilter are designed as given in (78) and (79). Finally, the coefficients $\alpha(n)$ are found from the prototype filter coefficients by relating (67) and (69) and the overall filter is synthesized by using any of the structures existing in literature [13]-[15] or [17].

Example 5. The following code example illustrates the design of a Type III Hilbert transformer with $\delta = 0.004$, $\omega_L = 0.01\pi$ and $\omega_H = \pi - \omega_L = 0.99\pi$ using the MATLAB Signal Processing Toolbox. The optimized value for Ω_L is $\Omega^*_L = 0.2237\pi$ and the lengths for the prototype filter and the subfilter are, respectively, $L_P = 14$ and $L_G = 31$. The value Ω^*_L has been optimized to minimize the number of coefficients in the structure of Figure 16. This code makes use of the MATLAB function ChebyshevPoly.m, which is available online [30].

```
%*********** INITIAL DATA ****************
L_g=31;  wl=0.01*pi;  L_p=14;   Om_L=0.2237*pi;
%************** SUBFILTER*********************
wH=pi-wl;   dG = (1/2) - (1/2)*sin(Om_L/2);
vd = (( 1 - sin(Om_L/2) )/2) + sin(Om_L/2);
g = firpm(L_g-1,[wl/pi wH/pi],[vd vd],'hilbert');
%*************PROTOTYPE FILTER******************
[p]=firpm(L_p-1,[Om_L/pi 1],[1 1],'hilbert');
%***************BASIC BUILDING BLOCK H1********************
r1=2*conv(g,g);
delay=[zeros(1,L_g-1) 1 zeros(1,L_g-1)];
h1=r1+delay;
%**************ALPHA COEFFICIENTS FROM CHEBYSHEV POLYNOMIAL **************
N = L_p/2
for mm=1:N;  d(mm)=2*(p((N+1)-mm)); end
D(N)=2*d(N);
for Mm=fliplr([3:N]);  D(Mm-1)=(2*d(Mm-1))+(D(Mm));   D(1)=d(1)+((1/2)*D(2));
end
tt=0;
for nn=fliplr([0:N-1]); tk=ChebyshevPoly(nn); T(nn+1,:)=[zeros(1,tt) tk'] ;
   tt=tt+1;
end
ll=sum((D'*[ones(1,N)]).*T);
alpha=fliplr(ll);
%**************OVERALL FILTER **************
upper_branch = g;   lower_branch = g*alpha(1);   h = lower_branch;
for ii=1:N-1;
upper_branch = conv(upper_branch,h1);
lower_branch = conv(h, [zeros(1,L_g-1) 1 zeros(1,L_g-1)]);
h=lower_branch + alpha(ii+1)*upper_branch;%Overall Hilbert transformer
end
[H w]=freqz(h,1,1000);
figure
plot(w/pi,abs(H))
```

Figure 17 shows the magnitude response of the obtained Hilbert transformer. The overall structure requires only 15 coefficients in total, i.e., 7 structural coefficients, $a(0)$ to $a(6)$, and 8 coefficients for the subfilter $G(z)$. Compared to a direct design, where the estimated length is 287 and which would require approximately 72 coefficients, The FT-based design achieves almost a 75% of reduction in the number of distinct required coefficients.

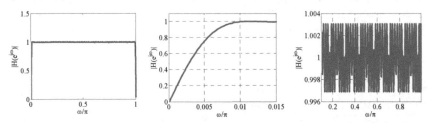

Figure 17. Magnitude responses of FT-based Hilbert transformer. From left to right: overall magnitude response, transition bandwidth detail and passband ripple detail.

5.3. Hilbert transformer design based on Piecewise Polynomial Sinusoidal technique

This method to synthesize Hilbert transformers, first proposed in [25] and then detailed in [11], is based on the previous method [31] and on a modification to the method [32]-[33]. The method stems from a windowing technique for Type III and Type IV FIR filters of order $2N$ and $2N-1$, respectively. The basic windowing technique for Type III filters is expressed as

$$h(n) = w(n)h_0(n) ,\tag{89}$$

where

$$h_0(n) = \begin{cases} 0 & \text{for } n \text{ odd} \\ \dfrac{1 - \cos((n - N)\pi)}{(n - N)\pi} & \text{for n even} \end{cases}\tag{90}$$

is an ideal impulse response, $w(n)$ is the window function and N is odd. Similarly, an ideal odd-order impulse response can be expressed as

$$h_0(n) = \frac{1}{(n - (2N - 1)/2)\pi} .\tag{91}$$

The overall transfer function can be expressed in the following way,

$$F(z) = \begin{cases} \displaystyle\sum_{n=0}^{2N} W(n)[1 - \cos((n - N)\pi)]z^{-n}, & \text{Type III} \\ \displaystyle\sum_{n=0}^{2N-1} W(n)z^{-n}, & \text{Type IV} \end{cases}\tag{92}$$

with

$$W(n) = \begin{cases} w(n-N)/[\pi(n-N)], \\ w(n-(2N-1/2))/[\pi(n-(2N-1/2))]. \end{cases} \tag{93}$$

$W(n)$ is an impulse response satisfying $W(2N - n) = -W(n)$ for $n = 0, 1, \ldots, N - 1$, $W(N) = 0$, and $W(2N - 1 - n) = -W(n)$ for $n = 0, 1, \ldots, N$, for Types III and IV respectively. Additionally, $w(n)$ is a positive and symmetric window function for all n.

A way to generate the piecewise-polynomial-sinusoidal transfer function $F(z)$ is to consider the following transfer function:

$$G(z) = \sum_{n=0}^{N_s} W(n)z^{-n}(e^{j(n-N)\pi}) = \sum_{n=0}^{N_s} W(n)\big[1-(\cos((n-N)\pi) + j\sin((n-N)\pi))\big]z^{-n}, \tag{94}$$

where N_s is $2N$ or $2N - 1$ for Types III and IV, respectively. From (92) it follows that $F(z)$ can be expressed as

$$F(z) = \text{Re}\left\{\sum_{n=0}^{N_s} W(n)z^{-n} + z^{-n}(e^{j(n-N)\pi})\right\} = \text{Re}\left\{\sum_{n=0}^{N_s} W(n)\big[1-z^{-N\pi}(z^{-1}e^{j\pi})^n\big]\right\}. \tag{95}$$

In [32] a wideband FIR filter is obtained by first generating the envelope filter with $W(n)$ for $n = 0, 1, \ldots, 2N$ [$2N - 1$] as the impulse-response coefficients. This impulse response is designed to become piecewise polynomial. The coefficient values of this envelope filter are modified by multiplying them with $[1-\cos(n-N)\pi]$ for Type III, which gives $F(z)$. From (92) it can be seen that for Type IV the piecewise-polynomial-sinusoidal impulse response coincides with the piecewise-polynomial impulse response, i.e., the constant part of the real part in (95).

Let us consider the simpler case Type IV filter. The overall transfer function, denoted by $H(z)$, is constructed as presented previously in sub-section 4.3. We will repeat the equation here for convenience,

$$H(z) = \sum_{m=1}^{M} z^{-N_m} H_m(z) + z^{-\hat{N}} \hat{H}(z). \tag{96}$$

Recall that the integers N_m in the delay terms z^{-N_m} satisfy $N_1 = 0$ and $N_{m+1} > N_m$ for $m = 1, 2, \ldots, M - 1$, and the order of $H_m(z)$ is $2(N - N_m) - 1$. The impulse response is given for $n = 0, 1, 2, \ldots, N - N_m - 1$ by Lth order polynomials as follows

$$h_m(n) = \sum_{r=0}^{L} a_m^{(L)}(r)n^r. \tag{97}$$

Additionally, $z^{-\hat{N}}\hat{H}(z)$ is a conventional [$2N - 1$]th-order Type IV direct-form transfer function with the additional impulse response coefficients at $n = N - c, \ldots, N - 1$, where $c =$

$\lceil T/2 \rceil$ and T is the number of additional coefficients at the center of the filter. The delay terms in (96) are used to shift the center of the symmetry at the desired location, which occurs at $n = (2N - 1)/2$.

In order to indicate that the overall filter has a piecewise-polynomial impulse response the time interval $[0, N - 1]$ is divided into the following M subintervals:

$$X_M = [N_m, N_{m+1} - 1] \text{ for } m = 1, 2, ..., M - 1 \tag{98}$$

and

$$X_M = [N_M, N]. \tag{99}$$

First, we have that $X_1 = [0, N_2 - 1]$ because $N_1 = 0$, Secondly, the overall impulse response can be studied up to $n = N - 1$ because of the odd symmetry. The impulse response on X_m can be expressed as

$$h(n) = \sum_{m=1}^{M} \tilde{h}_m(n), \tag{100}$$

where

$$\tilde{h}_M(n) = \sum_{k=1}^{m} \left[\sum_{r=0}^{L} \left[a_k^{(L)}(r)(n - N_M)^r \right] \right] \tag{101}$$

for $m = 1, 2, ..., M - 1$ and

$$\tilde{h}_M(n) = \sum_{k=1}^{M} \left[\sum_{r=0}^{L} \left[a_k^{(L)}(r)(n - N_M)^r \right] \right] + h'(n), \tag{102}$$

which equals the overall impulse response and where $h'(n)$ is a conventional direct-form Type IV filter with nonzero coefficients for $n = N - c, \ldots, N - 1$, in which $c = \lceil T/2 \rceil$ and T is the number of separately generated additional center coefficients. The slices N_ms should be chosen so that $|N_2 - N_1| \neq |N_3 - N_2| \neq ... \neq |N_M - N_{M-1}|$, where $N_1 = 0$ and M is the number of subintervals in the overall impulse response.

Based on the above equations, in each X_m for $m = 1, 2, \ldots, M$, a separate piecewise-polynomial impulse response can be generated. In addition, in the X_M, there are additional center coefficients, which are of great importance for fine-tuning the overall filter to meet the given criteria.

Given the filter criteria as well as the design parameters M, N, L, N_m's, and the number of center coefficients included in $\hat{H}(z)$, the overall problem is solvable by using linear programming.

6. Conclusion

In this chapter we have studied the Hilbert transform relations existing among the real part and the imaginary part of complex analytic signals. The importance of these signals has been highlighted in terms of spectral efficiency, i.e., the analytic signals do not have spectral components in their negative-frequency side. For discrete-time sequences, this characteristic holds for the negative-frequency side in every Nyquist period.

The Hilbert transformer has been introduced as a special type of FIR filter which is the key processing system to generate analytic signals. The design of such important filter is, of course, straightforward with the aid of an important filter design tool: the MATLAB Signal Processing Toolbox. However, this direct design method, shown as a very simple and convenient MATLAB code, cannot be efficiently applied for more stringent and realistic specifications. We have presented a concise explanation of the relation of Hilbert transformers and half-band filters because this relation, as has been observed from literature, is one of the most important characteristics to overcome this problem.

The efficient methods to design low-complexity FIR Hilbert transformers with strict specifications have been detailed. Three methods have been analyzed, namely, Frequency-Response Masking (FRM), Frequency Transformation (FT) and Piecewise-Polynomial Sinusoidal (PPS). These schemes are based on three different approaches to design efficient FIR filtering. FRM is a periodical subfilter based method, FT is an identical subfilter based method and PPS is a piecewise-polynomial based method. Additionally, it has been observed that FRM and PPS are fully parallel approaches and do not take direct advantage of hardware multiplexing. On the other hand, we have shown that FT allows area-efficient architectures by multiplexing a simple subfilter.

Finally, the FRM and the time-multiplexed FT approach have been illustrated in MATLAB, with the aid of the Signal Processing Toolbox. Even though the underlying theory on the efficient techniques to design FIR Hilbert transformers is specialized, the MATLAB codes have been preserved in a simple and as clear as possible presentation. The presented codes allow a clearer understanding on such specialized techniques and, at the same time, can serve as a basis for more elaborated algorithms and further research on this fertile area.

Author details

David Ernesto Troncoso Romero and Gordana Jovanovic Dolecek
Department of Electronics, Institute INAOE, Tonantzintla, Puebla, Mexico

Acknowledgement

Special thanks to Miriam G. Cruz Jimenez for her valuable assistance in the development of this chapter.

7. References

[1]   Andreas Antoniou (2006) Digital Signal Processing. McGraw Hill, USA.

[2]   Alan V. Oppenheim, Ronald W. Schafer (1989) Discrete-Time Signal Processing. Prentice Hall, USA.

[3]   R. L. C. Van Spaendonck, F. C. A. Fernandez, R. G. Baraniuk and J.T. Fokkema (2002) Local Hilbert transformation for seismic attributes. EAGE 64th Conference and Technical Exhibition.

[4]   Jose G. R. C. Gomes and A. Petraglia (2002) An analog Sampled-data DSB to SSB converter using recursive Hilbert transformer for accurate I and Q channel matching. IEEE Trans. Circ. Syst. II, vol. 49, no. 3, pp. 177-187.

[5]   Michael Feldman (2011) Hilbert transform in vibration analysis. Mechanical Systems and Signal Processing, no. 25, pp. 735-802.

[6]   R. Ansari (1987) IIR discrete-time Hilbert transformers. IEEE Trans. Acoust. Speech and Signal Processing, vol. ASSP-35, no. 8, pp. 1116-1119.

[7]   Ljiljana D. Milic and Miroslav D. Lutovac (1999) Approximate linear phase Hilbert transformer. IEEE International Conference on Telecommunications in Modern Satellite, Cable and Broadcasting Services, TELSIKS'99, pp. 119-124.

[8]   S. Samadi, Y. Igarashi and H. Iwakura (1999) Design and multiplierless realization of maximally flat FIR digital Hilbert transformers. IEEE Trans. Signal Processing, vol. 47, no. 7, pp. 1946-1953.

[9]   Yong C. Lim and Y. Yu (2005) Synthesis of Very sharp Hilbert transformer using the Frequency-Response Masking technique. IEEE Trans. on Signal Processing, vol. 53, no. 7, pp. 2595-2597.

[10] Yong C. Lim, Y. Yu and T. Saramaki (2005) Optimum masking levels and coefficient sparseness for Hilbert transformers and Half-band filters designed using the Frequency-Response Masking technique. IEEE Trans. Circuits and Sistems-I: Reg. Papers, vol. 52, no. 11, pp. 2444-2453.

[11] R. Lehto, T. Saramaki and O. Vainio (2010) Synthesis of wide-band linear-phase FIR filters with a piecewise-polynomial-sinusoidal impulse response. Circ. Syst. and Signal Process., vol 29, no. 1, pp. 25-50.

[12] Y. L. Tai and T. P. Lin (1989) Design of Hilbert transformers by multiple use of same subfilter, Electronics Letters, vol. 25, no.19, pp. 1288-1290.

[13] M. G. C. Jimenez, D. E. T. Romero and G. J. Dolecek (2010) On design of a multiplierless very sharp Hilbert transformer by using identical subfilters. In Proc. 53rd. IEEE Int. Midwest Symp. on Circ. and Syst., MWSCAS'10, pp. 757-760.

[14] D. E. T. Romero, M. G. C. Jimenez and G. J. Dolecek (2012) Optimal design of multiplierless Hilbert transformers based on the use of a simple subfilter (in Spanish). Computación y Sistemas, vol. 16, no. 1, pp. 111-120.

[15] D. E. T. Romero, M. G. C. Jimenez and G. J. Dolecek (2012) A new Pipelined-Interleaved structure for FIR Hilbert transformers based on frequency transformation technique. IEEE 5th Int. Symp. on Communications, Control and Signal Process, ISCCSP'12 (In press).

[16] Y. C. Lim (1986) Frequency-Response Masking Approach for the synthesis of Sharp Linear Phase Digital filters. IEEE Transactions on Circuits and Systems, vol. CAS-33, no. 4, pp. 357-364.

[17] T. Saramaki (1987) Design of FIR Filters as a Tapped Cascaded Interconnection of Identical Subfilters. IEEE Transactions on Circuits and Systems, vol. CAS-34, no. 9, pp. 1011-1029.

[18] S. M. M. Zanjani, S. M. Fakhraie, O. Shoaei and M. E. Salehi (2006) Design of FIR filters using identical subfilters of even length. In Proc. IEEE Int. Conf. on Microelectronics, ICM'06, pp. 83-86.

[19] Z. Jiang and A. N. Wilson (1997) Efficient digital filtering architectures using Pipelining/Interleaving. IEEE Transactions on Circuits and Systems- II: Analog and Digital Signal Processing, vol. 44, no. 2, pp. 110-119.

[20] Richard G. Lyons (2004) Understanding Digital Signal Processing. Prentice Hall.

[21] H. W. SchüBler and P. Steffen (1998) Halfband filters and Hilbert transformers. Circuits and Systems signal Processing, vol. 17, no.2, pp. 137-164.

[22] J. F. Kaiser and R. W. Hamming (1977) Sharpening the response of a symmetric non-recursive filter by multiple use of the same filter. IEEE Transactions Acoustics Speech. Signal Processing, ASSP-25, pp. 415-422.

[23] Sanjit K. Mitra, James F. Kaiser (1993) Handbook for Digital Signal Processing. John Wiley & Sons, USA.

[24] R. Lehto, T. Saramaki and O. Vainio (2007) Synthesis of wide-band linear-phase FIR filters with a piecewise-polynomial-sinusoidal impulse response. IEEE International Symp. Circuits and Systems ISCAS 2007, pp. 2052-2055.

[25] R. Lehto and O. Vainio (2008) Hilbert transformers with a piecewise-polynomial-sinusoidal impulse response, IEEE International Symp. Circuits and Systems ISCAS 2008, pp. 2450-2453.

[26] T. Saramaki, Y. C. Lim and R. Yang (1995) The synthesis of halfband filter using frequency-response masking technhique. IEEE Trans. Circuits Syst., vol. 42, no. 1, pp. 58-60.

[27] T. Saramaki, J. Yli-Kaakinen and H. Johansson (2003) Optimization of frequency-response-masking based FIR filters. Circuits, Syst. Signal Processing, vol. 12, no. 5, pp. 563-590.

[28] Y. C. Lim, Y. Yu, K. L. Teo and T. Saramaki (2007) FRM-based FIR filters with optimum finite word-length performance. IEEE Trans. Signal Processing, vol. 55, no. 6, pp. 2914-2924.

[29] K. Ichige, M. Iwaki and R. Ischii (2000) Accurate estimation of minimum filter length for optimum FIR digital filters. Circuits and Systems II: IEEE Trans. on Analog and Digital signal process, vol 47, pp. 1008-1016.

[30] Matlab Chebyshev polynomial function at http://www.mathworks.fr/matlabcentral/fileexchange/35051-2-dimensional-filter-design-using-mcclellan-transformation/content/Filter%202D%20McClellan/ChebyshevPoly.m (last accessed 7-5-2012)

[31] R. Lehto, T. Saramaki and O. Vainio (2007) Synthesis of narrowband linear-phase FIR filters with a piecewise-polynomial impulse response. IEEE Trans. Circuits and Syst. I, vol.54, no. 10, pp. 2262-2276.

[32] S. Chu and S. Burrus (1984) Efficient recursive realizations of FIR filters, Part I: The filter structures. IEEE Circuits, Syst. Signal Process. , vol. 3, no.1, pp. 2-20.

[33] S. Chu and S. Burrus (1984) Efficient recursive realizations of FIR filters, Part II: Design and applications. IEEE Circuits, Syst. Signal Process. , vol. 3, no.1, pp. 21-57.

Chapter 6

Position Estimation of the PMSM High Dynamic Drive at Low Speed Range

Konrad Urbanski

Additional information is available at the end of the chapter

1. Introduction

Permanent Magnet Synchronous Motors (PMSM) are widely used in industrial drives due to their high power density, high torque-to- inertia ratio, small torque ripple and precise control at low speed range, possibility to torque control at zero speed, high efficiency and small size. To exploit presented advantages, a vector control should be used. Vector control allows the drive a good dynamic, effective performance especially during transients and prevents overload of the motor by controlling the torque. However, a motor shaft position sensor is required to enable the effective vector control of a PMSM. Such sensors increase the overall cost of the drive and decrease its reliability. That sensor occupies usually the end of the shaft, so elimination of the need for its installation allows new applications of such drive. This scientific problem remains an open question for and is the subject for extensive research in many scientific centers. Several approaches to this problem are reported in the literature, which are based on state observers [1,2], various versions of the Kalman filters [3,4], sliding-mode observers [5,6] or methods of applying motor saliency [7,8,9]. State observers and Kalman filters based on a motor model require complex computational operations to obtain proper accuracy, which always causes problems in real time operation. Several approaches apply motor magnetic saliency and detect the rotor position by measuring phase inductances. These methods provide a real solution at small speeds and during standstill operation, but requirements with respect to hardware and software are high. The additional scientific problem is to obtain high dynamic sensorless drive [10,11]. Assumption of the limitation the applications up to speed control (without position control) gives possibility to achieve well performance of high dynamic sensorless drive for low speed operating range.

A simple and effective structure of an observer is proposed in this paper. The presented observer structure is based on a modified concept of back EMF detection [5] and introduces a more complex corrector function which differs from the traditional one. The structure contains a corrector with a proportional-multi integral function (PII²) instead of the proportional correction used in the Luenberger observer [12]. Prepared observer structure is applied to control structure presented at figure 1. The motor is fed by the PWM inverter, the control system includes vector control system of stator currents at dq independent axes (R_{iq} and R_{id}), speed controller (R_ω) and observer. The system is equipped with position and speed sensors which are used only to analysis of the estimation quality. The estimated value of the actual shaft position is used in transforming blocks of the coordinate system $dq\text{-}\alpha\beta$ and $\alpha\beta\text{-}dq$. The estimated value of the speed is used in control loop of the speed.

Presented structure gives possibility to test system in closed (observed values are used to control drive) and open (observed values are only considered) mode using manual switches as it is shown on figure 1. To achieve smooth observed values, a reference voltage can be used instead of measured ones.

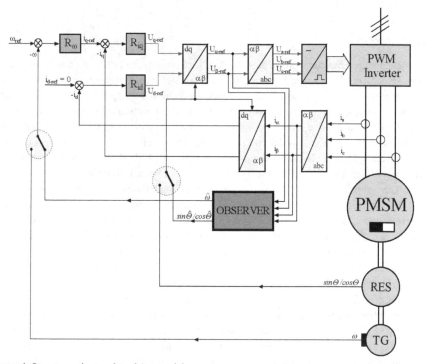

Figure 1. Structure of sensorless drive model

2. Inverter

For modeling the PWM converters can be used models with various complexity degrees. First approximation can be a usage of the inverter's transfer function equal to one. One can do that in the case of high carrier frequency of the inverter, since any significant delays occur in the measuring loops. At this case, the observer input signals may be smooth, and is easily obtained the proper observer performance. The other possibility to ease modeling transfer function of the inverter is zero order sample and hold block, usage the delay block or first order transfer function, which time constant or sampling interval is calculated depends on the proposed carrier frequency. These models do not require a very small simulation step size. In the case of the simulation where the effect of the inverter such as simply the impact the modulated voltage on generated state vector's waveforms and drive performance or inverter's dead time impact is taken into account, the more accurate model is inserted in place of the simplified one. Figure 3 presents used in this model simplified structure of the PWM inverter. Structure of this model is directly derived from the method of generating the states of the switches, the change of switch state is carried out at the intersection of the reference voltage and the carrier signal. This model does not take into account the dead time phenomenon.

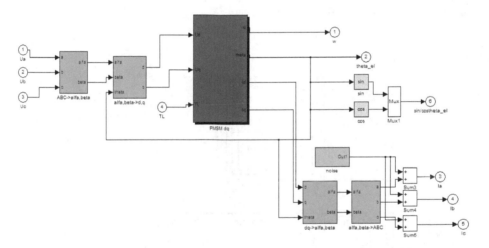

Figure 2. General view of PMSM model in *dq* axis expanded on *ABC* coordinates system inputs and outputs

The cost of the exact model of inverter usage is of course much smaller calculating step, from single microseconds up to dozens of nanoseconds (for range about 10 kHz carrier frequency) in place of dozens or hundreds microseconds for simple inverter model for presented drive parameters. The calculating step value is very important due to simulation time especially during optimization procedure (thousands or hundreds of thousands of repetitions). For example, the presented drive is simulated in normal mode, at 2.10 GHz dual core Intel processor at 8.3 s, (simulation stop time 0.12 s, fixed step size – 5 µs), but start simulation without opening the model (using only the command window), will reduce the simulation time to about 6.3 s.

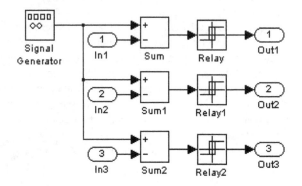

Figure 3. General view of simple PWM inverter model

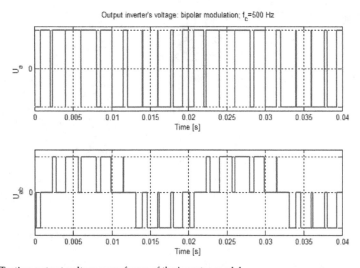

Figure 4. Testing output voltage waveforms of the inverter model

Presented at figure 3 inverter model generates the exemplary (for the ideal three-phase sinusoidal excitation) waveforms of the output voltage (the testing waveform obtained for carrier frequency f_c=500 Hz) for bipolar voltage modulation – as presented on figure 4. Figure 5 presents the carrier frequency influence for waveforms for the excited phase current for the stationary circuit.

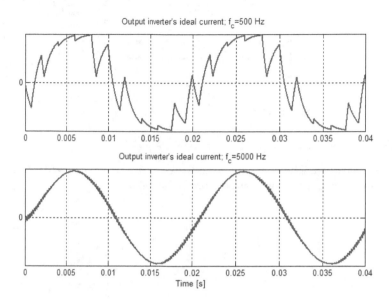

Figure 5. Carrier frequency influence for current Iₐ waveform

3. Speed controller structure

All the controllers and observer are implemented as a discrete structure. The used in this study structure of speed controller is shown in figure 6 (the currents controllers used in q and q axis are typical PI structure with anti wind-up and limited output). The signals used in a controller module are "Wref" – reference speed, "Wm" – measurement (or estimated) feed back speed value and speed controller output signal, "Iref" – reference current/torque. Choice of controller structure allows determining the impact of the control algorithm for ability to sensorless performance because of the transients. The tested structure of speed controller was the typical P/PI structure. To avoid integrator saturation for a controller with limited output level, a hard limit is imposed. It is easy and effective solution. The easiest way to set the integrator limit is to use the same value as in the output. Figure 6 shows the tested structure of PI controller. The structure is parallel. Block zero-order-hold in proportional gain branch is used to "synchronize" input signals of the adder. For fast integration switch-off a manual switch "s1" is used. This structure provides a stable performance of the system, and easy selection of settings using different methods. One of the methods used for setting the controller parameters was RWC method (that method will be discussed later), the same as used for settings the observer's parameters.

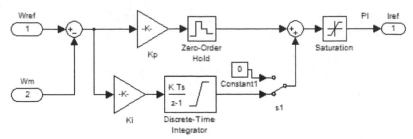

Figure 6. The speed controller structure

4. PMSM model

Assuming ordinary simplified assumptions, the general form of the PMSM model in $\alpha\beta$ stationary orthogonal coordinates can be expressed as follows:

$$\frac{di_\alpha}{dt} = -\frac{R}{L} \cdot i_\alpha - \frac{1}{L} \cdot e_\alpha + \frac{1}{L} \cdot v_\alpha$$
$$\frac{di_\beta}{dt} = -\frac{R}{L} \cdot i_\beta - \frac{1}{L} \cdot e_\beta + \frac{1}{L} \cdot v_\beta \tag{1}$$

and the mechanical part:

$$\frac{d\omega}{dt} = \frac{1}{J} \cdot \left(\Psi_\beta \cdot i_\alpha - \Psi_\alpha \cdot i_\beta - T_L \right)$$
$$\frac{d\theta}{dt} = \omega \tag{2}$$

The motor model with state variables i_α, i_β ω and Θ is non-linear. All state variables are measurable but in a concept without mechanical sensor ω and Θ should be estimated. The symbols i_α, i_β, Ψ_α, Ψ_β, e_α, e_β are stator current, stator flux linkage and induced back EMF in $\alpha\beta$ coordinates. Symbols v_α, v_β are the components of input stator voltage, R and L are the stator windings resistance and inductance. The symbols ω and Θ are the rotor speed and the position, J is the moment of inertia and T_L is the load torque treated as an external disturbance. Such model formula is used for easy derivation of the observer structure. The observer is prepared as a $\alpha\beta$ model because there is no need of conversion of the coordinates systems for calculation of the output values.

After simple conversion of the motor model, we get the model in the coordinates system rotating with the rotor - dq – electrical part:

$$u_d = R \cdot i_d + L_d \frac{di_d}{dt} - \Psi_q \cdot \omega$$
$$u_q = R \cdot i_q + L_q \frac{di_q}{dt} + \Psi_d \cdot \omega \tag{3}$$

$$\Psi_d = L_d \cdot i_d + \Psi_f$$
$$\Psi_q = L_q \cdot i_q \tag{4}$$

and the mechanical part:

$$T_e = \frac{3}{2}\Big[\Psi_d \cdot i_q - \Psi_q \cdot i_d\Big]$$
$$T_e - T_L = J\frac{d\omega}{dt} \tag{5}$$

where u_d, u_q means the components of input voltage, i_d, i_q, L_d, L_q mean currents and inductance of the motor in the dq-axis respectively, Ψ_d, Ψ_q, Ψ_f means flux in the dq-axis respectively and flux excited by permanent magnet. The electromagnetic torque is represented by a symbol T_e.

Such structure gives a possibility to ease analyze of the decoupled dq values of the currents and introduction of different forms of the nonlinear flux distribution. It should be noted that such simple model does not take into account the variable number of pole pairs.

Based on such general model, in simulation PMSM block expanded on nonlinearities in distribution of the flux, current measurement noise addition with control and simple model of friction are used. Model prepared in dq-axis gives simple solution to simulate salient pole motor by use the different values of the axis inductance. The dq model is equipped with external conversion modules, to get inputs and outputs as voltages and currents in *ABC* phases. It gives possibility to test the drive under various conditions. Outside the PMSM model in axis dq, the model is equipped with conversion block into *ABC* coordinates systems used to supply and measurement (Fig. 2). As a measurement noise source a uniform random number function may be used.

5. Observer structure

Proposed observer system calculates position information from back EMF estimated in $\alpha\beta$ coordinates (stator based). This coordinates system was chosen because of its simple form, and there is no need to convert the coordinate system by using the (estimated) shaft position. The sine and cosine of shaft position is calculated from back EMF values, and based on their modulus, is calculated the motor speed (Fig. 7). The inner structure of the observer depends on the correction function. As is shown in figure 7, the observer consists of the electrical part of the PMSM model and an additional correction loop. Different forms of correction functions are shown in the following equations.

According to the method presented in [13] it is convenient to use only first two electrical equations (1), in which the back EMF components are considered as disturbances. In such a case we can prepare an extended state formula, which can be described as:

$$\dot{x}_E = A_E x_E + B_E u, \qquad y = C_E x_E \tag{6}$$

where

$$x_E = \begin{bmatrix} i_\alpha \\ i_\beta \\ e_\alpha \\ e_\beta \end{bmatrix}, \quad y = \begin{bmatrix} i_\alpha \\ i_\beta \end{bmatrix}, \quad u = \begin{bmatrix} v_\alpha \\ v_\beta \end{bmatrix} \tag{7}$$

For presented system it is possible to use ordinary Luenberger observer with correction based on error between measured and calculated currents value. Assuming that derivative of disturbances is equal zero one can write the equations describing observer (8).

$$\frac{d\hat{i}_\alpha}{dt} = -\frac{R}{L}\hat{i}_\alpha - \frac{1}{L}\hat{e}_\alpha + \frac{1}{L}v_\alpha + K_{i\alpha}\left(i_\alpha - \hat{i}_\alpha\right)$$

$$\frac{d\hat{i}_\beta}{dt} = -\frac{R}{L}\hat{i}_\beta - \frac{1}{L}\hat{e}_\beta + \frac{1}{L}v_\beta + K_{i\beta}\left(i_\beta - \hat{i}_\beta\right)$$

$$\frac{d\hat{e}_\alpha}{dt} = \qquad\qquad +K_{e\alpha}\left(i_\alpha - \hat{i}_\alpha\right) \tag{8}$$

$$\frac{d\hat{e}_\beta}{dt} = \qquad\qquad +K_{e\beta}\left(i_\beta - \hat{i}_\beta\right)$$

or in matrix form

$$\dot{\hat{x}}_E = A_E \hat{x}_E + B_E u + K\left[\Delta i\right] \tag{9}$$

where **K** is a correction factor.

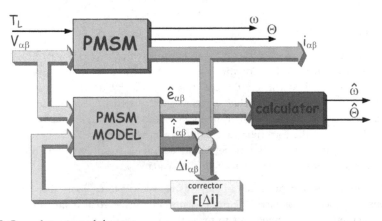

Figure 7. General structure of observer

Such solution generates acceptable observer's performance, however, a more accurate model was also taken into account [14].

The cost of that simplicity is required of the change of the observer's corrector parameters settings due to operating point (*gain scheduling*). Modifying the observer's parameters as a function of velocity only is sufficient at this case. Its proper change is very important in the case where the speed range is wide. At that case (low speed), the corrector parameters may be constant. Otherwise a scheduling mechanism based on the fuzzy logic or artificial neural network should be used [14]. Because observer estimates back EMF values, to achieve position and speed information one can use that transformation:

$$\sin\hat{\Theta} = -\frac{\hat{e}_\alpha}{|\hat{e}|} \qquad \cos\hat{\Theta} = \frac{\hat{e}_\beta}{|\hat{e}|} \tag{10}$$

where

$$|\hat{e}| = \sqrt{\hat{e}_\alpha^2 + \hat{e}_\beta^2} \qquad |\hat{\omega}| = \frac{|\hat{e}|}{k_e} \tag{11}$$

Multiplication of observer error by constant coefficient **K** (9) gives the observer structure with proportional correction equation. To modify observer operation it can be proposed a more complex function of observer error **F[Δi]** instead of a proportional one. By analogue to designing ordinary controller of P, PI and PID structure, one can propose instead of proportional correction more complex operation like PI or PID. This leads to a new general concept of observer, which formula can be written as:

$$\dot{\hat{\mathbf{x}}}_E = \mathbf{A}_E\hat{\mathbf{x}}_E + \mathbf{B}_E\mathbf{u} + \mathbf{F}\left[\Delta\mathbf{i}\right] \tag{12}$$

where **F[Δi]** is a function of observer corrector. So, the correction function may be a sliding mode corrector [15], an integrated sliding mode corrector [16] or e.g. any other correction function based on integration. Such idea of the observer structure may be used for position estimation also in other types of motor, e.g. SRM [17].

In the case of the proportional-integral (PI) correction the observer equations take the following form:

$$\mathbf{F}_1\left[\Delta\mathbf{i}\right] = \mathbf{K}_p\left[\Delta\mathbf{i}\right] + \mathbf{K}_i\int\left[\Delta\mathbf{i}\right]dt \tag{13}$$

On the basis of many simulation tests a more complex corrector structure with proportional-double integral (PII^2) correction was proposed [16]:

$$\mathbf{F}_2\left[\Delta\mathbf{i}\right] = \mathbf{K}_p\left[\Delta\mathbf{i}\right] + \mathbf{K}_i\int\left[\Delta\mathbf{i}\right]dt + \mathbf{K}_{ii}\int\left[\int\left[\Delta\mathbf{i}\right]dt\right]dt \tag{14}$$

The advantage of introducing integral and double integral components of the observer corrector is that they ensure the astatic character of observation (parameters estimation) even during the transient speed process, in which fast changes of speed and reference currents occur – when the back EMFs waveforms are not in sinusoidal shape. The estimation of back EMF signals by the observer enables the calculation of the new values of the rotor speed and position from (10) and (11) at each step of algorithm realization. In fact, the observed signals (back EMFs) are still changing its values (sinusoidal wave) when motor isn't at standstill and the astatic character of observer corrector is very important to follow up the position with small estimation error and small phase shift. The structure of the observer's parameters vector consists of six different elements due to symmetry of the equation (14) for current and back EMF calculation and the additional seventh k_e , which is used to scaling back EMF's estimated amplitude into speed value (11). The observer's structure is identical in both α and β component.

6. Observer parameters setting

The choice of observer parameters is an important task and should take into account dynamics in closed loop system as well as good accuracy of observation. The simulated drive is a compound object. Motor nonlinearity, discontinuity caused by the inverter structure and discrete structure of the control loop make it difficult to calculate the parameters of the observer. The solution presented in this paper is based on the special algorithm, which is used for automatic supervising the calculations, and after a certain number of cycles generates the results in form of the observer parameter set. The process of parameter synthesis was optimised by means on the base of random weight change (RWC) procedure [18] (Fig. 8). This algorithm is fast and insensitive to the local minimum of the optimized criterion. Depending on the value of the search step parameters, the effects of the algorithm performance   that we get are like for gradient algorithm or evolutionary algorithm (Fig. 9), the possibility to quickly find a local minimum or in longer calculations the searching and finding the global minimum. The searching process is supervised by the quality index. The quality function of observer optimization is formulated as:

$$Q = \int_{t_1}^{t_1+\tau} e_\Theta^2(t)\,dt + \Delta e_\Theta(\tau) \tag{15}$$

where e_Θ is the position estimation error, Δe_Θ is the range of the error value changes of the estimated position during the transient process, t_1 and $t_1 + \tau$ are the time boundaries of the integral calculation. The meaning of those parameters is explained in figure 10.

The optimization procedure is performing *off-line* by simulating a transient process (can also be performed *on-line* using real system, while motor drive is operating, in a case of significantly reduced range of coefficients change). According to the RWC procedure a new set of corrector settings is randomly selected at each step but only the set which gives estimation improvement (for quality index defined by (15) means smaller quality index

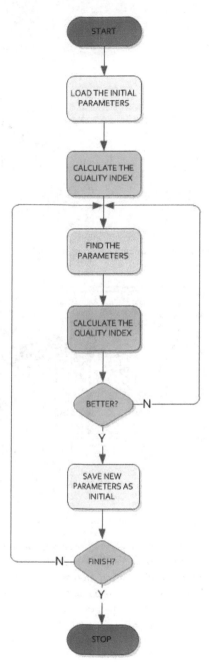

Figure 8. Adaptation of the RWC algorithm to the parameter selection of the observer procedure

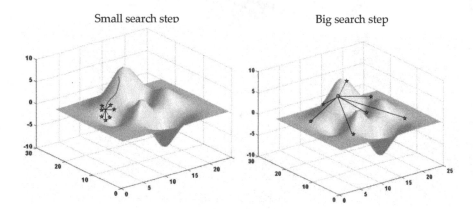

Figure 9. Features of the algorithm, depending on the search step value

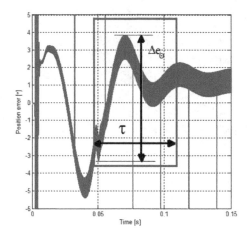

Figure 10. Explanation of the equation (15) parameters

value) is saved. In the procedure a dimension of search area (a range of randomly change of coefficient values) must be determined at each step. In the presented solution a wide area was assumed at the beginning of optimization process for fast quality index reduction and next at the final stage its dimension was reduced to achieve better accuracy. As a result of such *off-line* optimization a set of optimal values of corrector coefficients is found for the analyzed point of operation. If the speed is changed in a wide range, the modifying of the parameter set is needed. This procedure depends on search parameters, may be fast and insensitive to the local minimum of the optimized criterion. The optimization procedure may be performed *off-line* by simulating a transient process. The optimization procedure should be repeated for different points of operation, which were determined by the steady state speed value. At each step of optimization the transient process of the step response to speed reference changes in the selected point of operation was simulated, and during this process the value of the criterion was calculated. According to the RWC procedure a new set of corrector settings is randomly selected at each step but only the set which gives estimation improvement (smaller criterion value) is stored. In the procedure a dimension of search area (a range of randomly change of coefficient values) must be determined at each step. In the presented solution a wide area was assumed at the beginning of optimization process and next at the final stage its dimension was reduce to achieve better accuracy.

Because the optimization procedure of the observer parameters is based on random numbers generation, it is important to take care on proper initiation of that generator. It is very important to initiate generating values using such code:

```
rand('state', sum(100*clock))
```

It is used to eliminate the generation of the same values sequence, each time you start MATLAB.

7. Simulation results

The model of the PMSM control system was carried out in MATLAB Simulink ® environment. The motor was modeled with ordinary simplifying assumptions such as constant resistance and inductance in stator windings, symmetry of windings, and isotropic properties of motor (3, 4, 5). The motor model was connected with a model of a control system, which includes a vector control system of stator currents, a speed controller and a model of the analyzed observer (Figure 1). Drive model contains also a d-axis current control loop because even that current value is considered during sensorless mode operation.

The model of the observer was used as an element of feedback sending detected signals of rotor position and speed. The motor model was calculated with a very small step of integration, which simulates its continuous character. The step value was within the range of 0.02÷20 μs, depending on the simplification level of the inverter model. To reduce simulation time, the inverter may be neglected and calculation step 20 μs may be used. Contrary to that, the model of the control system with the observer was calculated with much higher step values (50÷200 μs), simply because it enables a better simulation of how the control system works on a signal processor with a real value of the sampling period. Presented waveforms are achieved for observer's parameter settings prepared for reference speed 5 rad/s.

Selected waveforms of speed, currents and position error are presented below. These images well illustrate the operation of observer compared with sensor mode. These waveforms were obtained as responses to the step change of speed reference, generated in the form of a step sequence starting from zero speed to 10 rad/s and to 5 rad/s at time 0.1 s. Motor load changes from zero to motor's nominal load value at time 0.16 s. In addition, figures 11 and 12 show ±2 % range of reference value. Waveform 11 and 12 prove the well performance of sensorless mode drive at low speed – even at 5 rad/s. That drive still remains robustness on disturbance (rapid reference speed and load change). Enlarged part of figure 11 (Fig. 12) shows clearly the setpoint achieving process. Figures 13 and 14 show waveforms of currents in q-axis and d-axis respectively obtained for test such as at figure 11. One can notice the d-axis current value in sensorless mode isn't close zero at transients – it is determined by temporary ripple in position estimation signal but the ripple quickly fades away. Figure 15 shows waveforms of the calculated position error (observer estimates only sine and cosine of the position). The steady state position error does not depend on motor load (which is seen at time 0.1÷0.2 s of that figure) but the operating point (determined as a motor speed). Presented in figure 16 sine and cosine of the estimated position waveforms proves that observer operates well at longer simulating time. Figures 17 and 18 present drive performance for additional difficulty: disruption of the "measured" phase currents by injection of the random signal. Reliable performance is considered even for such disturbance. Then observer was tested to determine its robust on inaccurate estimation of the motor parameters. Results are shown in figure 19 and table 1. For such system the parameters lower deviation range is about ±10 %. Motor parameters were stationary, only the observer's parameters were changed with factors presented below. Certain robust on inaccuracy parameter estimation is noticed.

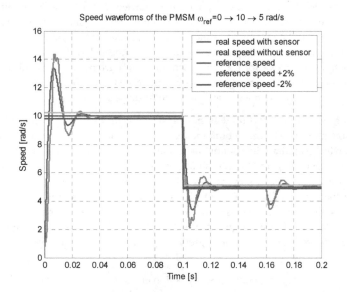

Figure 11. Waveforms of real and estimated speed involved by step changes of reference
0→10→5 rad/s
at t=0.16 s load changes from 0 to its nominal value

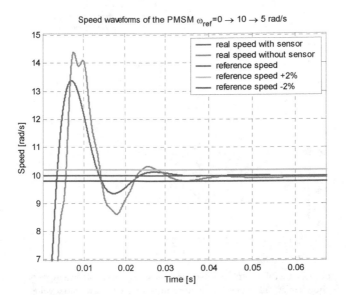

Figure 12. Waveforms of real and estimated speed involved by step change of reference 0→10 rad/s – enlarged part of fig. 11.

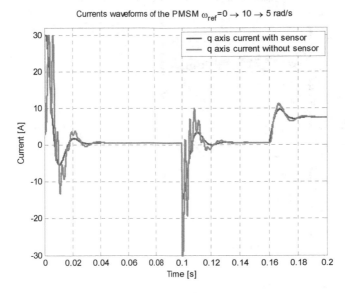

Figure 13. Waveforms of q-axis current in sensor and sensorless mode; step changes of reference speed 0→10→5 rad/s as shown in fig. 11. At t=0.16 s load changes from 0 to its nominal value

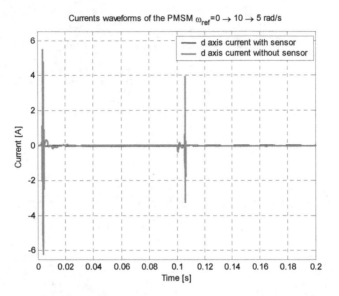

Figure 14. Waveforms of *d*-axis current in sensor and sensorless mode; step changes of reference speed 0→10→5 rad/s as shown in fig. 11. At t=0.16 s load changes from 0 to its nominal value

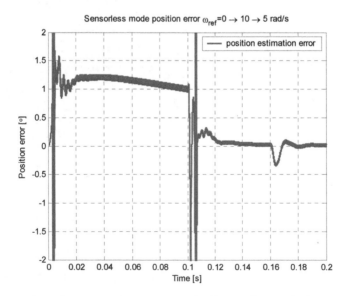

Figure 15. Waveform of position estimation error involved by step changes of reference speed 0→10→5 rad/s as shown in fig. 11
at t=0.16 s load changes from 0 to its nominal value

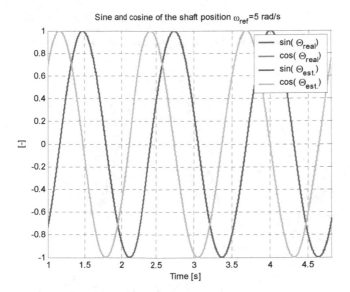

Figure 16. Waveforms of sine and cosine of the estimated and real position at reference speed 5 rad/ at steady state

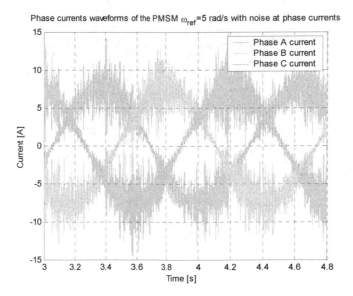

Figure 17. Waveforms of phase currents in sensorless mode for reference speed 5 rad/s with "measuring" noise at phase currents

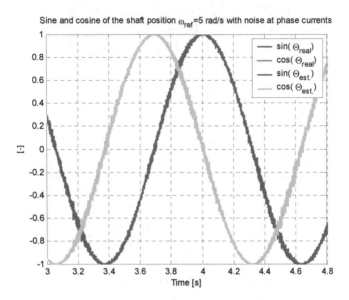

Figure 18. Waveforms of sine and cosine of the estimated and real position at reference speed 5 rad/s at steady state with "measuring" noise at phase currents as shown in fig. 17

In observer		Position error [°]		
R factor	L factor	loaded 5 rad/s	unloaded 5 rad/s	unloaded 10 rad/s
1	1	0.08	0.08	0.5
1.2	1	0.1	0.1	0.5
0.9	1	0.06	0.08	0.5
1	0.91	-0.2	0.05	0.5
1.1	0.91	-0.2	0.06	0.5

Table 1. Position error according to motor parameter inaccuracy

The final test was prepared to determine the robustness to the incorrect estimate of the initial position. The question was how big may be position difference between estimated and the real one, to prevent the motor startup. Tests have shown, that the possible range of the initial position error, for which the engine will start correctly, it is 80 degrees of arc (Fig. 24). Figures 20-23 show the sine and cosine waveforms of the estimated and the real shaft position. Corresponding to sine and cosine waveforms from figures 20-23, figure 24 shows the "measured" speed waveforms. The robustness on initial position error estimation is proven.

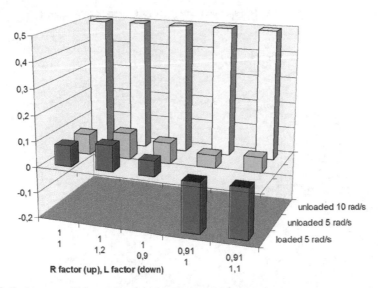

Figure 19. Position error [°] according to motor parameter inaccuracy

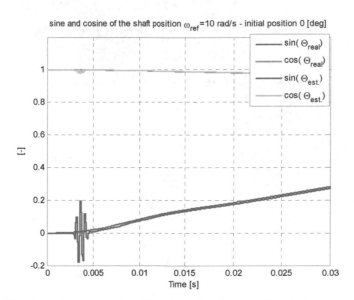

Figure 20. Waveforms of sine and cosine of the estimated and real position at reference speed 10 rad/s during startup – shaft initial position equal the estimated one

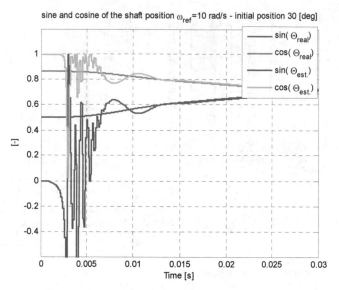

Figure 21. Waveforms of sine and cosine of the estimated and real position at reference speed 10 rad/s during startup – shaft initial position different than estimated one: 30 °

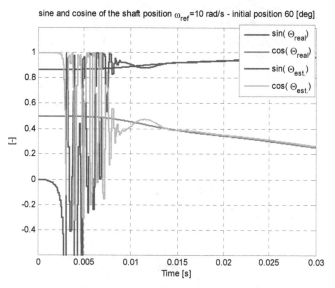

Figure 22. Waveforms of sine and cosine of the estimated and real position at reference speed 10 rad/s during startup – shaft initial position different than estimated one: 60 °

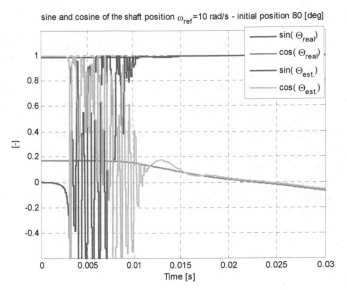

Figure 23. Waveforms of sine and cosine of the estimated and real position at reference speed 10 rad/s during startup – shaft initial position different than estimated one: 80 °

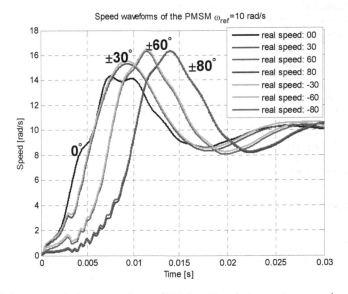

Figure 24. Robustness to the incorrect estimate of initial position during startup – speed waveforms for 0→±80 ° position variance

8. Conclusions

Stable performance of the sensorless drive with PMSM at low speed was noticed in the closed loop mode. Small position error and robust on inaccuracy motor parameter estimation were proven. The resistance tolerance is about 20 %, whereas inductance error tolerance is below 9 %. A wider range of resistance change could be achieved by using resistance observation. A test for robustness on the disturbance in the measured signal was passed: even a disruption of the phase currents by injection of the random signal does not disturb the performance of the sensorless drive. Such drive can achieve high dynamics according to the definition presented in abstract. Robustness to the incorrect estimate of initial position was also tested. The used PI controller discrete implementation gives possibility to use the same speed controller settings in both operating mode – sensor and sensorless. The sensorless drive using modified Luenberger observer gives possibility of the high performance of the high dynamic drive, where the "high dynamic" definition is introduced in this chapter. An additional effect of this work is to present the outline of how to create and how to operate the complex models of electrical motor drives in the context of the selection of model components of varying complexity which affect the calculation time and quality and accuracy of the results.

Notice

Motor parameters:

- stator inductance: $L = 5.7\,\text{mH}$
- stator resistance per phase: $R = 0.7\,\Omega$
- total moment of inertia: $J = 0.007273\,\text{kg·m}^2$

Author details

Konrad Urbanski

Institute of Control and Information Engineering, Poznan University of Technology, Poznan, Poland

Acknowledgement

This work was supported by grant N N510 325937.Appendix

9. References

[1] J. Liu, S. Hao, R. Ma, and M. Hao, "Research on Integer State Observer in Current Control for PMSM," 2008, pp. 228–231.

[2] L. A. Jones and J. H. Lang, "A state observer for the permanent-magnet synchronous motor," *IEEE Transactions on Industrial Electronics*, vol. 36, no. 3, pp. 374–382, Aug. 1989.

[3] T.-F. Chan, P. Borsje, and W. Wang, "Application of Unscented Kalman filter to sensorless permanent-magnet synchronous motor drive," presented at the Electric Machines and Drives Conference, IEMDC, 2009, pp. 631–638.

[4] S.-M. Gu, F.-Y. He, and H. Zhang, "Study on Extend Kalman Filter at Low Speed in Sensorless PMSM Drives," presented at the 2009 International Conference on Electronic Computer Technology, 2009, pp. 311–316.

[5] F. Parasiliti, R. Petrella, and M. Tursini, "Sensorless speed control of a PM synchronous motor based on sliding mode observer and extended Kalman filter," 2001, vol. 1, pp. 533–540.

[6] J. Vittek, P. Bris, M. Stulrajter, P. Makys, V. Comnac, and M. Cernat, "Chattering free sliding mode control law for the drive employing PMSM position control," 2008, pp. 115–120.

[7] A. B. Kulkarni and M. Ehsani, "A novel position sensor elimination technique for the interior permanent-magnet synchronous motor drive," *IEEE Transactions on Industry Applications*, vol. 28, no. 1, pp. 144–150, Feb. 1992.

[8] U. H. Rieder and M. Schroedl, "A simulation method for analyzing saliencies with respect to enhanced INFORM-capability for sensorless control of PM motors in the low speed range including standstill," in *Power Electronics and Applications, 2005 European Conference on*, 2005, p. 8–pp.

[9] Y. Ying, Z. Jianguo, G. Youguang, and J. Jianxun, "Numerical simulation of a PMSM model considering saturation saliency for initial rotor position estimation," in *Control Conference, 2008. CCC 2008. 27th Chinese*, 2008, pp. 114–118.

[10] F. Genduso, R. Miceli, C. Rando, and G. R. Galluzzo, "Back EMF Sensorless-Control Algorithm for High-Dynamic Performance PMSM," *IEEE Transactions on Industrial Electronics*, vol. 57, no. 6, pp. 2092–2100, Jun. 2010.

[11] K. Urbanski, "Sensorless control of PMSM high dynamic drive at low speed range," in *2011 IEEE International Symposium on Industrial Electronics (ISIE)*, 2011, pp. 728–732.

[12] D. Luenberger, "An introduction to observers," *IEEE Transactions on Automatic Control*, vol. 16, no. 6, pp. 596–602, Dec. 1971.

[13] Germano, F. Parasiliti, and M. Tursini, "Sensorless Speed Control of a PM Synchronous Motor Drive by Kalman Filter," in *Proc. of the 1994 International Conference on Electrical Machines*, 1994, vol. 2, pp. 540–544.

[14] K. Urbanski and K. Zawirski, "Adaptive observer of rotor speed and position for PMSM sensorless control system," *COMPEL: Int J for Computation and Maths. in Electrical and Electronic Eng.*, vol. 23, no. 4, pp. 1129–1145, 2004.

[15] F. Parasiliti, R. Petrella, and M. Tursini, "Sensorless speed control of a PM synchronous motor by sliding mode observer," in *Industrial Electronics, 1997. ISIE'97., Proceedings of the IEEE International Symposium on*, 1997, pp. 1106–1111.

[16] K. Urbanski and K. Zawirski, "Rotor speed and position detection for PMSM control system," in *Proceedings of 9th Int. Conference and Exhibition on Power Electronics and Motion Control*, Kosice, 2000, vol. 6, pp. 239–243.

[17] K. Urbanski and K. Zawirski, "Sensorless control of SRM using position observer," in *2007 European Conference on Power Electronics and Applications*, 2007, pp. 1–6.

[18] B. Burton, F. Kamran, R. G. Harley, T. G. Habetler, M. A. Brooke, and R. Poddar, "Identification and control of induction motor stator currents using fast on-line random training of a neural network," *IEEE Transactions on Industry Applications*, vol. 33, no. 3, pp. 697–704, Jun. 1997.

Chapter 7

Detection of Craters and Its Orientation on Lunar

Nur Diyana Kamarudin, Kamaruddin Abd. Ghani, Siti Noormiza Makhtar, Baizura Bohari and Noorlina Zainuddin

Additional information is available at the end of the chapter

1. Introduction

Craters are features commonly used as research landmarks compared with the other landforms such as rocks, mountains, cliffs and many others. Because of their simple and unique geometry and relatively established appearance under different conditions, the authors decided to select craters as ideal landmarks for detection and spacecraft localization. This chapter focuses on identification of craters in terms of their characteristics and detection of these visual features of the moon to determine a safe landing site for a lunar Lander. Cheng et al. proposed using craters as landmarks for navigation purposes because the geometric model grants a robust detection under different lighting conditions. Moreover, craters appear in enough density on most planetary system bodies of interest and they are also known to have fairly stable appearance or shapes over time or under different conditions and environments. These special features make them an appropriate type of landmark to observe. Currently, there is a lot of on-going studies mainly on craters detection and optical navigation systems for the moon and these studies still adopt a complex and similar approach such as detection using the Hough transform method. To part from this limitation, the authors decided to build a simple algorithm for detecting craters on the moon's surface which will detect the craters based on two important measurements including the distance and angle measurements. The advantages of using this approach are threefold: (1) its uncomplicatedness (2) fast detection (3) can be used further in ellipse reconstruction algorithm to determine the position and orientation of the crater. This chapter will discuss the method of employing MATLAB and image processing tool on an optical image as well as the morphological image detection fundamentals. In addition, some geometrical projection analysis in reconstructing an ellipse as a disc will be evaluated in order to obtain the orientation of the disc (crater) for an autonomous optical navigation system.

1.1. Background and context

The first lunar exploration spacecraft named Luna 1 was flown to the moon on January 1959 [21]. Nonetheless, this mission did not give too much impact as it did not land on the moon itself. Due to the enthusiasm to continue the journey of previous research pioneers, Luna 2 became the first spacecraft to land on the moon's surface in late 1959 [21]. These histories of moon explorations became a motivation for a new researcher and moon explorer to find out more about Lunar and its unique features.

A crater plays a vital feature to estimate the age of the moon's surface when any sample specimen is not available [10, 11]. An autonomous crater detection algorithm will help space research scientists to reduce their laboratory works of manually identifying those craters. Previously, several automatic and semi-automatic crater detection algorithms were proposed [12], but their accuracy was not enough for craters chronology and they have yet to be fully tested for practical uses (example: spacecraft navigation). Craters chronology means the history or the sequence of events that formed the craters on the moon's surface and the variety of its features. Optical Landmark Navigation using craters on the planetary surface was first used operationally by the Near Earth Asteroid Rendezvous (NEAR) mission [15, 16]. This mission is to determine the spacecraft orbits and the range of the body for close flybys condition and low attitude orbiting [13].

Many planetary missions such as SELENE (Selenological and Engineering Explorer) and Clementine take the images of the moon's surface for on-going research. This attention to the moon exploratory especially will help us divulge the unimagined information and characteristics of planetary science specifically on the moon's surface. In 2006, a Japanese Lunar Orbiting Spacecraft was launched and was expected to bring a large amount of useful data for on-going planetary research. However, it is known that the images taken under the low sun elevation, such as those from 'Lunar Orbiter' and 'Apollo' are suitable for crater detection as mentioned before to differentiate the 'light and dark patches' for sooner analysis.

Current descent and landing technology for planetary operations, such as those of lunar, is performed by a landing error ellipse greater than 30x100 kilometres without terrain recognition or hazard avoidance capability. Most of the previous research on lunar pin point landing specifically has a limitation such that requires *a priori* reference map describing the past and future lunar imaging and digital elevation map data sets in order to detect the landmarks on a particular planetary surface. Due to this drawback, the authors propose a landmark-based detection algorithm named craters detection algorithm to detect main hazards on the moon's surface independently from those references in order to produce a reliable and repeated identification and detection system. This intelligent imagery-based algorithm will detect craters based on their pointing direction relative to the sun and classification to differentiate between the light and dark patches. Furthermore, by making a match of those detected craters with the internal lunar atlas, the Lander can further determine the spacecraft motion and velocity relative to the lunar surface.

1.2. State of the art

A spacecraft mission on the moon involving Entry, Descent and Landing (EDL) requires precise and intelligent landing techniques. There were numerous previous research efforts and various methods used to determine such landing sites that are safe for a moon Lander. Trying to get a new technique that can search for free hazards locations, this paper will propose an intelligent algorithm described as craters identification algorithm in order to recognize and detect craters consistently and repeatedly over most of the moon's surface. In addition, using geometric recognition techniques, the authors we can also determine the position, attitude, velocity and angular velocity of the spacecraft; the four important parameters used to land safely on the moon by finding a match of those detecting craters to a database containing the 3D locations of the craters (internal lunar atlas).

The lunar surface consists of several hazardous characteristics such as rocks, mountain, boulders, slopes and mainly craters. Particularly, in this paper, the authors choose craters as primary hazard detection because of its geometric shape which makes it easy to identify using image detection codes. Over the years, craters are created as a result of a continuous bombardment of objects from outer space like meteorites, asteroids and comets. All of them strike the lunar surface at various speeds, typically 20 kilometres per second. In addition, unlike the earth, there is no atmosphere on the moon to protect it from collision with other potential impactors.

Previous researchers such as Cheng and Ansar [5] proposed a feature detector and tracker algorithm for detecting craters as mapped landmarks and matched those using applications during EDL for the spacecrafts. In a sequence, one can also determine the position and velocity of the spacecraft using the desired parameters achieved by the matched craters technique mentioned above. For this approach, craters are classified based on their size and orientation of their outlining ellipses. There are databases of previously matched craters to detect the desired impact craters. Position is estimated using subset middle values of at least three matched craters in a linear pose estimation algorithm [6]. By combining the average velocity between two image based position and computed velocity by integrating the accelerometer reading, the actual velocity is dictated by the output of the image processing algorithm.

Continuously, there were preceding research on On-board hazard detection and avoidance for a safe landing which has aimed to autonomously detect the hazards near the landing site and determine a new landing site free from those hazards [7]. In order to detect the potential hazards on the moon's surface, there are specific requirements as agreed by the ALHAT project which will detect the hazards that are 0.3 meters tall or higher and slopes that are 5 degrees or greater mainly for the craters. Moreover, the requirement is not just to detect the hazards with the above mentioned criteria but also must be able to find a safe landing site with a diameter around 15 meters over most of the moon's surface. This proposed system is achieved by using the imaging LIDAR sensors to get the direct measurements of the lunar surface elevation from high altitude. Besides, the probability of the existence of a hazard free landing site is determined as a function of a Lander diameter, hazard map area and rock coverage, and together these procedures are used as guidance for LIDAR sensors and the overall Navigation and Control Architecture.

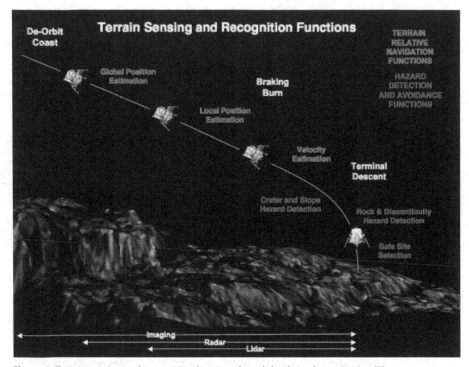

Figure 1. Terrain sensing and recognition functions for safe land site determination [5].

Hazard Detection Avoidance (HDA) and Terrain Relative Navigation (TRN) are on-board capabilities that use sensing and computing technologies to achieve optical safe and precise terrain navigation within 100 meters of a predetermined location on the lunar's surface [8]. They are based on three methods including global position estimation, local position estimation and velocity estimation as illustrated in Figure 1 above. All these functions can be realized using passive imaging or active range sensing. One of the TRN approaches is by using pattern matching which requires *a-priori* reference map describing past and future imaging and digital elevation map datasets (map-dependant system). Pattern matching approach applies landmark (Craters) matching instead of patch correlation and employs passive visible imagery system. There are several parameters required such as diameter of craters, relative distances and angles between landmarks. Craters are usually distinguished in a map of the landing site and then stored in a database. During landing process, craters are detected in descent imagery and are matched as well as compared to the database. Then only the position of the Lander is determined.

Continuous research in developing the greyscale imagery mainly on detecting landform is still being explored within these past few years. In order to detect craters of any particular planetary bodies, one of the approaches is by using the Hough Transform shape detecting assignments [9]. The proposed algorithm focuses on detection of the (sensor independent) geometric features of the impact craters (i.e centre position, craters radius) as well as identification of sensor dependant geometric features such (i.e rim height) as a following task. The use of a simple model (circular shape) for craters detection makes it possible to exploit the algorithm in different operational environments (i.e recognition of Earth and other planetary craters in the Solar System) using data attained by dissimilar sensors such as Synthetic Aperture Radar (SAR). Because of its complex algorithm, Hough Transform is not directly employed to the original image. Some pre-processing steps are necessary to obtain better result and performance of the system as illustrated in Figure 2 below. The Hough Transform has been built by Paul Hough (1962) for the identification of lines in pictures. Describing a circle represented by lines, if the radius is r and centre coordinates represent (a, b), then the parametric representation of a circle:

$$R(x, y) = \{x = a + r \cos \theta, y = b + r \sin \theta\} \tag{1}$$

where $\theta = [0, 2\pi]$

Each point (x, y) represents a, b and r parameter is mapped in a cone surface that has the following representation:

$$H(a, b, r) = \{a = x - r \cos \theta, b = y - r \sin \theta\} \tag{2}$$

where $\theta = [0, 2\pi]$

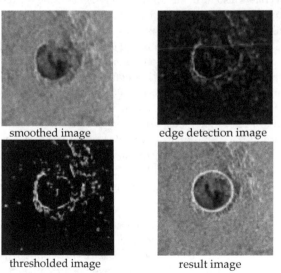

smoothed image   edge detection image

thresholded image   result image

Figure 2. Result obtained using Hough Transform in SAR (Synthetic Aperture Radar) Image [7].

There is also multiple approach algorithms in detecting craters on the lunar's surface as proposed by Sawabe, Matsunaga and Rokugawa, 2005. It is known that the crater's feature changes according to its size. Small craters form a simple circle, and the larger its size, the more complex its shape becomes [3]. This change in feature poses difficult problems to detect craters with different sizes by a single approach. In their data-dependant based algorithm, they defined that a crater is a circular topographical feature in images and a minimum detection crater size is two pixels in radius [13] and it uses data from SELENE (Selenological and Engineering Explorer) to visualize the surface geological settings and the subsurface structure of the Lunar. These approaches are different to the authors' research as they consider the crater to bean ellipse for their detection algorithm. The authors also propose the data independent based algorithm. Four different methods were used with the crater detecting algorithm to find (1) 'shady and sunny' patterns in images with low sun angle, (2) circular features in edge images (3)curves and circles in thinned and connected edge lines, and (4)discrete or broken circular edge lines using fuzzy Hough transform. Besides, the detected craters are also classified by spectral characteristics derived from Clementine UV-Vis multi-spectral images [13]. The main advantages of the proposed algorithm compared to the previous one are that the detection algorithm is uncomplicated and it has an outstanding successful rate of detections. These methods of detection and their determination of accuracy will be evaluated in the experimental results afterwards.

In Landmark Based Pinpoint Landing Simulator (LAMPS) by Cheng and Ansar, a robust yet complex crater detection algorithm has been developed for autonomous spacecraft navigation. Based on their research, craters might have a random appearance based on their ages and sizes. For example, younger craters may have sharper and regular rims [14]. Spatial densities of craters also form the primary basis for assessing the relative and absolute ages of geological units on planetary surfaces [14]. However, typical craters will have ellipse shape in their rims, with a light to dark pattern that is dictated by the sun azimuth and elevation as well as its own topography. In fact, this statement is very similar to the authors' own approach in defining a crater as a composition of light and dark patch. Technically, Cheng and Ansar approach algorithm consists of five major steps which are edge detection, rim edge grouping, ellipse fitting, precision fitting and crater confidence evaluation. Another important property of landmark based detection system is the use of spacecraft pinpoint landing (PPL) for autonomous navigation method. To decrease the probability of landing on a hazard surface, one of the two safe landing proposals must be taken into account: craters hazard detection avoidance, which will detect all hazardous craters upon landing on the moon's surface or pinpoint landing which determines the Lander's position in real time and guide the spacecraft to a safe and free landing site, away from those hazards (craters).

According to recent studies on the size and frequency of the craters on a Mars' surface [17], a sufficient number of adequately sized craters for determining spacecraft position are very likely to be found in descent imagery. For an instance, if the image was taken using a camera field of 45 degrees and is taken from 8km above the surface, there will be an average of 94 craters of less than 200m in diameter. Ideally, from this situation, these craters can be used as landmarks to match a pre-existing crater database and therefore to determine the position of the Lander. This approach of pattern matching will be further used as future works in the authors' research. For the time being, the authors have proposed to use a projection geometry concept in determining the orientation and position of the spacecraft using two vital equations that were discussed later.

As in Figure (3) below, the proposed pinpoint landing is as follow. First, the landing site is pre-determined on the targeted body (moon's surface, Mars' surface, etc) on the earth using orbital imagery, and the landmarks within the landing ellipse (red ellipse) are mapped. During EDL, its preliminary position prior to the landmarks and selected landing site is determined. The Lander's position is then frequently tracked and guided using continuous updates of the Lander's position and the velocity all the way through the descent.

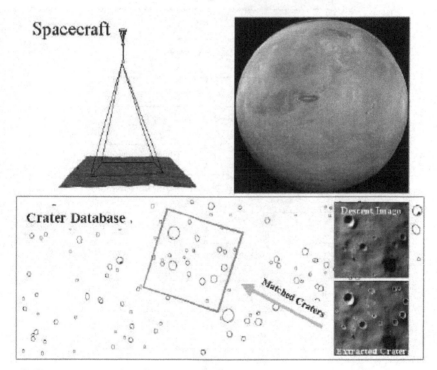

Figure 3. Craters pattern matching for position estimation of the spacecraft during EDL [14]

2. Methodology

2.1. Real time craters detection algorithm

This reliable topography-based Craters Detection Algorithm that the authors are proposing in this chapter is mainly based on a real image (optical image) analysis and morphological

Image Analysis. There are various stages of coding in order to get a satisfactory result, provided that the sun's elevation angle is known. This algorithm is suitable for any optical images taken from 'Lunar Orbiter' or 'Apollo' sources. The Algorithm flowchart is presented in Figure (4) below:

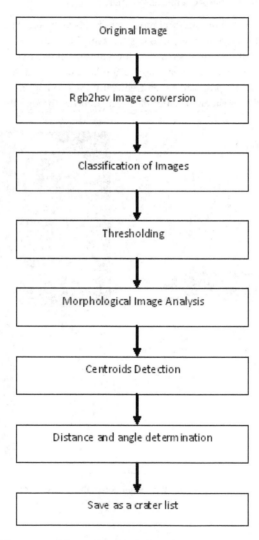

Figure 4. Flowchart of the proposed Craters Detection Algorithm

In the proposed craters detection algorithm, the authors used the original image (3D optical image) of the moon's surface. Originally, this image is a coloured image. For pre-processing step, the authors invented a colour conversion technique which started/originated from RGB (red,green,blue) image to HSV (hue,saturation,value) image using rgb2hsv function in MATLAB. Converting the RGB image to HSV image is basically the transformational of colours from RGB space into HSV space. Value (brightness) gives the amount of light in the colour; hue describes the dominant wavelength which determines the colour type while saturation indicated the vibrancy of the colour. The vital reason for this colour conversion is that the authors want to analyze only one of the entities that is Value entity in HSV component range 0(tend to be dark) to 1(tend to be light) which is then further used in the thresholding calculation. Besides, HSV plane is more popular in analyzing images because of its similarities to the way human intends to recognize colour. RGB and CMYK (Cyan, Magenta, Yellow and Black) colour models are additive and subtractive models respectively, defining colour in terms of the combination of primary colours whilst HSV encapsulates information about a colour in terms of its familiarity to the human adaptation such as; what colour is it? How light and dark the picture is? Or what is the colour vibrant?

For thresholding purposes, a similar approach as Sawabe et al's [13] has been implemented and is discussed thoroughly in the technical section. The purpose of applying a threshold is to distinguish the craters on the moon's surface to light and dark patches groups. Thresholding is the simplest method of image segmentation. This segmentation procedure is to classify the pixels into object pixel (light and dark patch) and non object pixel (background). In this classification of images, it is clearly seen that a crater is formed by two different patterns that are light and dark patches under a different angle of sun beam. The authors use this property of craters in order to analyze and detect them on a lunar's surface. These light and dark patches pattern is distinguished based on the values of pixel's intensity for both images. For an instance, alight patch is determined by a pixel value that is below the threshold brightness calculated whilst a dark patch is determined from a pixel by a pixel value that is above the similar threshold brightness calculated.

Furthermore, in morphology image analysis, erosion and dilation is applied as a combined analysis to the tested image. These two operations can be described simply in terms of adding or removing pixels from the binary image according to certain rules which depend on the pattern of neighbouring pixels. Erosion removes pixel from features in an image or equally turns pixel OFF that were originally ON [20]. Fundamentally, erosion can entirely remove extraneous pixels representing point noise or line defects which are only a single pixel wide. The image that is processed using erosion and dilation are shown in Figure (9) below for better visualization. These two methods are discussed entirely in the experimental results section (craters detection algorithm results) later. Another method is called dilation, which is widely used to add pixels. The dilation rule is that for erosion, is to add (set to ON) any background pixel which touches another pixel that is already part of a foreground region [20]. This will add a layer of pixels around the periphery of all regions which results in dimension increment and may cause images to merge or expand.

In centroid determination, the authors use 'regionprops' function to get every centre for each light and dark blob classified previously. After that, the authors then have to link the blobs together in a single picture. As a result, the final image will comprise a group of clusters or patches that correspond to craters on the moon's surface. These groups of blobs (light and dark patches) will then be used to measure the minimum distance and angle between each of them. First, the algorithm will calculate all the distances of every patch and will pick only the minimum distance. The light patches with minimum distances that are attached to the dark patches will be considered craters as a first step. Second, every angle between the known input sun vector and pairing patches vector is calculated using a scalar product or dot product. Technically, all these methods will be elaborated further in the technical section and experimental results section.

2.2. Geometrical analysis

In the geometric analysis, there are several stages that can be determined as Figure 5 below:

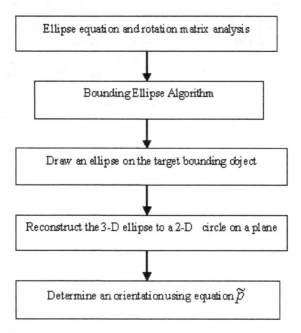

Figure 5. Flowchart of Geometrical Analysis

Users must consider a crater as an ellipse in a real image. This method of consideration will convert an ellipse in a 2D image into a circle on a plane using Conical Projection Analysis. Any ellipse will appear to be a circle from a certain point of views. In other words, an ellipse will be projected into a circle at a certain projection point. At the final stage, this method will be able to calculate the orientation and position of a crater (disc in shape) that is being detected before through the proposed detection algorithm.

2.2.1. Fundamentals of ellipse and rotation matrix

Mathematically, an ellipse can be defined as the locus of all points on the plane whose distances R1 and R2 (as Figure 6 below) to two fixed points added to the same constant and can be notified as:

$$R1 + R2 = 2a \qquad (3)$$

where a = semi major axis and the origin of the coordinate system is at one of the foci (-c,0) and (c,0). These two focis are chosen to be identical with the bounding ellipse algorithm equation. It is sometimes defined as a conical section from cutting a circular conical or cylindrical surface with an oblique plane. There are five vital parameters in ellipse including semi-major axis denoted as **a**, semi-minor axis denoted as **b**, centre, **c** of ellipse in X-coordinate, **Xc**, centre of ellipse in Y-coordinate, **Yc**, and an angle of rotation denoted as ω. The ellipse with all the parameters can be illustrated as below:

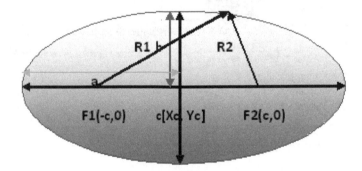

Figure 6. Ellipse

An ellipse that lies along the horizontal X-axis with foci points F1 (-c, 0) and F2(c, 0) as can be shown in Figure (6) above, will have an equation of

$$x^2/a^2 + y^2/(a^2-c^2) = 1 \text{ where a > c for the ellipse} \qquad (4)$$

For an ellipse, the distance c between the centre and a focus is less than the distance a between the centre and foci, so a^2-c^2 is positive and a new constant b>0 is introduced by setting [2]:

$$b^2 = a^2 - c^2 \text{ for ellipses} \qquad (5)$$

Hence the equation of an ellipse with F1 (-a, 0) and F2 (a, 0) is simplified to

$$x^2/a^2 + y^2/b^2 = 1 \text{ where } 0 < b < a \qquad (6)$$

For both the hyperbola and the ellipse, a number e, called the eccentricity is introduced by setting [2]:

$$e = c/a \text{ or } e = \sqrt{(a^2-b^2)}/a \tag{7}$$

In this mathematical and geometrical analysis, the authors started to brief in ellipse equations and rotation matrix first which are going to be analyzed soon in the bounding ellipse algorithm and for the reconstruction of ellipse to a circle on a 2-D plane. These methods are beneficial to determine the orientation and the position of the spacecraft during Entry, Descent and Landing (EDL) applications. In this case, the rotation matrix for an ellipse can be illustrated as Figure 4 below:

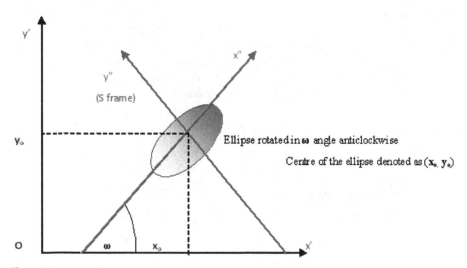

Figure 7. Rotation Ellipse

In S frame as in figure 7 above, it can be shown/demonstrated that using a standard ellipse equation, the x" and y" can be expressed as

$$(x'')^2/a^2 + (y'')^2/b^2 = 1 \text{ where } 0 < b < a \tag{8}$$

Where

$$\begin{pmatrix} x'' \\ y'' \end{pmatrix} = \begin{pmatrix} \cos\omega & \sin\omega \\ -\sin\omega & \cos\omega \end{pmatrix} \begin{pmatrix} x' \\ y' \end{pmatrix} \tag{9}$$

$$= \begin{pmatrix} x'\cos\omega & y'\sin\omega \\ -x'\sin\omega & y'\cos\omega \end{pmatrix} \tag{10}$$

and

$$\begin{pmatrix} x' \\ y' \end{pmatrix} = \begin{pmatrix} x - xo \\ y - yo \end{pmatrix} \tag{11}$$

After substitution of these three vital equations, new formula for the rotation ellipse, which is also the bounding ellipse equation:

$$\frac{((x-xo)\cos\omega+(y-yo)\sin\omega)^2}{a^2}+\frac{((-x+xo)\sin\omega+(y-yo)\cos\omega)^2}{b^2}=1 \qquad (12)$$

Again, the rotation ellipse can also be expressed through this formula:

$$(\tilde{x}-\tilde{c})^T A(\tilde{x}-\tilde{c})=(x-xo)^2 A_{11}+((x-xo)(y-yo))(A_{21}+A_{12})+(y-yo)^2 A_{22}=1 \qquad (13)$$

Where $A_{11}, A_{21}, A_{12}, A_{22}$ is the E matrix that is determined from the bounding ellipse algorithm following the form of

$$A=\begin{pmatrix} A_{11} & A_{12} \\ A_{21} & A_{22} \end{pmatrix} \qquad (14)$$

Thus, by comparing the equations of 12 and 13 above, the authors express all the ellipse parameters a,b,c (Xc and Yc) and ω in terms of this $A_{11}, A_{21}, A_{12}, A_{22}$ entities when drawing the bounding ellipse around the target patch which:

$$a=(\frac{2\sin 2\omega}{(A_{11}+A_{22})\sin 2\omega+2A_{12}})^{1/2} \qquad (15)$$

$$b=(\frac{2\sin 2\omega}{(A_{11}+A_{22})\sin 2\omega-2A_{12}})^{1/2} \qquad (16)$$

$$\omega=\tan^{-1}(\frac{-2A_{12}}{A_{22}-A_{11}})/2 \qquad (17)$$

Furthermore, the other two ellipse parameters Xc and Yc values can be determined straight away from the bounding ellipse algorithm.

2.2.2. Bounding ellipse algorithm

This is the first method used in the geometrical analysis and the reason of using it is to get the bounding ellipse around the targeted patch. This is further used in a final stage of this section that is reconstruction or projection of the ellipse to a circle in a 2-D plane. The bounding ellipse takes five inputs of the ellipse parameters described previously, which are semi-major axis a, semi-minor axis b, centre of ellipse in x-coordinate Xc, centre of ellipse in y-coordinate Yc and rotation angle ω. These five parameters are embedded in the A matrix produced by this algorithm as an output along with the Xc and Yc values. In order to draw the bounded ellipse the authors need to express all those ellipse parameters in terms of the entities $A_{11}, A_{21}, A_{12}, A_{22}$ of the A matrix. The derivations of these terms are comprehensively described in the previous section. The results of this bounding ellipse algorithm will then be used to reconstruct this 2-D ellipse to a 2-D circle in a plane using Reconstruction Ellipse Algorithm. There are two vital equations of reconstructing a disc that will be used in this algorithm to determine the orientation of the spacecraft which is described below [18]; nonetheless in this chapter the authors will only determine the orientation:

$$\tilde{q} = \frac{B}{\sin\alpha}\left\{\cos\beta\tilde{R}_1 \pm_1 \cos\alpha\sin\beta\sqrt{\tan^2\alpha - \tan^2\beta}\tilde{R}_2\right\} \tag{18}$$

$$\tilde{p} = \pm_2 \cot\alpha\left\{\frac{\sin\beta}{\cos\alpha}\tilde{R}_1 \pm_1 \cos\beta\sqrt{\tan^2\alpha - \tan^2\beta}\tilde{R}_2\right\} \tag{19}$$

Where:

$\tilde{q}$ = is the position of the reconstructed ellipse
$\tilde{p}$ = is the orientation of the reconstructed ellipse
B = is the radius of a disc (craters that the authors model as a disc)
α= is the arc length of the semi-major axis
β= is the arc length of the semi-minor axis
$\tilde{R}_1$ = Rotation matrix of the column vector
$\tilde{R}_2$ =Rotation matrix of the column vector

This is the reconstruction or projection ellipse equations where the authors consider an ellipse as a half-length along the axis symmetry, which is taken to 0 that is **A**=0. In this case, the authors need to model the crater bounded as a disc. That is the reason for the half-length along the axis symmetry **A**, is taken to 0. **A** in this case is not the attributes of the matrix determined previously. The authors have to deal with those two equations above where as can be seen the equation $\tilde{p}$, the orientation of a disc, is independent of parameters B (the radius) which means that the authors are able to determine quickly the reconstruction algorithm in order to identify the orientation of the spacecraft relative to the moon's surface. There is the ambiguity case in equation $\tilde{p}$ which is the negative and positive case of $\pm_2$ sign. In this case, the $\tilde{p}$ equations always takes a positive value instead of negative as the crater's orientation is just pointing upward towards a camera or in other words, a disc will only be seen if its outward face points towards the camera rather than away from the camera [18]. This is a discerning case; when one considers how human calculates an object's position, its exact size is needless in finding the direction of neither its centre nor its orientation. In contrast, the equation $\tilde{q}$ is dependent on the radius of a disc, B which the authors have no knowledge of the radius of the craters and how far it is from the moon's surface. Therefore, searching for a solution q is actually an interesting future work that needs to be achieved if the authors want to find the position of the spacecraft during the EDL operations.

3. Technical sections

There are different mathematical equations and fundamentals applied during this project development. In order to make the project runs smooth as planned; the authors have divided the logical structures of the project into three different sections:

3.1. Craters detection algorithm

This project involved the development of the detection algorithm using MATLAB image processing tool and an image of the moon's surface. It is mainly based on the binary image and morphological image analysis. At the first stage, the authors introduce the concept of HSV (Hue, Saturation, and Value) as well as morphology image investigation such as dilation and erosion to exploit the real image. The Hue is expressed as an angle around a colour hexagon mainly using the real axis as 0° axis. The Value is measured along the cone and has two different conditions. If V=0, the end of the axis is represented by black and white if V=1at the end of the axis is represented by white [4]. The Saturation is the purity of the colour and is measured as the distance from the V axis looking at the hue, saturation and value hexagonal cone.

The HSV colour system is based on cylindrical coordinates. Mathematically, converting form RGB (Red, Green and Blue) image to HSV is actually developing the equation from the Cartesian coordinates to cylindrical coordinates. To reduce the complicatedness of analysis on image detection, the authors analysed a 2-D optical image. The threshold for the image is set using intelligent approach from Sawabe, Natsunaga and Rokugawa in classifying the images as can be shown in equations (20) below. By using this approach, images were classified into two components that are light and dark patches or obviously known as 'sunny and shady patches'. Ideally, these two groups of patches are easily recognizable if the image was taken under low sun elevation. These patterns of light and dark patches were detected when all these equations [13] are satisfied:

$$R_{min} < R_m - \sigma$$

$$R_{max} > R_m + \sigma \tag{20}$$

$$P_{min} < P_{max}$$

Where R_{min} indicates the minimum pixel value, R_{max} indicates the maximum pixel value; R_m indicates the average pixel value and σ indicates the standard deviation in the small area including the targeted patches. P_{min} and P_{max} indicate the positions at the minimum and maximum value pixels from the direction of the sun radiation or sun vector [13].

Apart from that, there are two basic fundamentals on morphological operation applied in the algorithm which are dilation and erosion. Dilation is an operation that grows or expands objects in a binary image. This can be represented by a matrix of 1's and 0's but usually it is convenient to show only the 1's group. The dilation between two images A and B, is denoted by $A \oplus B$ and is defined as [1]:

$$A \mathring{\oplus} B = \{z \mid (\mathbf{B})_z \cap A \neq f\} \tag{21}$$

Nevertheless, erosion shrinks or thins objects in a binary image, which is the opposite case of the dilation operation. The mathematical definition of erosion can be expressed as [1] and the result of eroded and dilated image is shown in Figure 8 as below. This can be compared to the original image in Figure (9):

$$A \ominus B = \{z \mid (B)_z \cap A^c \neq f\} \tag{22}$$

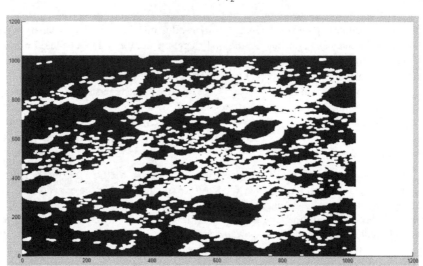

Figure 8. Image after dilation and erosion were applied

The previous stages are then followed by another image analysis methodology that is *regionprops* function and this region indicates the patch that the authors want to analyze. The reason for using this region descriptors function is to plot the centroids of each light and dark patch and gather them (light and dark patches) back together in a single picture which will then be used to further calculate the desirable minimum distance and angle between them to the known sun direction. *Regionprops* takes the labelled matrix as an input and uses axis-x and axis-y to describe horizontal and vertical coordinates respectively.

To classify and consider this region of interest as a crater, the authors proposed two ways of detection which are minimum distance measurement and angle detection based on the known sun vector. In the distance measurement, the minimum distances between each of the centroids calculated previously are determined using this formula:

$$|\textbf{Distance}| = \sqrt{[(x^2-x^1)^2 + (y^2-y^1)^2]} = |\textbf{r}| \tag{23}$$

where |**Distance**| is the measurement of distance between two pairing patches (light and dark), x^2 and x^1 are the x-component of the centroids and y^2, y^1 are the centroid's component of the y-axis respectively. In the angle determination, the authors give an input for the sun vector which is known by looking at the sunray effect at those craters (the position of the light and dark shades). This algorithm will then compute each of the angles of every pairing blob with their minimum distances to the sun vector added input using scalar product or dot product in the vector analysis which is:

$$\textbf{r.s} = |\textbf{r}| \, |\textbf{s}| \cos \theta \tag{24}$$

Where   **r** = vector of each pairing blobs

s = sun vector

|**r**| = distance/length of each pairing blobs

|**s**| = distance of sun vector = unit vector = 1

θ = angle between sun vector and vector of each pairing blobs

Each of the pairing blobs angle is calculated using the above equation and those who has a minimum angle to with known sun vector and has a minimum distance calculated previously will be considered and stored as a crater. Oppositely, those who are against the direction and have the maximum angles to the sun vector will be scrapped and considered noise. At the end of these two measurements (distance and angle), the authors managed to get the best eight craters using this reliable craters detection algorithm.

3.2. Geometrical analysis

3.2.1. Bounding ellipse algorithm

The geometrical part is mainly based on the mathematical analysis on vector calculus, the rotation matrix, ellipse equations and also the mathematical applications to determine two major features that is the orientation of a crater that has been modelled as a disc and the position of the disc after projection. These two features make a vital solution to have a safe landing on the moon's surface. Firstly, from the previous codes, the authors choose one of the best eight in a crater's list to run a bounding ellipse algorithm around the targeted crater. The bounding ellipse algorithm input the P matrix which is composed from the targeted crater itself. The tolerance of the bounding image is set to get more precise result. As discussed above in the methodology section, the output of this algorithm will be the A

matrix and c, the centre of the ellipse. A matrix is in the form of $A = \begin{pmatrix} A_{11} & A_{12} \\ A_{21} & A_{22} \end{pmatrix}$. The reason

the authors highlighted this is to show that another important parameter in ellipse is embedded in this A matrix. They are semi-major axis **a**, semi-minor axis **b**, and angle of rotation ω. As a result, the final equations (equations 13, 14 and 15) are used to draw the ellipse to bind the targeted patches as derived from the previous methodology section. The next step is to draw the ellipse using another algorithm and all those parameters above and also the centre of the ellipse that can be determined straight away from the bounding ellipse algorithm. Statistically, after the algorithm has calculated all the values of the parameter, the authors have the same value for semi-major axis **a** and semi-minor axis **b** which suggests that a circle is formed. This important knowledge tells the authors that the camera is actually pointing straight around 90 degrees vertically to the targeted crater on the moon's surface. If the authors have an ellipse instead of a circle, it means that the camera is not pointing straight 90 degrees downward away from it (crater). That is the first assumption the authors made before doing the third stage algorithm that is Reconstruction of an Ellipse to a circle in a 2-D plane.

3.2.2. Reconstruction of an ellipse on image plane

First, the input of this algorithm is the five primary parameters of the ellipse that are **a**, **b**, **Xc**, **Yc**, ω, the half-length of the semi major axis is denoted as capital **A**, and the half-length of the semi-minor axis is denoted as capital **B**. This reconstruction vision is to model the craters or projected ellipse as a disc. Mathematically, the concepts are adapted by taking the focal point as an origin of a camera frame and the x-axis is aligned with the focal axis of the camera and x > 0 is what the camera is looking for. Furthermore, the image plane is always assumed to be in front of the focal point rather than those in practice. Taking this objective into account, the half-length of the semi major axis **A** is taken to 0 because it is a disc. In comparison, the half-length of the semi-minor axis **B** is actually the radius of the crater or a disc. This reconstruction or projection ellipse algorithm is based on Stephen's proposed complex method on reconstruction spheroid. The authors will use the equation 17 previously to determine the orientation of a disc or crater that the authors modelled from the reconstruction algorithm.

$$\tilde{p} = \pm_2 \cot\alpha \left\{ \frac{\sin\beta}{\cos\alpha} \tilde{R}_1 \pm_1 \cos\beta \sqrt{\tan^2\alpha - \tan^2\beta} \tilde{R}_2 \right\} \tag{25}$$

$\tilde{p}$ equation describes the orientation of the reconstructed disc (crater) and equation $\tilde{q}$ describes the position of a disc (crater) after reconstruction or projection. As the above two equations, there are four possible solutions (regardless of the ambiguity case of $\pm_2$ as discussed before in the methodology section), two of them are from equation $\tilde{p}$ and another two from equation $\tilde{q}$. The equation $\tilde{p}$ is independent from the half-length semi minor axis B as can be seen from the equation. Therefore, the authors can determine the orientation of a disc straight away from the algorithm. Unfortunately, the equation $\tilde{q}$ is dependent on the half-length of semi-minor axis B which the authors are not aware of the radius of a crater because the authors are not able to determine the distance to the moon's surface. This is the main challenge. But getting the value of $\tilde{p}$ will then lead the authors to get the position of $\tilde{q}$ by some means because they are related. The position $\tilde{q}$ of the disc will then be a greater future work to be explored.

4. Experimental results and discussion

4.1. Craters detection algorithm result

In this section, some experimental results are reported which were obtained by applying craters detection algorithm. In particular, the authors choose real images (optical images) of the moon's surface and develop the codes mainly based on the binary image analysis and morphological techniques. As mentioned before, this is the independent algorithm which does not depend on the data elevation map as well as past and future imaging data, which is the advantage compared to other detection algorithms proposed previously. There are seven stages to develop this algorithm as mentioned in the methodology (refer to the flowchart). The authors will discuss the results from the first stage until the last stage by attaching the result image for a better view and understanding of the concept used for analysis.

Erosion and dilation are two fundamentals in Morphological Image Analysis. In Figures 10 and 11, the erosion and dilation are experimented in a combined process for dark patches and light patches. For an ideal result, the authors just used the eroded image for both light and dark patches by adding them together in a single picture for centroid detection later. If the authors take consideration of both the dilation and erosion process as a combined process, the image itself will produce too much noise as shown in the figure above. For centroid determination, therefore, the authors want the noise to be kept at a minimum level in order to attach valid pairing patches and in order to produce minimum small blobs or patches that do not have their pairs (light and dark patch). This is also to reduce the processing time (running time) and complexity of centroid calculation.

Figure 9. Real Image of Craters (Optical Image)

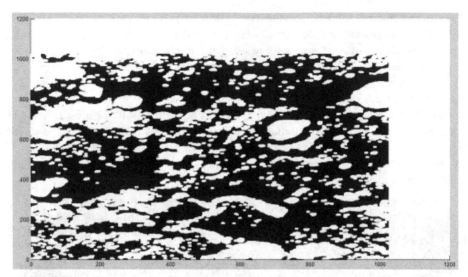

Figure 10. Erosion and Dilation for dark patches

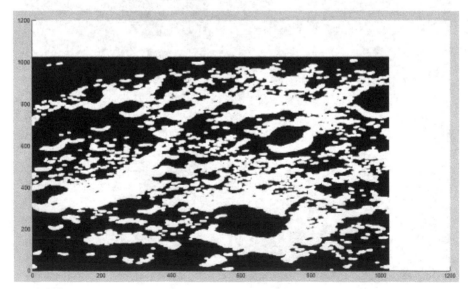

Figure 11. Erosion and Dilation for light patches

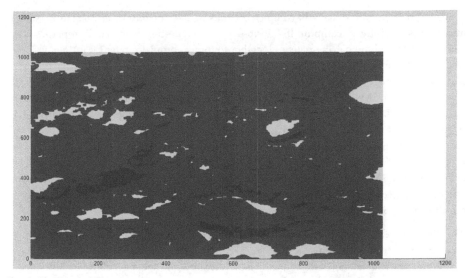

Figure 12. Threshold Image

Secondly, after converting the RGB image plane to HSV image plane and taking into consideration only the *'Value'* from the HSV image plane, thresholding is then used for image segmentation proposal. Thresholding is used firstly to differentiate the object (foreground) from the background. The targeted foreground is ideally the craters themselves that are composed by light and dark patches pattern. The light patch occurs when the pixel value is more than the calculated threshold brightness using the same approach that is fully described in the technical section. Whilst the dark patch is detected when the pixel value is less than the same threshold brightness calculated before. The threshold image can be shown in Figure (12) above.

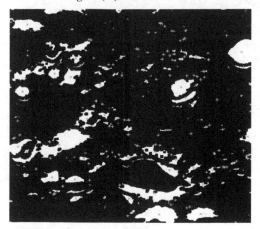

Figure 13. Centroid Determination using 'regionprops' function

Centroid determination stage is completed by using the 'regionprops' function in Matlab and this is basically to compute the desired region properties or targeted properties. This step also attached the pairing patches together to form a complete crater for further analysis. Regionprops only takes the label matrix as an input. Therefore, the authors have to pre-process the image by labelling it first using 'bwlabel' function along with regionprops function later. In MATLAB, bwlabel is used to label the connected components in binary image and bwlabel also supports the 2-D inputs only. After labeling the entire target then only the authors can use them in a memory with regionprops. Regionprops takes this labelled component as an input and return them with an image of centroid determination labelled as a cross (*) symbol as in Figure (13) above. For a smoother image, the authors apply another function in MATLAB called bwareaopen to remove all of the unnecessary objects or all connected components (objects) that are fewer than P pixels set, producing another binary image.

The final stage of this craters detection algorithm is minimum radial distance and angle calculation. The authors have tested the algorithm with two different image conditions (different sun angles and background noises). According to the algorithm, the authors can select the number of craters to be detected by the system. The users can choose how many craters to be detected by the system based on the original image taken. As for this case, it will select the eight best craters that satisfy the minimum distance and angle conditions by assuming that the sun direction is known. An image of the landing site on the moon's surface has to be captured first and the amounts of craters needs to be detected are calculated manually. Based? on the original image, the authors have assumed the sun direction by identifying the shade and sunny pattern locations that formed the craters If the image has less than eight craters, then the system will choose the maximum number of craters on the image. If one deals with the image with many craters, he/she can choose any number that he/she wants to detect based on the original image, which has to be captured first prior to the detection. Although sometimes the system will detect the craters with wrong pairing patches (light patches connected to the wrong dark patch and vice versa) the Lander should understand that one of them might still be one of the hazards that have to be avoided during landing application. The radial distance is calculated for each of the pairs detected in green lines as in Figures (14) and (15) below and using the equation (23) and, the shortest distance between adjacent pairs (light and dark patch) is chosen as a preliminary result for further angle calculations.

After the light patches were connected to the dark patches with a minimum distance between them, then the system will calculate the minimum angle by inputting the direction of the sun (assuming that the authors know the sun's angle) and later comparing it with the pairing patches angle using the dot product (equation 24) as has been thoroughly described in the methodology section. By taking into account both techniques (minimum distance and angle), the authors can determine the best craters that they want on an image. The final craters detected will be denoted in yellow lines as shown in Figures (14) and (15) below.

Ideally, this algorithm will work on any images that have a clear pattern of light and dark patches and the authors do not even have to know the important parameters such as radius, gradient and etc of the craters. Unfortunately, this algorithm will work effectively on the image that has a clear pattern of these light and dark patches only. A crater with a clear pattern in this context will have clear features of light and dark patches that constitute one crater. To determine the accuracy of the algorithm created by the authors, the authors will provide a figure taken from two separate images tested by this algorithm. The final results have to be compared with the real image in order to determine which craters are true. In a real scenario, all craters detected will be considered hazards even though they are connected to the wrong pair of light or dark patches.

Comparing the results taken from Image 1to the original image (real image of the moon's surface), there are eleven valid craters or true craters after pre-processing (after erosion and noise reduction (*bwareaopen* function), labelled by BW label). Valid craters or true craters in this context means that the craters have a clear pattern of light and dark blobs regardless of the size and other features. Over these eleven valid craters, eight of them are successfully detected using this craters detection algorithm; this suggests that the authors have a 73% successful rate. The authors have tested this craters detection algorithm into two different optical images with different sun angles which are 10 degrees, > 10 degrees and with a noisy image as mentioned below. These evaluations below are to measure the accuracy of the algorithm based on the two images proposed and how robust the algorithm is. The determination of accuracy of the algorithm is based on how often craters are detected and the calculations are shown below:

Based on the original Image 1 as can be illustrated in Figure (14) below

Sun direction: 10 degrees
Manual Detection (number of craters after pre-processed): 11
Automatic Detection (number of craters detected): 8
8/11 x 100 = **73% accuracy**

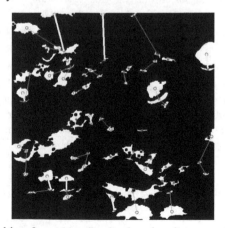

Figure 14. Craters detected from Image 1 in yellow line based on distance and angle measurements

Based on the original Image 2 as can be illustrated in Figure (15) below

Sun direction: > 10 degrees
Manual Detection (number of craters detected after pre-processed): 10
Automatic Detection (number of craters detected): 8
8/10 x 100 = **80% accuracy**

Figure 15. Craters detected from Image 2 in yellow line based on distance and angle measurements

In Figure (15) above, yellow lines, which denote as craters are detected with a minimum distance and angle detection while green lines, which denote as craters are detected with a minimum distance only prior to the minimum angle detection. This angle detection will be a final stage in defining the craters based on the light and dark patch pattern (sometimes denoted as sunny and shady parts) and the final craters are those with yellow lines. By comparison, the accuracy of the algorithm based on these two images with different types of craters, angle (Sun) and lighting condition is said to be 77% and it is quite a satisfactorily accurate.

This accuracy factor can be improved if the authors know exactly the sun elevation angle since in this research; the authors just assumed the angle and the value is not really accurate. In a real application, this sun angle can be measured separately using the satellite, altimeter or radar prior to this detection process and the value will be more accurate. Besides, this algorithm will detect the craters that are above 0.0265 meters in image size (100 pixels). This can be vouched by using the *'bwareaopen'* function where it will remove the entire blobs pixel which is less than 100 pixels.

4.2. Bounding ellipse algorithm results

In the geometrical analysis section, the authors start with the bounding ellipse algorithm using the information from the previous proposed craters detection algorithm to bound the targeted blob as shown in Figure 18 above. The blob is selected randomly from the true craters detected by the detection algorithm such as in figure (16) above by labelling the targeted output using 'bwlabel.' This function numbers all the objects in a binary image. By using this information, the user can select the true matching pair that can be selected for further research (to determine its position and orientation) by using the function 'find' in MATLAB and this step can be repeated for all of the true matching pairs detected by the algorithm. This is the first step before the authors can draw the ellipse around the target (figure 16) to bound it and to reconstruct the crater selected as a disc using ellipse reconstruction algorithm. This reconstruction is beneficial to later determine the orientation and position of a Lunar Lander using the equation $\tilde{p}$ and $\tilde{q}$ as proposed before during EDL of the spacecraft. There are some mathematical fundamentals and equations that need to be understood before one can apply the bounding ellipse algorithm to a certain targeted object. They are fundamentals of the ellipse and also the rotation matrix fundamentals. This knowledge is used to extract the embedded entities from the output of bounding ellipse algorithm in terms of basic ellipse parameters such as **a**, **b**, **Xc**, **Yc** and ω which are further used to draw an ellipse around the targeted object (target patch). Generally, the authors want to express all those ellipse parameters in terms of E matrix which is the output of bounding ellipse algorithm. This E matrix takes a form of $E = \begin{pmatrix} A_{11} & A_{12} \\ A_{21} & A_{22} \end{pmatrix}$. Finally, the authors want to express the ellipse parameters in terms of $A_{11}, A_{21}, A_{12}, A_{22}$ in order to draw the bounding ellipse and further to reconstruct it as a disc.

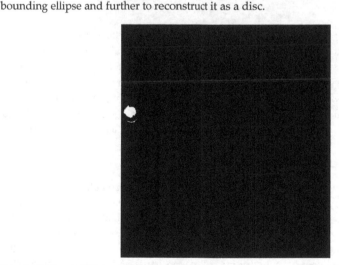

Figure 16. Targeted blobs chosen randomly from the matched true pairs in distance and angle measurement using bwlabel function.

After the authors obtain the bounding ellipse around the targeted patch as in shown in the figure below, the next step is to reconstruct the bounded crater using ellipse reconstruction algorithm. As a result, the authors will get a circle which suggests that the camera is pointing straight vertically to the lunar's surface.

Figure 17. Bounded crater using bounding ellipse algorithm and Image plane ellipse algorithm in green circle line

As can be seen in Figure (17) above, a circle, instead of an ellipse, appeared after the authors ran the bounding ellipse algorithm along with the image plane ellipse algorithm. This is because the semi major axis **a** is actually similar to the semi minor axis **b**, so a circle is produced. In fact, this means that actually the camera is pointing down vertically straight to the moon's surface providing an angle of around 90 degrees relative to the moon's surface. Next, the reconstruction ellipse algorithm took the input of **a**, **b**, centre (Xc,Yc), A , B and produced the output of the orientation $\tilde{p}$ of the ellipse after reconstruction or projection.

4.3. Ellipse reconstruction algorithm results

This algorithm is about to model a crater as a disc and reconstruct an ellipse to a circle in 2 dimension (2-D) plane in order to determine the position and orientation of a crater relative to the spacecraft. For the first case, the authors used a real image which is an optical image. To realize the above purposes, the authors have assumed several altitudes from the spacecraft to the moon's surface. As mentioned before, after the authors performed the bounding algorithm and drew the bounding ellipse on a particular targeted crater, the authors have an image of a circle that bound a targeted crater rather than an ellipse, and therefore the authors have an assumption that the camera on the spacecraft is pointing vertically, almost 90 degrees from above in angle if measured from a flat lunar's surface. From bounding ellipse algorithm, the authors have determined the image plane ellipse parameters and the results show that the semi-major axis, *a* is similar to the semi minor axis, *b*. Taking advantage of this idea, a circle will only have one solution in order to determine the position of a crater and the ambiguity case (an ellipse has 2 solutions) can be eliminated. The reconstruction algorithm [18] described in the methodology and technical sections previously is then used to reconstruct a possible disc (crater) positions and orientations after taking into account of the camera's parameters [18] below where Xc and Yc is the coordinate of the centre of an ellipse. The authors use an optical image dimension of 1024x1024 pixels.

In real applications, the lunar's surface is not flat, and the crater is not straight below the camera. In this case, the authors had determined a circle in bounding ellipse algorithm that bounds a certain target; hence the authors made this assumption as the above figure. By looking at the figure above, the focal axis line is not really parallel to the centre of the disc hence the perspective distortion would have an effect as being described further in the next section. When the authors set A = 0 it is important to bear in mind that the ellipse will become a disc and this means that $\bar{p}$ is parallel to $\bar{q}$ and the authors should obtain a circle. Contrary to this, if $\bar{p}$ is perpendicular to $\bar{q}$, the authors will get a line rather than a circle.

In a real situation, the altitude assumptions above are measured prior to the landing purposes. This altitude is usually measured by the altimeter or the satellite. Before the authors can construct the position a disc, they must determine the orientation first. This orientation and position of the disc is obtained from the equations (18) and (19) previously. As being mentioned before, the orientation equation is free from the term B and can be determined fully from the reconstruction algorithm. The orientation of the disc can be described as a unit vector that gives the direction of the centre of the disc. It is a positive value since the crater can be seen positioned upwards rather than downwards (negative side).

An ellipse will be detected on the image plane for each disc that is visible on the camera's view. For each ellipse detected, there will be two discs reconstructed in 3-D space in terms of its orientation and position as well; one is pointing away from the plane which is a true direction while the other will be pointing in the wrong direction. As can be seen in the result above, the authors have the orientations of (1.0000,-0.0000, 0.0000) and (1.0000,-0.0049,-0.0007). This ambiguity case can be removed by taking into consideration that from a camera's perspective, a disc will only be seen if they are orientated upwards (positive values) rather than downwards (negative values). So, using the information above, it is clear that the image plane is one unit away (P (1, 0, 0)) from the origin (of a camera at the spacecraft) which is the orientation of the spacecraft itself. The readers should be also reminded that in this case, the orientation vector is the unit vector that gives the direction of the centre of the crater. Hence, this orientation vector is also considered the normal vector of the crater that is pointing upward.

As can be seen in this second solution of these orientations, there is an error when the authors calculate the vector unit of this orientation which has to be 1. One of the drawbacks when the authors use MATLAB is that it will always round the value, for example 0.99995 to

1. That is why those (1.0000,-0.0049,-0.0007) values when squared, summed them all and squared root them back, the authors will have more than 1. By theory, this value should be 1 and the reason for this error is maybe due to MATLAB that has rounded the value of 1.0000 that lies on the x axis.

Furthermore, in order to evaluate the error of the ellipse that the authors reconstruct, the ellipse itself has an error on the image. This is because of the digitization of a real shape that has an inherent loss of information c compared with the original shape. One should notice that there is no possibility that the original ellipse can be recovered from the digital ellipse but the errors can be optimized by increasing the picture resolution of an image. If the image is unclear or has a poor resolution, the authors can pre-process the image to reduce the presence of noise in the original image by using a smoothing technique [9]. This smoothing technique is carried out by implementing the low-pass filter to the original image. The main purpose is to attenuate the high-spatial frequencies by keeping the low spatial frequencies of the signal strength [9].

Besides, what cause the error are the uncertainties that appear from hardware (altimeter, satellite, or radar), software (MATLAB) and also the landing site topography itself. In a real situation, the sensor noise that comes from the altimeter also has to be considered a noise as it will affect the accuracy of the results determined by the system.

5. Under what conditions the craters are not detected

The higher the successful detection rate is, the lesser the false alarm rate will be. When the detection rate is 80%, the false alarm rate is just 17% whereas for the detection rate of 73%, the false alarm rate increases to 25%. The authors have plotted the graph of successful rate detection versus the false alarm rate as can be shown in Figure (18) below. The FAR (False Alarm Rate) is the percentage of non-signals that were detected as signals (craters) and is calculated based on the number of false alarms and the correct-rejections which can be formulated as [19]:

FAR = Num. Of False alarms/(Num. Of False alarms + Number of Correct-Rejections)   (26)

The number of false alarm in this case can be referred to as a signal that was not presented but was mistakenly detected by the system whilst correct rejections can be referred to as a signal that was not presented and not detected by the system at all. The lesser false alarm rate in the system is, the better the system/algorithm will be. The main reason that brought these false alarms is the assumption of the sun angle that will lead to a faulty detection of true crater pair (true light patch connected to a true dark patch) hence will decrease the accuracy of the detection rate.

As in any true scenario, an image has to be captured first before the system can detect the safe landing sites that are free from hazards (craters). As mentioned before, this algorithm is assuming that the authors know the sun's direction and will be using the sun angle as one of the steps to detect the craters on the moon's surface. But, there will be some errors when the authors assume the sun angle without knowing its true direction. This assumption will affect the algorithm to pick up the wrong pairs (light patches will be connected to wrong dark patches and vice versa). Nowadays, the authors can obviously determine the sun elevation by many ways from the satellite system or LIDAR.

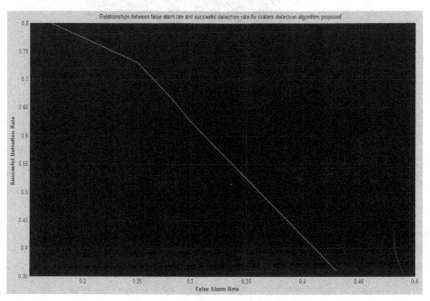

Figure 18. Relationship between successful detection rate and false alarm rate for the proposed craters detection algorithm

This algorithm is not effective on a noisy image with lots of tiny craters, undesired features that look like a crater, the craters' rims which are overlapping and segmented as well as a blurry image. Besides, an image with a too high or too low of sun elevation angle will make the system unable to differentiate the pattern (the light and the dark patches/blobs) and thus, influence the craters to be rarely detected by the system/algorithm. The algorithm will work accurately/efficiently with a sun elevation angle between 10 degrees to 50 degrees based on the experimentations under different image conditions earlier. With noisy image, the only way to reduce the tiny blobs is by using the function in MATLAB called 'bwareaopen'. As discussed before, this function removes from a binary image all connected components (objects) that have fewer than G (set by the authors) pixels, producing another binary image. Figure (21) below is an example of the image if the algorithm does not apply the 'bwareaopen' function to eliminate tiny blobs which makes the algorithm becomes ineffective while Figures (14) and (15) above show the detected craters after the function 'bwareaopen' is applied. The detection rate falls to only 36% and the difference of accuracy is very obvious which is about 37%. To capture an image with a clear pattern of light and dark patches, it is vital as it is one of the most important features to improve the accuracy of the system detection.

Therefore, the image has to be taken by the spacecraft's camera under ideal sun elevation angle (not too low and too high) and a low noise image is a bonus.

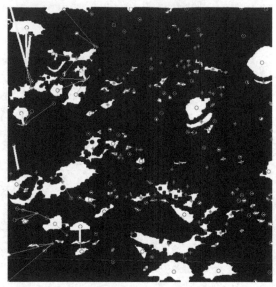

Figure 19. Low detection of craters by the algorithm because of too many unnecessary blobs (tiny blobs)

However, for the advantages, the algorithm itself can detect the craters without knowing the main parameters such as the size (radius/diameter or the gradient of the craters). It is an uncomplicated detection algorithm and has a fast detection performance. Under a clear image (low noise, good lightning condition and ideal sun elevation angle) where the pattern is easily distinguishable, the accuracy will be much higher. Besides, the craters detection is independent of the shape detection whether it is a circle or an ellipse.

6. Comparison with other previous detection method

In comparison to other techniques in terms of performance, this craters detection algorithm also has an understanding performance in terms of accuracy measurement to the previous algorithm proposed by Sawabe, Matsunaga and Rokugawa in 2005. As highlighted and calculated above, it is proven that the craters detection algorithm has an accuracy detection of 77% based on the two images tested above. This understanding percentage measurement is based on how much craters are detected compared with the pre-processed image as in Figures (14) and (15) above. The detected craters are measured from groups of pairing patches (light and dark) with minimum distances and angles detection.

This proposed craters detection algorithm by the authors can be improved by introducing more approaches like edge detections of each crater and evaluating more techniques from the morphological image analysis. To experiment more with the image morphology, the authors have tested the edge detection method using *prewitt* and *canny* on the original Image 2 using the algorithm and the results are shown in Figures (22) and (23) below. As can be seen b, *canny* method has detected the edges more precisely than the *prewitt* method. There are some previous craters detection algorithms implemented in this edge detection method as proposed by Yang Cheng and Adnan Ansar in their proposed craters detection technique [5]. Edge detections are usually used in a pre-processing step to obtain better results before the shape of the crater can be detected.

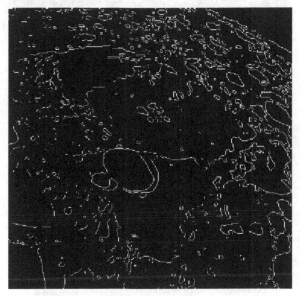

Figure 20. Edge detections using 'prewitt' detector

In comparison to the multiple approaches craters detection and automate craters classification algorithm proposed by Sawabe, Matsunaga and Rokugawa in 2005, the algorithm has an accuracy of 80%. Four approaches are implemented in the craters detection algorithm to find shady and sunny patters in images with low sun angles, circular features in edge images, curves and circles in thinned and connected edge lines and discrete or broken circular edge lines using fuzzy Hough transform. In this particular research, they have considered a crater as a circle and used circular Hough transform to detect circular feature of a crater. The detected crater is then classified by spectral characteristics derived from Clementine UV-Vis multi-spectral images. Although it has more percentage of accuracy compared with the algorithm proposed by the authors, it has a limitation such as the crater has to be assumed to be a circle before it can be used to detect a crater. If the authors have an ellipse in the image, then it will be difficult to use this method of detection.

Figure 21. Edge Detection using 'canny' detector

Previously, there were quite a number of craters detection algorithms using Hough Transform especially using circular features detection as proposed by E.Johnson, A.Huertas, A.Werner and F.Montgomery in their paper [7]. As emphasized above, a camera will capture an ellipse if the image is taken from a certain angle and certain distance relative to the moon's surface. An ellipse will have five dimensions that have to be considered in the Hough algorithm when detecting shapes. An ellipse is more complicated to be detected than a circle because a circle just has 3 dimensions to be considered. It will certainly have a complex codes hence will take a longer time to construct. That is the reason why the authors have created an uncomplicated and robust algorithm in detecting hazards mainly craters on the moon's surface for easy implementation.

7. Ellipse reconstruction algorithm using artificial image

To test the algorithm with various image types, the authors have created a two dimension (2-D) image as given in Figure (22) using Adobe Photoshop with its axis of symmetry of a half-length A=0 (to model it as a disc) and degenerate axes of a half-length, B=48. The objective is to determine the position of the centre of the disc reconstructed from the reconstruction algorithm and to compare it with the known centre position determined by the Bounding Ellipse Algorithm. The ellipse created has a position of q = (168.5469, 140.0172).The image generated is 494x494 pixels. The image plane ellipse determined by the Bounding Ellipse algorithm is described as:

a = 133.998 pixels
b = 48.934 pixels
Xc = 168.5469 pixels
Yc = 140.0172pixels
omegha degrees, ω = -0.0017 degrees

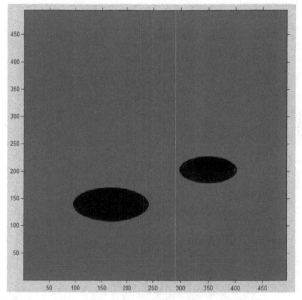

Figure 22. Artificial Image in 2-D created using Adobe Photoshop

To centralize the coordinate system and scale the image, it requires a translation of half of the image dimensions. The reconstruction algorithm is then used to determine the position and orientation of the modelled disc after taking into account the camera's parameter as below:

$Xc = (X_{Cimage} - 247)/494$
$Yc = (Y_{Cimage} - 247)/494$
a (semi major axis) $= a_{image}/494$
b (semi minor axis) $= b_{image}/494$

The ellipses generated in Figure (23) above will undergo the same process as the authors performed on the real image (optical) previously using the same method of detection. For the reconstruction results, the authors will be judging two planes namely plane y and plane z to determine the position of the disc reconstructed. This is because, as being set in the algorithm, the centre coordinate of the 2-D plane is at [Zc,Yc]. Thus, the results of the position of the disc will be analyzed in two dimensions only namely Zc and Yc. This reconstructed position will be compared with the centroid's position calculated by the bounding ellipse algorithm. At the end of the experiment, the results from the reconstructed algorithm are satisfactory and similar to the results from the bounding ellipse algorithm. The positional error evaluated for both two solutions are shown in the table below. The one which has a low error will be taken as a true position. As can be seen in the results below, the positional errors are quite high from both solutions that are 8.8722 and 8.8715. Therefore, the authors take the solution 2 as a disc reconstructed position.

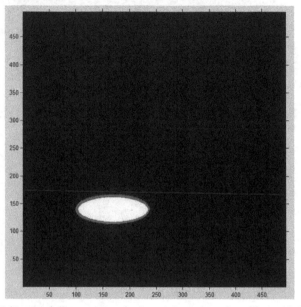

Figure 23. Artificial image of ellipse processed using minimum bounding ellipse with Khachiyan Algorithm

The positional errors are evaluated as shown in Table (3) below. Unlike before, the causes of the errors in the disc position are something similar to what were discussed in the previous 4.1.2.4 section. The positional error can be in any circumstances such as pixellation, the bounding ellipse algorithm error, MATLAB rounding figures as described before, uncertainties from the hardware and the like. These are the reasons why the authors tend to have quite a high number of errors on the position determination part. Besides, when the authors have the ellipse that is too eccentric, both the outputs of the reconstruction algorithm will become complex.

The ellipse bounding algorithm also has an error in bounding the targeted patch. As can be seen in the Figure (26) above, the targeted ellipse is not totally bounded by the red lines and this will affect the output of the image plane ellipse parameter such as semi major axis and semi minor axis. Hence, these parameters will also affect the output of the reconstruction algorithm and will cause errors in the disc's position. In practice, the way to overcome this problem is by reducing the eccentricity of the image plane ellipse or by increasing the eccentricity of the spheroid to be reconstructed. The results of this disc reconstruction algorithm are shown in the table below:

Reconstruction possible results	Solution number 1	Solution number 2
Position, q Taken A=2; B = 6 ;	Xc = 163.2225 Yc = 147.1142	Xc = 163.2224 Yc = 147.1137
Positional error	8.8722	8.8715
Orientation, p Where A=2 and B=6	1.0000 0.0038 0.0016	1.0000 -0.0085 -0.0036

Table 1. Reconstruction algorithm results for disc position tested in artificial image

As for the orientation part, the authors will take the positive one which has to be (1.0000, 0.0038, 0.0016) similar to those in the real optical image. As discussed before, the orientations for the crater will only be seen if they are orientated upwards (positive values) rather than downwards (negative values). Therefore, after taking into account the above condition, the authors can eliminate the negative orientation. Further, the evaluation of error in the orientation part is similar to the one with the real image as discussed in previous section.

8. Conclusion and recommendation

This paper focuses primarily on the identification and detection of craters on a lunar's surface. To realize these goals, an algorithm to detect craters which happen to be the main hazardous features on lunar is proposed. The authors divided the evaluation of this algorithm into a flowchart as presented in the methodology section. First, using the original image of craters on the moon's surface, the authors convert the RGB image plane to HSV image plane and analyze only the Value parameter of a HSV plane. Further, the thresholding is applied to the image for classification using this Value and thresholding approaches by Sawabe et al. After these classifications of images between light and dark patches, the authors have labelled them and determined the centre of each patch using 'regionprops' function. This stage is then followed by a vital stage in determining the best craters of all using two proposed methods: the minimum distance determination and angle measurement. This is a new and simple method proposed by the authors in detecting craters as main hazardous features on the moon's surface.

For precise moon landing, the authors then proposed the geometrical analysis consisted of projection or reconstruction of the ellipse to a 2-D circle on an image plane. At this stage, the authors applied the bounding ellipse algorithm as a first step in modelling a crater as a disc. The authors then calculated all the ellipse parameters using the information embedded in the output of bounding ellipse algorithm, then drew the bounding ellipse around the targeted patch. This output will then be used in ellipse reconstruction algorithm in order to get the orientation, $\tilde{p}$ and further position, $\tilde{q}$ of the disc (crater) from the camera's projection.

There are some limitations that have to be stated here for further extension and modification. For the craters detection algorithm, it is dependent on the sun angles and these assumptions will lead to an error of detecting a true pair (light and dark pairing patch). In addition, there are uncertainties as discussed before from the software (MATLAB) and the hardware itself in a real application (altimeter to measure the altitude). The Hough method seems to give more precise results but have a constraint in the shape of a crater itself. For an instance, the reconstruction needs to analyze a crater as an ellipse model instead of a circle. In Hough ellipse transformation, the authors have to analyze the ellipse in 5 dimensions instead of 3 dimensions in a circle. These limitations make the Hough Transform method to be unreliable and make its computational method a burden to use together with this craters detection algorithm

For future works, this useful research can be extended to a crater pattern matching as described in the Literature Review section above. Craters Pattern matching is proposed by previous researchers to attain the position and velocity estimation of a spacecraft and a Lander during Entry, Descent and Landing (EDL) purposes and also for autonomous precision landing purposes. By making a pattern matching, one can get the differentiation between the position determined by the pattern matching and those from the reconstruction algorithm. The errors in the crater's position between these two methods can be evaluated to determine which is better in a real application. In reality, the lunar's surface is not flat and the camera parameters will not usually estimate perfectly. The image does require scaling, but the true amount is impossible to be identified without also knowing the camera's specifications (focal length and field of view). In most cases, the picture is not usually taken straight at the centre of the image and perspective distortion will have an effect as discussed before. As none of these are true in real applications, the need of the reconstruction algorithm to find the position of the crater is high. The crater's position determination and evaluation of this reconstruction algorithm were discussed in detail in the previous section. Then, the authors can determine the velocity of the spacecraft based on the position and the orientation of the crater. The idea is, if the authors can find the position and orientation in a single frame, then the velocities are the difference from one frame to the other one. Therefore, this research has a great valuable for future works. In addition, this research is a very worthy research indeed and has valuable benefits to any spacecraft missions in order to avoid the hazardous craters (feature proposed) and for a moon Lander to have a precise landing on a Lunar. Besides, the authors can compare the position determined using equation $\tilde{q}$ and the position determined using the craters pattern matching and this will be a noble future work for new researchers.

Author details

Nur Diyana Kamarudin, Kamaruddin Abd. Ghani, Siti Noormiza Makhtar, Baizura Bohari and Noorlina Zainuddin
National Defense University of Malaysia, Malaysia

Acknowledgement

We would like to express our gratitude to our supervisors Dr Phil Palmer and Dr David Wokes from the University of Surrey, United Kingdom for their guidance and support. This academic article is also dedicated to our new supervisor, Associate Professor Major (R) Ir. Kamaruddin Abd. Ghani, co-supervisors, our beloved families and university. This chapter is fully supported by the Department of Electrical and Electronic Engineering, Universiti Pertahanan Nasional Malaysia, Malaysia.

9. References

[1] C. Gonzalez, E. Woods, and L. Eddins (2004).*Digital Image Processing Using MATLAB*. Prentice Hall, New Jersey.

[2] Randolph J.F. (1967). *Calculus $\cup$ Analytic Geometry $\cup$ Vectors*. Dickenson Publishing Company, California.

[3] Heiken, G.H., Vaniman, D.T., French, B.M. *Lunar Source Book*. The University of Cambridge, 1991.

[4] M. Seul, Lawrence O'Gorman and J. Sammon (2000).*Practical Algorithms for Image Analysis, Description, Examples and Code*. Cambridge University Press, United Kingdom.

[5] Cheng, Y. and Ansar, A. (2005). Landmark Based Position Estimation for Pinpoint Landing on Mars. In *Proceedings of the 2005 IEEE International Conference on Robotics and Automation (ICRA)*, pages 4470-4475, Barcelona, Spain.

[6] Ansar, A. And Daniilidis, K. (2003).Linear Pose Estimation from Points or Lines.*IEEE Transactions on Pattern Analysis and Machine Intelligence*, 25 (5): 578-589.

[7] E. Johnson, Andres Huertas, A. Werner and F. Montgomery (2008).Analysis of On-Board Hazard Detection and Avoidance for Safe Lunar Landing.*IEEEAC Paper*, pages 1-8, California.

[8] E. Johnson and F. Montgomery (2008).Overviewof Terrain Relative Navigation Approaches for Precise Lunar Landing.*IEEEAC Paper*, pages 1-9, California.

[9] L. Bruzzone, L. Lizzi, P.G. Marchetti, J. Earl and M. Milnes.*Recognition and Detection of Impact Craters from EO Products*. University of Trento, Italy.

[10] Neukum, G., Konig, B., Arkani-Hamed, J. A Study of Lunar Impact Crater size-distributions. The Moon 12, 201-229,1975.

[11] Neukum, G.,Ivanov, B., Hartmaan, W.K. Cratering Records in the Inner Solar System, Chronology and Evolution of Mars, vol. 55-86. Kluwer, Dordecht, 2001.

[12] Honda, R., Iijima, Y., Konishi, O. Mining of Topographic feature from heterogeneous imagery: its application to lunar craters. Progress of Discovery Science, LNAI pp. 395-407, 2002.

[13] Sawabe, Y., Matsunaga, T., Rokugawa, S. Automated detection and classification of lunar craters using multiple approaches, COSPAR (Advance in Space Research), 2005.

[14] Cheng Y., Ansar, A. A Landmark based Pinpoint Landing Simulator, Jet Propulsion Laboratory, California Institute of Technology, USA.

[15] Williams J.K. Navigation Results for NASA's Near Earth Asteroid Rendezvous Mission, AIAA/AAS Astrodynamics Specialists Conference.

[16] Miller, J.K. Determination of Shape, Gravity and Rotational State of Asteroid 433 Eros, Icarus,155, vol. 3-17,2002.

[17] Bernard, G., Golombek, M. Crater and rock hazard modelling for Mars Landing, AIAA Space 2001 Conference, Albuquerque, NM.

[18] Wokes, D.S. and Palmer, P.L. (May 2009). Perspective Projection and Reconstruction of a Spheroid onto an Image Sphere.*SIAM Journal on Imaging Science*, 2009.

[19] Coombs, C. H., Dawes, R. M., and Tversky, A. (1970) Mathematical Psychology, Englewood Cliffs, pp. 165-201, NJ: Prentice-Hall.

[20] http://www.engnetbase.com/ejournals/books/book_summary/summary.asp?id=792

[21] http://science.nationalgeographic.com/science/space/space-exploration/moon-exploration-article.html

Permissions

The contributors of this book come from diverse backgrounds, making this book a truly international effort. This book will bring forth new frontiers with its revolutionizing research information and detailed analysis of the nascent developments around the world.

We would like to thank Vasilios N. Katsikis, for lending his expertise to make the book truly unique. He has played a crucial role in the development of this book. Without his invaluable contribution this book wouldn't have been possible. He has made vital efforts to compile up to date information on the varied aspects of this subject to make this book a valuable addition to the collection of many professionals and students.

This book was conceptualized with the vision of imparting up-to-date information and advanced data in this field. To ensure the same, a matchless editorial board was set up. Every individual on the board went through rigorous rounds of assessment to prove their worth. After which they invested a large part of their time researching and compiling the most relevant data for our readers. Conferences and sessions were held from time to time between the editorial board and the contributing authors to present the data in the most comprehensible form. The editorial team has worked tirelessly to provide valuable and valid information to help people across the globe.

Every chapter published in this book has been scrutinized by our experts. Their significance has been extensively debated. The topics covered herein carry significant findings which will fuel the growth of the discipline. They may even be implemented as practical applications or may be referred to as a beginning point for another development. Chapters in this book were first published by InTech; hereby published with permission under the Creative Commons Attribution License or equivalent.

The editorial board has been involved in producing this book since its inception. They have spent rigorous hours researching and exploring the diverse topics which have resulted in the successful publishing of this book. They have passed on their knowledge of decades through this book. To expedite this challenging task, the publisher supported the team at every step. A small team of assistant editors was also appointed to further simplify the editing procedure and attain best results for the readers.

Our editorial team has been hand-picked from every corner of the world. Their multi-ethnicity adds dynamic inputs to the discussions which result in innovative outcomes. These outcomes are then further discussed with the researchers and contributors who give their valuable feedback and opinion regarding the same. The feedback is then collaborated with the researches and they are edited in a comprehensive manner to aid the understanding of the subject.

Apart from the editorial board, the designing team has also invested a significant amount of their time in understanding the subject and creating the most relevant covers. They scrutinized every image to scout for the most suitable representation of the subject and create an appropriate cover for the book.

The publishing team has been involved in this book since its early stages. They were actively engaged in every process, be it collecting the data, connecting with the contributors or procuring relevant information. The team has been an ardent support to the editorial, designing and production team. Their endless efforts to recruit the best for this project, has resulted in the accomplishment of this book. They are a veteran in the field of academics and their pool of knowledge is as vast as their experience in printing. Their expertise and guidance has proved useful at every step. Their uncompromising quality standards have made this book an exceptional effort. Their encouragement from time to time has been an inspiration for everyone.

The publisher and the editorial board hope that this book will prove to be a valuable piece of knowledge for researchers, students, practitioners and scholars across the globe.

List of Contributors

Mohammed Z. Al-Faiz
Computer Engineering Department, Al-Nahrain University, Baghdad, Iraq

Abbas H. Miry
Electrical Engineering Department, AL-Mustansiriyah University, Baghdad, Iraq

Ramy Saad, Sebastian Hoyos, and Samuel Palermo
Department of Electrical and Computer Engineering, Texas A&M University, College Station, Texas, USA

S. Chountasis
Hellenic Transmission System Operator, Greece

V. Katsikis
Technological Education Institute of Piraeus, Petrou Ralli & Thivon 250, 12244 Aigaleo, Athens, Greece

D. Pappas
Department of Statistics, Athens University of Economics and Business, Greece

Momoh-Jimoh E. Salami, Ismaila B. Tijani and Za'im Bin Ismail
Intelligent Mechatronics Research Unit, Department of Mechatronics, International Islamic University Malaysia, Gombak, Malaysia

Abdussamad U. Jibia
Department of Electrical/Electronic Engineering, Bayero University Kano, Kano, Nigeria

David Ernesto Troncoso Romero and Gordana Jovanovic Dolecek
Department of Electronics, Institute INAOE, Tonantzintla, Puebla, Mexico

Konrad Urbanski
Institute of Control and Information Engineering, Poznan University of Technology, Poznan, Poland

Nur Diyana Kamarudin, Kamaruddin Abd. Ghani, Siti Noormiza Makhtar, Baizura Bohari and Noorlina Zainuddin
National Defense University of Malaysia, Malaysia